Law For You
PRACTICAL
LAW

Law For You
PRACTICAL
LAW

Law For You

PRACTICAL
LAW
for the
layman

Foster Furcolo, L.L.B.
Federal Administrative Law Judge
FORMER GOVERNOR AND CONGRESSMAN

FOREWORD BY
EUGENE V. ROSTOW
FORMER DEAN, YALE LAW SCHOOL

Illustrations by **Robert Gormley**

ACROPOLIS BOOKS LTD.
Washington, D.C. 20009

ACROPOLIS BOOKS LTD.
Colortone Building, 2400 17th St., N.W.
Washington, D.C. 20009

Printed in the United States of America by
COLORTONE PRESS
Creative Graphics Inc.
Washington, D.C. 20009

OTHER BOOKS BY FOSTER FURCOLO
LET GEORGE DO IT
PILLS, PEOPLE, PROBLEMS
RENDEZVOUS AT KATYN

*The publication is designed to provide accurate and
authoritative information in regard to the subject matter covered.
It is sold with the understanding that the publisher is not engaged in
rendering legal, accounting or other professional service. If legal advice
or other professional assistance is required, the services of a competent
professional person should be sought.*

Library of Congress Cataloging in Publication Data

Furcolo, Foster, 1917—
  Practical law for the layman.

  Earlier ed. (© 1975) published under title:
Law for you.
  Includes index.
  1. Law—United States—Popular works. 1. Title.
KF387.F87   1980   349.73   80-14617
ISBN 0-87491-612-7 (pbk.)

Contents

Foreword

Foster Furcolo's book, LAW FOR YOU, is a useful and perceptive guide to the law. Technically accurate, it is still simple and easy to read. The book discusses law in exactly the right way for the non-lawyer; yet lawyers will not find the treatment superficial. The author has done a grand job and one that is badly needed.

Eugene V. Rostow
Former Dean,
Yale Law School

CERTAINTY AND CLARITY ARE THE HALLMARKS OF LAW.

1
The Past Is Prologue

THE LAYMAN WHO WOULD like to understand law should be aware of its history. As a wise man once said, the past is prologue. To know the past often enables us to foretell the future. So let's take a look at the law of the past: what it was, when it began and where.

Law is undoubtedly as old as mankind itself—yet no one can point to an exact time and place when it all began. We can be sure, however, that wherever human beings of intelligence lived together, there soon developed some kind of law. Whenever the age, wherever the place, and whatever the type of society—simple or complex, sophisticated or savage, tribe or metropolis—it inevitably formulated some code of conduct that we think of as the law. It might have been law by custom, tradition, practice, taboo, rule, or some combination of usages, but whatever it became, it was The Law.

Just as we cannot point to an exact date when law began, neither can we name a specific originator. Nor can we spell out certain words and say, "These constituted the first law." Whatever we now have as The Law has come from many forgotten sources, and from many unnamed ancestors. It has grown, changed, progressed, backtracked, and evolved. It has been praised, damned, blessed, cursed, and lived. It has been helpful, harmful, clear, confusing, constant, uncertain, and eternal.

It is because law is all those things that the law will always be fair and just—*according to the prevailing moral code and beliefs of society at a given time.* That clause is essential because the mores and beliefs of society have always changed and always will change. For the same reason, the law is always just a little behind society, although eventually the law always becomes what society wants it to be. So the law is always fair and just, not necessarily at this particular

13

moment and in this particular case, but for these times and these cases. The question is not: On May 10, was John Jones treated fairly in his case? It is rather: In that decade were people in general treated fairly in their cases?

Was it fair and just to hang someone for picking pockets? It was, according to the moral code and beliefs of the people at that time. What about sentencing someone to ten years for smoking marijuana? It was fair and just according to the moral code and beliefs of the people at that time.

In recent years we had the death penalty for scores of felonies—today it is doubtful if we have it at all. By the time you read this, the death penalty may have vanished completely. Were we right then, a few years ago, or are we right now? Is there anything that is "right"—or is it "right" only if we add the words, *according to the moral code and beliefs of the people at that time*?

Like it or not, we must live with the law, and it is easier to live with it if we understand it. So perhaps a little history (which may include legend) will help us to better understand the law. In addition to satisfying our curiosity, such knowledge will also help explain why the law is what it is, and aid us in understanding the future changes that may occur in the law.

SOURCES OF MODERN LAW

There are many sources of our modern law, and each source played a role in fashioning law as we know it. Let us begin with the realization that wherever there is any kind of civilization, be it the simplest or the most sophisticated, there always has been, and always will be, a form of law. At various times it has been called custom, tradition, taboo, rule, regulation, ordinance, statute, case, and decision. Whatever it was called, whenever mankind turned to it as a standard of conduct for social relationships, it became the law.

One of the fascinating aspects of law is that it is never a dead letter. Whatever the law has been at any time, no matter how ancient or even absurd according to present-day standards, once something has been the law, its influence and effects may be seen in whatever more sophisticated thinking has replaced it. The various doctines of law in ancient times—the codes of Hammurabi, Solon, Draco, Justinian, Moses—still creep into the most modern legal thought. The most modern courthouses still harbor ancient wisdom along with new reforms; there is truly nothing completely new under the legal sun.

14

For example, in the early 1970's, the legislatures of Massachusetts and California began to experiment with the legal innovation of compensating victims of crime. This "new, radical, and revolutionary idea" (as it is usually described) had been forgotten for centuries—but at one time the criminal who murdered a man had to undertake the support of the victim's family. Fines went, not to the state, but to the person who had been injured by the criminal act. The practice was not called "compensation to the victims of crime," but what else could it have been?

Our present-day emphasis on the accused's right of silence, our insistence that no person has to incriminate himself, may be found in the teachings of the Talmud and Catholicism. Our jury, with its virtually sacred number—twelve—has its roots in the number of Christ's Apostles, according to some scholars, while others attribute it to sources even deeper in the mists of time.

Modern legislatures are constantly "codifying" or "recodifying" the law—cutting out the legal deadwood, streamlining terminology, clarifying decisions, and putting the law in simplified language. But the idea of codification is not new. Centuries ago, a long-forgotten ruler actually had tablets erected with all the laws of the time engraved upon them for all to see.

Over the last few thousand years of civilization, the codes of law have been numerous and diverse. Under Hammurabi, the Babylonians developed laws dealing with murder, adultery, divorce, and other social problems, as did the Hebrews in the Mosaic Law. Certainly the principles on which the Ten Commandments were based are still in vogue in every modern legal system.

The golden age of Greece saw the rise of various legal doctrines: the best known is probably the code of Draco, which imposed severe penalties. This was followed by the Solonian Law, which eased the Draconian penalties. Later, of course, there was Roman Law.

Most European law is based on Roman law, particularly on the Justinian Code, which had almost five thousand statutes. Roman law became so widespread that it has been said that although Rome failed to conquer the world with her armies, she did so with her laws.

Most of Latin America followed Roman law. Here in the United States, traces of Roman law can still be seen in Louisiana, Texas, Arizona, New Mexico, and California, where there are remnants of old French and Spanish law which originated in Roman law. However, most law in the United States is based directly on English law, which is very distinctive from Roman law or any other. Let us start

15

with what is now known as the First English Code, formed in the seventh century.

Modern English law began mostly with customs and rules which were unwritten and were passed down from generation to generation. The elders and the clergy in a community were the real governing body. Some time in the early seventh century, an English king (Ethelbert, King of Kent), attempted to codify all the known English laws. The result was the First English Code, a short, somewhat unsophisticated document, but the beginning of our system of codified law. Other rulers added to it from time to time. Penalties, prescribed right in the Code, were more severe for offenses against royalty than for offenses against commoners.

In later years, a King's Court was established. This court, however, was only to protect the rights of royalty and nobility. The common people had no right to seek justice in it. They were heard in the older local courts, called Hundred Courts or County Courts, where the judges might be freeholders, or a bishop or sheriff.

The influence of the French came into England with the Norman Conquest in 1066. We see Gallic traces in such legal words as judge, jury, debt and tort—but the English laws themselves remained the same.

In the twelfth century, under Henry II, full-time regular judges began to decide cases. They wrote decisions and followed precedents to establish the doctrine of *stare decisis*: stand by decisions; follow decisions. There began to be some system and certainty to the law. The decisions of these judges were backed up by the King and, since there was as yet no legislative body of any kind, the law was made by the judges. The cases are recorded in the names of the parties involved. These cases became known as the Common Law.

Another innovation of Henry II was the opening of the King's Court to the common people. They could have a jury trial there or, if they preferred, trial by ordeal. In trial by ordeal, the law determined that the "right side" would win. The usual procedure was to subject the accused party to fire, to water or even to battle, a test so severe it often resulted in the death of the accused. This type of trial was generally prohibited in 1219. A jury was normally composed of twelve knights, but in some cases the jurors could be commoners. At this time the judicial system was still primarily to uphold royalty, the nobility, and land owners, but the masses were at least beginning to enjoy some of its benefits. They also had some benefits (and punish-

16

ments) from the Canon Law of the Catholic Church, which had its own courts of law on religious matters.

The law was being more precisely recorded, and becoming so complicated that it was increasingly difficult for non-legal minds to comprehend or for them to present their rights in court. As a result, before the beginning of the fourteenth century, a class of professional legal experts had come into being. These eventually became the fraternity variously known as lawyers, barristers, solicitors, attorneys, and squires (esquire). Thus it was that, by the thirteenth century, England had come a long way in providing her people with courts, juries, judges, lawyers, recorded cases, and other trappings of a fairly sophisticated judicial system.

Although most modern American law is based on English law, another important source of law is something we call the constitution. We have to be concerned with two constitutions: the United States Constitution, which is the supreme law of the land, and the state constitutions, which are supreme so far as state matters are concerned.

A third source of law is statutory law. A statute is simply a law that has been passed by a federal or a state legislature: it is legislation. A statute may merely recognize law that has been created by judicial decisions, or it may be a brand new creation by the legislature. Statutes that have been passed by Congress are collected in many volumes known as the *United States Code Annotated*. The statutes of every state legislature are compiled in volumes for the individual state and are known by such titles as *General Laws* or *Annotated Statutes*. A sort of miniature form of statutory law may be found in the ordinances and by-laws of cities and towns.

A fourth source of law is known as "case law." This consists of decisions rendered over the years by the highest court of each state. There is a similar body of law from the federal courts. The well-established doctrine of following decisions is recognized in the above mentioned Latin phrase, *stare decisis*.

Another sometimes recognized source of law may be found in the rules of court (each court issues them), and in the rulings by various regulatory boards, commissions, agencies, and similar bodies.

We must remember that law is not there simply to regulate conduct or punish transgressions. The legal system is there to help mankind live under the best possible conditions, to serve the purposes of the community, and to try to direct conduct into channels that will avoid clashes, friction, and disputes of any kind.

The legal system is of vital importance. However, social control does not rely on the legal system alone. Controls are exercised by many private forces: the family, the church, educational institutions, professional associations, labor unions, clubs, and organizations. All are very influential and effective. Another control, very subtle but extremely powerful, is public opinion. The legal system comes into play when all these private sources fail.

There are other forces that seem to be semi-legal. Perhaps the best illustration of these is the collective bargaining agreement that plays a major role in the lives of so many people. Collective bargaining agreements govern millions of employees and employers. In 1975 there were over eighty thousand such agreements covering wages, pensions, insurance, seniority, grievances and many other matters. These semi-legal controls often play a much greater role in the lives of people than the law itself.

In trying to understand what law is and what it does, we must recognize certain basic attributes that have always characterized every legal system at any time and place in the world—and particularly in the United States.

BASIC ATTRIBUTES OF THE LEGAL SYSTEM

The first one is that law is not an exact science. It is impossible to have a rule of law, a statute or a decision that will always apply to every case. There are exceptions to everything in law. Consequently, when we say that something is "the law" we must be always ready to accept the fact that eventually an exception will arise. Perhaps in mathematics two and two always equals four, but in law one of the two's may occasionally contain a mitigating factor—perhaps a drop of mercy—that means it is not quite a mathematical two. The easiest way for the layman to understand law is to be satisfied with generalities that are ninety-five percent accurate and not to worry about the other five percent. So, one attribute of law is that it is not an exact science and there are exceptions to everything in law (probably even to this statement).

Another basic attribute is that the law is not a static substance but a living and growing thing that changes and develops as society changes and develops and as mankind's ideas of justice change. Law does not exist in a vacuum: it is a part of our social and economic structure; and we all are familiar with the fact that any social and economic structure changes. Of course the law must adapt to such shifts—which means the law itself must change.

18

To cite a few obvious examples, we might point to such recent inventions as the airplane, radio, and television. Of course there had to be new laws to meet situations arising from such new facets of life. The development of banks, insurance companies, and the stock market called for a new set of rules and regulations to protect the people. The creation of railroads, telephones, gas, electricity, and other utilities brought into being various regulatory bodies with new protective measures for those who would be affected by them. The automobile, too, carried with it the necessity for many new laws.

As society became more sophisticated, more civilized and more compassionate, we began to change our ideas about such things as sweat shops, child labor, and other social evils. And as we changed our thinking, we changed our laws. We were growing and the law was growing.

Another attribute of law is that it has at least two inconsistent goals. These goals, which tend in exactly opposite directions, are certainty and growth. The law cannot be certain and exact if it is to grow—and yet we want it to grow to keep pace with a changing society. The law cannot grow if it is to be exact and certain—and yet we want it to be exact and certain so we will know just what is the law to which we are supposed to conform. Thus, we can imagine one train of law heading east, its destination exactness and certainty; and another train heading west, its destination change and growth. Both trains reach their destinations: eventually the law grows and changes with society, and eventually we all know what the law is on a given point (but only at a given time).

We cannot completely reconcile these two inconsistent functions of the law, but we do and must have both; as a result, there is an occasional injustice in the law when someone is unfortunately caught at a time when the certainty of law is overtaken by a need for change. For example, a businessman pursuing some custom that was permissible, who was relying on the law, is caught by the growth of society that outlaws that particular custom. At one time it was perfectly permissible to use child labor. Back in the early twentieth century the Congress tried to stop the practice with a statute forbidding children's employment at certain hours. But the United States Supreme Court, in the case of *Hammer v. Dagenhart* (247 U.S. 251),* declared the child labor law unconstitutional. This

*Chapter 8, on bibliography, tells the reader how to find and interpret these citations of authority.

meant it was perfectly legal for the employer to employ children at such hours. Any employer could do so in the knowledge that the law permitted him to do it. A few years later, in *United States v. Darby* (312 U.S. 100), that decision was overruled—which meant that the employer could not so use child labor. Society had grown; its ideas and beliefs had changed, and so the law had grown and changed, too. What about certainty? What about the employer's reliance on his knowledge of the law? That had been lost, but only for the moment, because now he knew what the new law was, and the new law was exact and certain.

The case of *Lochner v. New York* (198 U.S. 45) held that a state statute that limited the hours of bakery shop employees to sixty a week was unconstitutional because it infringed liberty of contract. Years later that decision was reversed in *Nebbia v. New York* (291 U.S. 502).

Another illustration may be found in the legal dispute over the question of equal educational facilities for whites and blacks. The question came up in the United States Supreme Court in the case of *Plessey v. Ferguson* (163 U.S. 537) in 1896. The court held that it was permissible for a state to have separate educational facilities for blacks and whites provided equally good education was given in each. This was the "separate but equal" concept which continued in effect until 1954. In that year the United States Supreme Court overruled that concept when the case of *Brown v. Board of Education of Topeka* (347 U.S. 483) held that the doctrine of "separate but equal" has no place in public education.

Those who had relied on the certainty of the law (as stated in *Plessey v. Ferguson*) had been caught in the growth of society—the law had grown and the old certainty had changed to a new one.

Once we recognize that the law grows and changes, we also become aware that occasionally the dissent of a minority becomes the law of the majority. The fact that this might happen should give us pause to consider any dissenting opinion that is expressed in any legal decision. History shows that most reversals in thinking that changed dissent to majority are found in cases that were decided by five-to-four decisions of the nine-member United States Supreme Court. However, in the Plessey case cited above, the decision was eight-to-one, with only Justice John Harlan dissenting. Regrettably, he never had the satisfaction of seeing his judgment vindicated many years later.

Another attribute of the law is that it is administered by human beings. We constantly tell ourselves that we have a government of laws and not of men—and that is true. But it is equally true that our laws and our system of justice are administered by men; and, being human, they are subject to all the human frailties. I am not referring now to idiosyncrasies in individual cases, but rather to basic human differences in education, background and general viewpoint in judges who are otherwise equal in temperament, intelligence, judgment, and other such qualities. Of course, judges are affected by such things as emotion or illness in exactly the same way that all of us are. And they are human in another sense: they die and they retire. When that happens, another judge takes the bench, providing another point of view which could change the minority of four to a majority of five. It has happened.

Another attribute of the law is that courts function in a society, not in a vacuum. The judges are constantly influenced by what goes on in that society. They are a part of it; associate with others in it; see its newspapers and television; are aware of what their fellow human beings are thinking and doing; and are influenced either directly or indirectly, openly or subtly, consciously or unconsciously, by society's viewpoint. It is because courts function in a society that we see the judicial pendulum swing between the poles of conservatism and liberalism. For example, if society becomes angry at what it regards as excesses of labor, we are apt to see the courts make interpretations of law that will be adverse to labor's position. Is the country at war when someone is charged with improper treatment of the flag? It makes a difference in the attitude of the court. If crime becomes rampant, the courts tend toward severity in sentences—if rights of the individual have been interpreted in such a way that society becomes outraged at the loss of its own protection, we will find the court leaning against the defendant. And so the pendulum swings—not completely out of kilter, but within acceptable poles of conservatism and liberalism.

I have not tried to list even a fraction of the many complex principles, doctrines, and attributes of the law that play a role in our legal system. They are for law students and lawyers whose function it is to probe philosophical depths and to analyze legal pettifoggeries. Those laymen who wish to plunge into the murkier depths are free to do so. But for now, LAW FOR THE LAYMAN merely seeks to present a few relatively simple concepts: the law tries to be exact and certain, but of course it is continually changing and growing; it is

21

administered by judges who are human beings; and the legal system functions in a society, not in a vacuum. Once the layman understands these truths, the legal system becomes less of an Alice-in-Wonderland labyrinth.

OF COURSE, WE DON'T <u>HAVE</u> TO HAVE LAWS!

2
The Constitution Guarantees Your Rights

EVERY CONSTITUTION THAT EVER existed reflects the fact that injustice once prevailed against those who drew up its articles. When people have been tyrannized and oppressed beyond bearing, eventually they rebel; and their terms of reconciliation with the tyrant oppressor are spelled out in a written document that has come to be called a constitution. The oppressed insist on the guarantee to them of certain rights or privileges. The guarantees that are agreed upon by the oppressed and the oppressor are then handed down to posterity as "constitutional rights." Historically, this is how oppressed people rid themselves of such infamous practices as Bills of Attainder (obtaining a conviction by legislation and not by a judicial trial), the Star Chamber Court, and the Inquisition. It is how they secured the right to public trials, confrontation of accusers, elimination of confessions by torture, and other guarantees of justice. The United States Constitution, and the later state constitutions which were usually modeled after it, followed this pattern.

Although it was based on some of the earlier state constitutions, our own Constitution probably can be traced back to the Magna Carta of England. In the year 1215 A.D. the twenty-five barons of Great Britain wrung from King John the great charter which guaranteed rights that had been trampled on by British rulers for many generations. In the meadow called Runnymede, King John capitulated to the powerful barons, and the document known to history as the first bill of rights came into being. The Magna Carta provided that justice shall not be sold, denied, or delayed, and that an accused shall be tried by a jury of his peers. Our own Bill of Rights is modeled after this document. Magna Carta, and other reforms that followed it, may have been intended to guarantee rights solely to the barons or other privileged classes but history decreed otherwise; and soon the people were demanding rights for the rank and file, and demanding them from whomever their rulers might be.

Our Constitution, drawn up in the eighteenth century, was written and adopted within the framework of what the writers of the Constitution knew and wanted *at that time.* In general, constitutions contained only what was necessary and desirable at that stage of the needs and knowledge of the particular society for which that constitution was intended. They were sufficient for their own time—but with the growth and development of society, new problems would arise. Lawgivers would then have to amend a constitution so that the constitution itself would live and grow right along with society.

THE TWENTY-SIX AMENDMENTS

The U.S. Constitution explains why our forefathers decided to write a constitution, spells out certain truths that were declared to be basic, and then outlines the terms under which those who reside here will live and be governed. Over the years some twenty-six amendments have been added to it, the earliest being in 1791, shortly after its adoption, and the most recent being the Twenty-sixth in 1971, providing for the vote for eighteen-year-olds. While all the amendments are important, of course, the ones most apt to affect us directly are the First, guaranteeing freedom of speech and freedom of religion; the Fourth, guaranteeing freedom from unreasonable searches and seizures; the Fifth, protecting everyone from double jeopardy and self-incrimination; the Sixth, giving an accused the right to confront witnesses and the right to counsel; and the Fourteenth, guaranteeing every person due process of law and equal protection of the laws.

No citizen of the United States can be deprived of his constitutional rights by any other person; nor can the police or even the government, whether that government be local, state, or federal, abridge or negate our rights under law. We are protected against many wrongs and injustices by two simple words: "It's unconstitutional." The Constitution forbids certain laws, the Constitution protects certain rights. The great bulwark of our rights and the impenetrable mantle of our defense is the Constitution, and the most important of our constitutional rights are found in the several

24

amendments that are our shield against tyranny and oppression: the Bill of Rights.

Volumes have been written about virtually every clause in the Constitution; and the cases that have been decided, interpreting and re-interpreting each clause, sustaining and overruling points raised about every word, would fill more volumes and law books than any of us could read in a year, though the actual words of the entire Bill of Rights could be read by any of us in five minutes.

So, the words of the Constitution are simple, but the interpretation of those words is not. In law, words rarely have a simple meaning; or, for that matter, even a single meaning.

To illustrate, take the simple words "vehicle" or "means of communication." Might they not include something in 1974 that was never even imagined in 1910? We have statutes in which the word "person" is used. Does this word include corporations or business organizations? If the statute concerns marriage and divorce, the word "person" in it obviously does not include corporations or business organizations; but if the statute concerns taxes or property, the courts have ruled that the word "person" does include such entities.

Thus, there can be many meanings and interpretations of even such simple words; and the language is replete with thousands of complicated words and phrases with every shade of meaning. Law deals with varying circumstances at widely separated times and the interpretations are made by different judges and for different reasons.

Let's examine some of the constitutional amendments, and the problems involved in their interpretation.

1825   1925   1975   2000

THE CONSTITUTION NEVER CHANGES.

3

The Fourth Amendment Protects You, Your House, and Your Possessions

ALTHOUGH EVERY AMENDMENT TO the Constitution is of vital importance, we are all usually concerned primarily with the First, Fourth, Fifth, Sixth, and Fourteenth Amendments. The First Amendment reads as follows: "Congress shall make no law respecting an establishment of religion, or prohibiting the free exercise thereof; or abridging the freedom of speech, or of the press; or the right of the people peaceably to assemble, and to petition the government for a redress of grievances."

While we are all concerned with freedom of speech and religion and the other freedoms guaranteed by the First Amendment, the ordinary individual does not usually himself have the burden of enforcing these rights. Cases involving pornographic books and movies are usually fought by publishers and exhibitors; matters concerning distribution of pamphlets or the exercise of religion normally come within the province of religious groups or school committees or other organizations; and the press and other media of information are especially sensitive to any abridgment of freedom of the press. There are, of course, occasions when the individual is pretty much on his own in matters concerning the First Amendment, but they are still few. The Fourth Amendment, on the other hand, is one with which the average person or his family is almost certain to come into direct contact.

The Fourth Amendment says: "The right of the people to be secure in their persons, houses, papers, and effects, against unreasonable searches and seizures, shall not be violated, and no warrant shall issue, but upon probable cause, supported by oath or affirmation, and particularly describing the place to be searched, and the persons or things to be seized."

26

WHAT CONSTITUTES "YOUR HOUSE"?

Those are fairly simple words and no one should have any trouble understanding them. A house is a house and what's more, mine is my castle; so if someone tries to search my house, I've got certain rights that are protected by the Fourth Amendment. But I just rent. Does that make a difference? What about the garage? The woodshed in the backyard—is that a part of the "house" the Fourth Amendment protects? What about a trash barrel in the yard? Or a tool shed out beyond the fence? Suppose it were inside the fence? After all, it's my house and yard.

Suppose it's a two-family house—does that make a difference? What about an apartment? Suppose I live in a room in a rooming house or boarding house. Suppose it is in a hotel or motel. Even if they are covered, does it make a difference whether I'm a transient or rent by the week or month?

The Fourth Amendment only says "house." This is where the courts come in: they interpret the Constitution and its amendments, and although, over a period of years, different questions would arise concerning what is included in the word "house," the courts are empowered to answer them. Thus, the courts decided that "house" does include everything within the curtilage, which is defined as the area about the house, including the barn, garden, woodshed, and other area customarily used by occupants, but which probably does not extend to fields or meadows stretching out considerable distances beyond the house. An apartment or hotel room is a "house," and so is a transient's motel room, but the porch outside the motel room probably is not protected by the Fourth Amendment.

What about my office or the desk that is used solely by me at business? Both enjoy the protection of the Fourth Amendment. What about a locker in the shop where I work or, if I am a student, my school locker? These cases begin to enter a gray area that is usually shaded even more by the circumstances. If we have a clear-cut case where the locker is exclusively mine and no one else has any right to open it or to use it, then the Fourth Amendment probably protects me. But one of the terms of my employment, a company rule, part of the union agreement, or some other condition may have reserved all rights to it in the employer.

The case of a student's school locker is even more tenuous, so much so that no one can say definitely what protection it may enjoy. Such cases are complicated by inconsistent doctrines of law: one is that if the school is public, no one can impose on the student conditions about search of his locker (as might be done in private industry); another is that the school owes a duty to all the students, not just to the one using the locker, and that duty to all transcends any exclusivity to any one student. The area is so confused, the various courts are in such conflict, and the possibility of fluctuations in the law are so great that it is foolhardy to state what the law is on the point. Whatever it is may have changed by the morrow.

"UNREASONABLE SEARCHES"

The next important clause in the Fourth Amendment tells what the person is protected from: "unreasonable searches and seizures." The key word here is "unreasonable." It is not a prohibition against *any* search. It's only a protection against an *unreasonable* search.

What is unreasonable? It's the interpretation of the courts that will tell us that. The interpretation has changed and will continue to do so because of changes in the judges who decide, or because of changes in our society, such as new inventions, scientific progress or social progress. The use of electronic equipment, the advent of the automobile, and the other scientific innovations of a sophisticated society have all had an impact on questions that have arisen concerning interpretation of the words "unreasonable search."

We think we know what "reasonable" means, but do we really? Does it differ with different circumstances? A person says, "I'll see you if you don't mind waiting a reasonable time." What does "reasonable" mean? Could it depend on the relationship of the speaker to you? The subject matter? Will it make a difference whether the speaker is your roommate, a teacher, your doctor or the President? Could a "reasonable time" vary from five minutes to five weeks?

The Fourth Amendment goes on, "...no warrant shall issue but upon probable cause." We know what a warrant is: an authorization to do a certain act. A search warrant is an authorization to search. But what is "probable cause?" Would we agree that it is "reasonable belief"? If so, we're right back to the word "reasonable"; and the words "probable cause" must be interpreted and understood in a variety of circumstances.

"PROBABLE CAUSE"

Without doubt it means that a warrant cannot issue merely because a policeman asks for one: there must be something called "probable cause" for his belief that a warrant should issue. And, equally without doubt, there does not have to be proof positive or absolute certainty: the amendment merely says "probable cause," which is certainly a lot less than absolute proof. So we find ourselves in the never-never land between *some* cause and *absolute* cause, in the mists of *probable* cause. We know what we mean in casual conversation when we say "probably": a little more certain than "maybe" or "perhaps," but a lot less than "absolutely" or "positively." So it is with "probable cause" when the court is called upon to decide whether it does or does not exist in a particular set of circumstances: there is no general rule, and each case must stand or fall on its own peculiar facts.

WHAT MAKES A SEARCH WARRANT VALID?

There are many legal ways of making a proper search and one of them, by a search warrant, is described in the next clause, which says, "...particularly describing the place to be searched..." These words mean exactly what they say, and the warrant had better describe the premises exactly or it will be declared invalid and thrown out of court.

The practice by which a search warrant is issued is intended to protect the individual from overzealous police officers. To that end, the law requires that an officer who seeks to obtain the right to search must apply to the court for permission to search a particular place and for a specific object. He does this by means of an affidavit (a written statement under oath) in which he spells out not only why he wants to search a certain place, but why he believes the object he seeks is there. His "probable cause" to believe is based on his own observations or on those of someone whose information he reasonably believes to be good—and there are criteria which must be met before he can act on the word of the so-called "reliable informant." The officer seeking the search warrant must spell it all out in the affidavit that constitutes his application, and the warrant's validity is determined very strictly by what is within the four corners of that affidavit. The courts are very strict in insisting upon this and generally everything in contest about it is construed (interpreted or understood) favorably to the accused and against the officer. Why?

29

Because the individual has a right not to have any search warrant issued except under conditions that the law has determined will protect both his rights as an individual and society's rights as an entity.

A good test of whether the search warrant will be valid or not (as concerns the description of the place to be searched and the article to be seized) is whether someone who knew nothing about the case could look at the affidavit and see if, *from it alone*, he would know exactly where to go and exactly what to search for. The place must be identified exactly. The address should be given so accurately that no one could possibly go to the wrong place. And the description of the premises should be precise: an apartment described as consisting of four rooms is not a five-room apartment. A warrant authorizing the search of the first floor does not allow a search of the second floor.

Also, the item to be searched for must be described with particularity. If the officer cannot so describe it in his application for a search warrant, then we have no reason to believe he will be able to identify it on the premises.

In executing—carrying out—the search warrant, there are similar safeguards to guarantee that the individual is protected against any excesses by the police who are conducting the search. First, a search warrant is normally executed only in the daytime. While there may be an occasional night-time warrant, a police officer who desires to search at that time has the heavy burden of persuading the court of the necessity for a search after sunset. If officers have begun a search in the daytime, it may be extended into the night if it is reasonable to do so.

The length of time for the search, and its scope, are determined by the type of premises and the size of the article being sought. If a stolen television set is the object of the search, the officers may not open drawers of furniture—the TV set is too big to be there. On the other hand, if a stolen ring is the item being sought, the officers may open drawers and even small containers in the drawers. The length of time of the search may likewise vary depending upon the premises and the size of the article sought. The law merely says that the officers may search only for a reasonable time. It is the court that must determine what is a reasonable length of time, and that depends upon the circumstances and the facts of the particular case.

30

"NO-KNOCK" LAWS

Parenthetically, let me touch on the controversy surrounding the so-called "no-knock" laws that are praised by law enforcement personnel and castigated by civil liberties advocates. In the absence of statutes to the contrary, the police officer serving the search warrant is supposed to knock on the door and announce himself and his purpose. He is then supposed to wait a reasonable time for the occupant of the house to admit him; if the occupant delays or refuses, then the officer may break the door down. The problem has been that, when police officers followed such a procedure, often it gave the occupant of the premises time to destroy the evidence (for example, drugs are easily flushed down the toilet) or to arm himself and thus endanger the officer. As a result, law enforcement people periodically urge the enactment of "no-knock" legislation that eliminates the requirement of such warning in strictly limited cases where there is good reason to believe evidence could be destroyed or the officer's life put in danger. There is no good answer to the arguments on both sides. The very idea of "no-knock" is reprehensible to those who believe in the sanctity of the home; yet, the very idea of allowing evidence to be destroyed or lives of police officers endangered cannot be accepted by those who believe in law and order. Perhaps the only solution is to limit "no-knock" cases to those where the police officer's application for a search warrant satisfies the court that there is a virtual certainty that evidence will be destroyed or a police officer's life endangered otherwise. In addition, the court probably would allow them only in specified types of cases. Even so, there seems to be no satisfactory resolution of the "no-knock" problem.

LAWFUL SEARCH WITHOUT A VALID SEARCH WARRANT

Could there ever be a lawful search without a valid search warrant? Yes, there are several ways allowable under proper circumstances. But, in addition to other criteria, as a general rule they all are allowed only if there has been no opportunity to obtain a search warrant.

Search incidental to a lawful arrest is one exception to the rule that there must be a search warrant. The pendulum of judicial decisions swings back and forth regarding the circumstances under which such a search is permissible, so no exact answer can tell us

31

when such a search is valid. At one time the law stated that the search was limited in scope by the type of crime for which the arrest was made, on the theory that the officer could search only for such things as weapons or something connected with the crime. Thus, in an arrest for a traffic offense, the usual search was probably invalid because there is no evidence associated with a traffic violation. Later the law was changed to allow a search after any valid arrest, traffic or otherwise.

Assuming the case of a valid arrest followed by a permissible search, is there any limit to the scope of the search? The court has always held that there is, although the degree of limitation has varied at different times and under different courts. For example, at one time the law limited the search to whatever was in the direct and immediate control of the person arrested; that is his person, any suitcase or article he was carrying, or anything within his control. For the arrest of a bartender, for example, probably the search would extend all along the bar. At another time, the court held that the search might extend to the entire room in which the accused was arrested. So there can be no absolutely certain answer as to the extent of the search that is permitted after a valid arrest. We know what the law has been at various times and we also are reasonably certain that, as the pendulum swings, the law will change. Probably the best we can do is to understand the underlying philosophy of the law and to conclude that, depending upon the personnel of the court at any given time, after a valid arrest some degree of search will be allowed. If the court is liberal (that is, a court favorable to the individual who is accused), the search will probably be limited to the clothing of the accused and anything within his reach. If it is a conservative court (a law-and-order court favorable to the police), search may be allowed of the entire premises where he is arrested. The pendulum of permissible search incidental to arrest will swing between those two poles.

Emergency or exceptional circumstances may be another exception to the necessity of obtaining a search warrant. The question here is always whether the officer reasonably believed that a crime had occurred or was being committed, and whether there was time to get a search warrant. For example, if a police officer hears a pistol shot from a house, immediate action is required and he does not need a search warrant to enter the house. In the Massachusetts case of *Commonwealth v. Cohen* (268 NE (2)) the police officer answered a complaint about a noisy party in an apartment. While in the corridor outside the apartment, he smelled marijuana coming from the apartment and heard statements indicating that drugs were being used. The court held that he had probable cause to enter the apartment and he could do so without a search warrant.

The so-called emergency or exceptional circumstances cases are all based on the fact that there is no time to get a search warrant. In addition, the court carefully checks the question of whether the police officer's actions were reasonable. And the courts take the position that the prosecution has the burden of sustaining both points.

Another exception to the rule that a search warrant is necessary is where there is search by consent. The courts do not look with approval upon any police claim that the accused consented to a search without a warrant. The court is particularly skeptical where the person who consented is very young or very old, uneducated, a member of a minority group, or someone who might be easily intimidated or not understand his rights. In addition, if the police engage in any sort of coercion, fraud, trick, or other artifice, it will invalidate the consent. The coercion does not have to be direct: if there are many officers with guns that might frighten the occupant of the house, the court is very apt to conclude that there was indirect coercion. In brief, the courts frown upon cases where the police rely on "consent" rather than a search warrant. If the police have a warrant, the courts take the position that any "consent" was forced by the showing of the warrant, even if it later appears that the warrant was technically invalid.

Even if there is a consent that is apparently valid on its face, in the sense that there was no coercion or other improper conduct on the part of the police, there are still many technical questions that may invalidate the "consent." The first is: did the person who gave the consent have any legal standing to do so? A landlord usually has no right to give consent to the police to search a tenant's premises. The mere fact that the landlord has a key is not controlling: his right to inspect or repair does not give him the right to consent to a search. Technical questions arise when a parent or child gives the police permission to search the living quarters of the other. A parent probably may give consent for the search of a room occupied by a dependent child, but even this is not certain. If the child is emancipated (working and paying his own way), it would seem that a parent's consent in such a situation is invalid. It seems to be agreed that a child cannot authorize a search of the parent's premises.

33

What about consent by a husband or wife? It is questionable, but there have been cases that held that a wife's consent is valid. Again, there never will be any answer that will be certain at all times and under every court—the pendulum will swing.

What about the employer-employee relationship? Here we have many varying circumstances and, before the answer can be given in any case, we have to know whether the situation was covered by the employment contract, or the union bargaining agreement, or a company rule that the employee accepted, or any one of a dozen or more possibilities. The most we can conclude is that, in the absence of anything to the contrary, if an employee has a locker for his exclusive use, his employer cannot give a valid consent to its search by the police.

Where school students are concerned, the question of consent is even stickier, because the student has a right to public education. Any enforced consent he might have given to some rule or regulation may be null and void, which would not be the case for a private employee.

The host-guest relationship has problems, too. Certainly the host has a greater right to consent to a search of the guest's quarters than the guest does to authorize a search of the host's premises. But again questions arise. Was the guest a transient, or a house guest for several months? Did he have exclusive possession of his room? There is no all-conclusive and all-embracing answer to the host-guest situation; it will depend on the circumstances of the particular case.

When we consider the validity of a claim of consent as an exception to the rule that there can be no search without a search warrant, the only absolute certainty we have is that the courts do not favor search by consent.

Articles in open view are considered an exception to the rule requiring a search warrant but, if we take the position that there is actually no search because the articles were in open view, it really is not an exception. The police often rely on a position that the articles taken were in open view. Sometimes this claim is greeted with considerable skepticism or even laughter; however, there are countless cases where it has prevailed. The law says that if the initial entry of the police was lawful, and if the discovery of "the articles in open view" was inadvertent (not planned and not known about in advance), then they may be seized.

Search of motor vehicles is more or less in a class by itself as far as treatment by the courts is concerned. The police are given much more leeway because the automobile can be driven away if the officer leaves the scene in order to get a search warrant. The ticklish cases are those where the officer searches in the trunk after the car is safely in custody and there is obviously time to get a warrant. The best way to analyze the law concerning motor vehicles is to realize that, if there is time, a search warrant must be obtained; and that, as a practical matter, the courts are not as strict in construing the question against the police as they are in other situations.

BORDER SEARCHES

Border searches are invariably treated with much more leniency than any others. Practically any kind of search is regarded as permissible. The question of thorough search of the person comes up most frequently in border searches. How far can the police go in conducting a "strip search"? Pumping out the stomach? Exploring the cavities of the body? In a border search the police can go pretty far. They are not supposed to conduct any search in such a way that it "shocks the conscience." They are also required to show some concern for the feelings of the person; that is, the search should be in private and conducted by persons of the same sex as the suspect. Lastly, and undoubtedly the most important criterion, if there is to be some medical action taken—pumping the stomach, withdrawing blood, and similar acts—it should be done under sanitary conditions and by a properly qualified person (a doctor or nurse).

The question of what is a border arises occasionally. Obviously, the customs point is a border; and in another case, a "check point" some sixty-five miles away was also held to be one. The rights of the individual in a border search are certainly far more limited than in any other kind of search. As a practical matter, most questions will be decided in favor of the government and against the suspect. The border search is in a class by itself—practically anything goes, including the Fourth Amendment.

Law cases involving search and seizure and other individual rights are often misunderstood by the general public when the press reports that the court dismissed (threw out) a case because of some "mere technicality." The so-called technicality is usually a defect in the search warrant or in the procedure followed by the police in ransacking someone's home. The layman should realize that the fatal defect is by no means a "technicality"—it is rather a violation of the most sacred substantive legal rights we possess. And the

35

"we" means you and I and some two hundred million other Americans—not just some "criminal." We should remember that if the courts do not protect the rights of every single accused person, including that criminal, then they do not really protect the rights of any of us. Consequently, we must appreciate that any defect in the search warrant or its execution is a violation of a substantive right of the most precious kind, which must be protected at all costs. It is most emphatically not a "mere technicality." If policemen and other minions of the law are allowed to overlook procedural safeguards the result is the erosion of our constitutional guarantees until they no longer exist. In protecting the rights of an accused person, we really are protecting society—the accused person *is* a member of society, and any injustice to him is an injustice to society. We should remember this in all cases, but especially in search and seizure situations. It is here, as a practical matter, that the Constitution really comes to life to protect the average person in daily life. In the next chapter we explore the reasons why.

HEY!....SHE SEZ SHE WON'T STOP US FROM LOOKIN'!!!

4

If a Search Was Illegal, File a Motion to Suppress

WHY HAS THE QUESTION of whether a search is legal or not become of such overriding importance? Because a finding of guilt or innocence of the accused may depend completely on whether or not the search was legal or illegal. If it was illegal, the defendant often wins his case simply by filing a paper called a Motion to Suppress—a request for the court to rule that any evidence seized in the search cannot be used against him at the trial. If the court allows the motion, the prosecution usually finds itself without a case, since the evidence that was the basis for the accusation is suppressed and consequently there is no proof of the commission of the crime.

The case that started the rush for Motions to Suppress in state courts—they had always been used in federal courts—is the now-famous case of *Mapp v. Ohio* (367 U.S. 643). That case, decided in 1961, held that evidence taken in an unreasonable search cannot be used in *any* court, state or federal. Until this decision, it was believed that the federal Fourth Amendment applied only to federal cases in federal courts. As a result, the courts of many states did not exclude evidence that had been seized as the result of a search in violation of the Fourth Amendment. In Massachusetts, for example, evidence was admissible whether obtained by an illegal search or not. The only remedy the injured party had was a lawsuit against the officers—not a very practical solution and one that was rarely followed.

Since the Mapp decision, the courts have been flooded with Motions to Suppress evidence seized in allegedly illegal searches. The decision on the motion has become more important than anything else in the case; in fact, the judge's ruling on the question usually decides whether there will be a trial or not. If the judge rules that the evidence was illegally seized, the case is usually thrown out because the prosecution has no evidence to present. If the judge rules against the defendant's contention—that is, if he rules that the evidence is admissible—the defendant usually simply pleads guilty. It is easy to see that, as a practical matter, the decision on the Motion to Suppress usually decides the case.

A question that sometimes arises in Motions to Suppress is: who has standing to file the motion? In other words, who is so concerned that it is his business? At one time the courts held that a person could not object to an illegal search of a house, for example, unless he first acknowledged that he owned the house. Or he could not move to suppress illegally seized drugs unless he first admitted that he owned the drugs. Of course, in effect this deprived the defendant of the motion, because in order to avail himself of it, first he practically had to admit the substance of the charge against him. The courts eventually recognized the unfairness of this rule, and soon changed their decisions so that anyone aggrieved or hurt by an illegal search could present a Motion to Suppress, without admitting any criminality. While there are still some technical situations that may prevent someone from having "standing" to protest, the general situation is that anyone who is hurt by an illegal search may contest its legality.

THE "FRUIT OF THE POISONOUS TREE" DOCTRINE

A legal defense that is closely related to illegal search is the "fruit of the poisonous tree" doctrine. This simply means that if evidence has been obtained by some illegal or improper act of the prosecution, the accused may have it excluded from the trial. The theory is that, since the original act was improper or "tainted," this poison extends to and infects anything that springs from it. An example is the Massachusetts case of *Commonwealth v. Spofford* (343 Mass. 703). In that case, the police had made an illegal search of the defendant's home and had seized some pornographic pictures. When they were shown to the defendant at the police station, he said he had more at home that he would be glad to show to the police. Under this consent, the police went to the home, obtained the second batch of pictures, and later tried to introduce them in evidence at the trial. The court held that, since the first search was illegal, anything obtained in the second search was tainted by that illegality. It was the "fruit of the poisonous tree." If there had been no illegal first search, the pictures in the second search would have been legally obtained on the grounds of a search by consent. (If the police could have shown that the second search was independent of the first, and not based on anything learned from it, the second search might have escaped the "fruit of the poisonous tree" doctrine.)

The Fourth Amendment is a bulwark of strength to anyone accused of crime. It is a refuge for the guilty on occasion; but it is also the greatest shield the innocent have. And, like every constitution, amendment, and law, whatever protection is afforded is given to *everyone*. That's what the law is all about.

5

Before Police Interrogation, You Must Be Advised of Your Rights

THE LAW ALSO CONCERNS the right to counsel. This had all been spelled out for scores of years in the Sixth Amendment to the Constitution but the right was never really fully enforced until 1963, when the United States Supreme Court ruled in the case of *Gideon v. Wainright* (372 U.S. 335) that a defendant accused of crime had a right to have an attorney at the trial and, if he could not afford one, the court should appoint one for him.

It all began when Gideon, who had been convicted of the crime of burglary, sent a pencilled note to the United States Supreme Court complaining that he had been tried without an attorney in violation of the Sixth Amendment to the Constitution.

The Sixth Amendment states: "In all criminal prosecutions the accused shall ... have the assistance of counsel for his defense."

Gideon's note, written in pencil, contained poor spelling, grammatical mistakes, and other defects, but it also contained a message of truth. The truth was that he had been deprived of his constitutional rights when he had been forced to go to trial without the benefit of counsel. The United States Supreme Court, the highest tribunal in the land, responded to that appeal by a poor, uneducated drifter who had no standing or influence of any kind. Abe Fortas (who later himself became a Supreme Court Justice) was appointed to represent Gideon on the point of law he had raised. Gideon carried the day and won a Supreme Court decision that he had been entitled to counsel at his trial. Up to this time, a defendant had a right to a lawyer only if he could pay for his services or if it was a case where the penalty might be death. The Gideon case changed all that.

A humorous sidelight to the Gideon case is that after Gideon had been granted a new trial, with counsel to be appointed—which was the right he had claimed—Gideon decided to refuse counsel on the ground that, if he could convince the Supreme Court, he could certainly handle the case himself. He was persuaded to change his mind.

The Gideon case was the first in a line of cases making it clear that when the Sixth Amendment guaranteed the right to counsel, it meant exactly that. The case of *Escobedo v. Illinois* (372 U.S. 375), decided in 1964, established that someone accused of crime is entitled to counsel *before* the trial, if the investigation has begun to focus on him as a particular suspect. In the Escobedo case, when the accused was being interrogated at the police station, he requested to see his lawyer. The police refused, even though the lawyer remained at the police station for hours. The Gideon case had merely decided that an accused is entitled to counsel *at* the trial; the Escobedo case went one step further.

The next case went even further in assuring an accused the right to counsel. *U.S. v. Wade* (388 U.S. 219) held that the right to counsel arises at any "critical stage." The period from arraignment (the formal accusation in court when the defendant enters his plea) to trial is critical. The Wade case established that a so-called "critical stage" may be at the identification line-up, at first contact with the police, or at other times.

THE "MIRANDA WARNING"

The Gideon, Escobedo, and Wade cases were all landmark decisions establishing constitutional rights of anyone accused of crimes. They were soon followed by the case that established the necessity of warning the accused of his constitutional rights—the so-called "Miranda warning." The facts of *Miranda v. Arizona* (384 U.S. 436) showed that Miranda had not been given any warning about the fact that whatever he said might be used against him in court. The United States Supreme Court held that an accused is entitled to be given certain warnings if he is to be interrogated while in police custody. He must be told that he has a right to remain silent; that anything he says may be used against him in a court of law; that he has a right to an attorney; that if he is unable to employ an attorney, the court will appoint one for him; that if he does begin to answer questions he may stop any time that he wishes; and that he does not have to waive any of his rights if he does not wish to do so. If the prosecution alleges that the accused waived any of his rights, the court said that the prosecution has a heavy burden of clearly proving such waiver.

The Miranda case plays an important role in all cases that have been tried since that time. One question defense lawyers always ask is: "Did the police advise you of your constitutional rights?" Many police departments have adopted the practice of having their officers carry a card bearing the Miranda warnings so that the police officer may be certain he has properly advised an accused of his rights. There have been many technical decisions involving the question of the time and place when the accused was so alerted, and if he was given sufficient warning. A change in circumstances after he has been taken into custody has often required that the accused be given a second or even a third and fourth warning when he was being interrogated on the subject. As a result, there have been many cases when statements made by an accused were excluded from evidence and the accused had to be found not guilty or the case had to be dismissed. It seems certain that the Miranda case will be reviewed and probably amended to some degree. The decision in the case found the Justices split by the usual five-to-four margin and there has been a change in the makeup of the Court since that time. While it seems likely that the basic elements of the Miranda decision will be retained, it is probable that the Court will adopt an interpretation that will be slightly more favorable to the prosecution.

The important thing to remember about the thrust of the Miranda decision is that the courts are going to insist that any person accused of crime be given fair warning of his rights. It is sometimes forgotten that the Miranda decision refers only to in-custody interrogation by the police. If the accused is not in custody, the Miranda warnings do not protect him from the consequences of any admission he might make under such circumstances.

FELONIES AND MISDEMEANORS—THE DISTINCTION IS IMPORTANT

Legal questions may arise even before any interrogation by the police: there may be some doubt about the legality of the arrest itself. To determine whether an arrest is legal and valid in most states, we must be familiar with the distinction between felonies and misdemeanors. The dictionary we consult will probably define felony as "a crime that is more serious than a misdemeanor." So now we look up "misdemeanor" and learn that a misdemeanor is "a crime less serious than a felony." The best way to get off this semantic merry-go-round is to overgeneralize by thinking of felonies as more serious crimes, such as murder, assault with a dangerous weapon, robbery, rape, burglary, and so on; while misdemeanors are less serious offenses, such as driving under the influence of alcohol, assault, petty larceny, and other minor crimes.

Misdemeanors are usually considered by a judge without a jury in a lower court usually called Traffic Court or District Court; whereas felonies are presided over by a judge in Superior Court, sitting with a jury that determines the facts.

The various states have different definitions covering the two types of offenses. In Massachusetts, for example, a felony is defined as a crime for which the punishment can be confinement in state's prison, and a misdemeanor is any offense calling for a sentence less than prison. Other states may make such distinctions on the basis of duration of the sentence, defining a misdemeanor as an offense calling for a jail sentence of less than a year and a felony as any other crime. Every jurisdiction regards felonies as the serious offenses and misdemeanors as the minor ones. The distinction is important in many ways, one being the law of arrest.

A VALID ARREST

In most jurisdictions, in order to have a valid arrest, the arresting officer must have authority to arrest; his words and actions must indicate a purpose to take the person into custody; and the person must be taken into custody, either actually or constructively. An easy rule of thumb is that, if the situation is such that a person cannot leave without the officer's consent, he is under arrest.

There are three basic methods of arrest: with a warrant, without a warrant, and by a summons. In most states, the summons is not really an arrest. The officer merely gives the offender the summons, a document commanding him to appear in court on a certain day to answer the charge.

Where there is an actual arrest by warrant, the officer has been authorized by some court to take into custody the person who is being charged with the crime stated in the warrant. A warrant is a document containing the order, authority or command by a court to an officer of the court to perform some act—in this case, an arrest. Few legal problems arise when arrest is made by a warrant—but such arrests are decidedly in the minority.

The usual arrest is made by a police officer without a warrant. In such a situation, the officer must have "probable cause" to believe that the person he is arresting is violating, or has violated, the law. "Probable cause" is usually understood to mean that the circumstances were such that a reasonable man would believe the arrestee was probably guilty of the crime for which he is being arrested. There is no single definition of it, and thousands of words have been written covering the philosophical and technical distinctions that legal authorities find in the phrase. It means more than mere suspicion and less than certain guilt; and the best the layman can do is to think of it as some degree of belief between the two.

There are different criteria governing the validity of an arrest without a warrant depending on whether the arrest is for a felony or for a misdemeanor. If the offense is a felony, the officer may arrest without a warrant if a felony was committed in his presence or he had reasonable grounds to believe the arrestee had committed a felony. If the offense is a misdemeanor, the officer cannot arrest without a warrant unless the offense was committed in his presence *and* it amounted to a breach of the peace. There are usually some exceptions to this general rule. Most states by statute will authorize an arrest without a warrant for various motor vehicle offenses such as driving without a license or under the influence of alcohol, shoplifting, prostitution, booking or gambling, and other crimes that may not constitute a breach of the peace. Most exceptions are based on the practical reason that there would not be time to obtain an arrest warrant in such situations.

The place to contest the legality or validity of an arrest is the courtroom, not the street. The layman who challenges the policeman's right to arrest him may find that he is "fighting city hall." When a policeman arrests someone, he usually holds all the cards; the accused has very little chance in court if it is simply his word against the policeman's. Rightly or wrongly, the judge usually assumes that the policeman is not looking for trouble and is not going out of his way to arrest an innocent person on a whim. While the judge may often rule that the person is innocent, he will rarely find that the arrest itself was illegal. The layman may win in court by quoting decisions to the judge, but he should not try his legal wings on the street by arguing with the man in blue. He starts out with two strikes against him and the judge will usually throw the third one against a "wiseacre" who has given the police officer a bad time.

The layman would do well to remember another point—not a legal one but an extremely practical one. Maybe the policeman is within his rights in arresting you and maybe he isn't—but you can bet your bottom dollar that he will be technically correct about the circumstances when the case reaches court. It's sometimes also not a bad idea to acknowledge gracefully that you may be in the wrong; maybe that's all the cop wants.

What are the consequences of an arrest? From your point of view, the best it can mean is a newspaper item and the case thrown out of court—but in most states it's an arrest on the police blotter from that point on, and it will probably involve credit reports, employment interviews, and your general reputation.

From the policeman's point of view, once an arrest has been made, he must make a formal accusation against you or run the risk of a false-arrest civil suit. So he will accuse you and he will try to make the accusation stick. In his mind you may be the one who "forced" him to do it.

Oral argument with a policeman can be foolish, but physical resistance is even worse. The person who *physically* resists an arrest may end up with a broken head and some technical legal arguments that the judge will dismiss with a wave of the hand. Most courts will take the position that, regardless of whether the arrest is technically illegal or unauthorized, the person has no right to resist physically as long as the police officer was in good faith. The point is very clear: do not resist on the street. Wait until you get to court to contest the validity of the arrest. You're probably going to lose—but at least you won't also have a broken head.

Closely allied to arrest are police practices called "threshhold inquiry" or "stop and frisk." Most states give policemen authority to stop and question all persons whom they have reason to suspect for being "abroad"; and if the answers are not satisfactory, they may arrest. "Abroad" usually refers to persons who at night are in places where they have no legitimate business or purpose—usually a stranger in a residential neighborhood. Yes, the streets are public—but the law feels that society has a right to be protected, too. As a practical matter, the person who can satisfactorily identify himself will usually have no problems, but the vagrant or the stranger with a screwdriver and a criminal record may find himself in custody.

If the police officer reasonably believes the person may have a weapon, he may detain him while he pats down the outer garments

45

of his clothing to see if he can detect it—the "stop and frisk." While the police sometimes use this legal device as an improper search, the courtroom testimony rarely identifies it as such. A full-scale search on the street occasionally shows up before the judge as a mere "frisk."

Private persons also have authority to arrest but under much more limited circumstances. Most states say that a private person may arrest someone who has *in fact* committed a felony—reasonable belief is not enough. A private person may also (like a police officer) arrest for a misdemeanor committed in his presence. He should remember that a private person arrests at his own risk.

The law of arrest has many technicalities, and the layman is well advised to shun testing any of them. He also should be aware that most states have laws requiring a private person to assist when a policeman calls on him for help in a difficult situation.

The main thing to remember about arrest is this: once arrested, you should *maintain absolute silence until your lawyer arrives.* When arrested, after giving your name, your ONLY answer to ANY question should be: "I'm glad to answer, but when I had a lawyer in an automobile case some years ago, he made me promise that I would never discuss ANY legal matter unless he was present. And I know you wouldn't want me to break that promise. So I'll answer any question you ask as soon as he's here — BUT NOT BEFORE," (that puts you in a better light than simply refusing to talk).

These are some of the many questions that arise before or during an arrest. As we will see in the next chapter, things can get even more complicated later on.

6
Your Rights after the Arrest

THERE ARE MANY QUESTIONS that may arise after an arrest, depending upon what the police did or failed to do. One question is: For identification purposes, may the police take a person's fingerprints? His clothing? Cut his hair? In general, the answer is "yes" to all those questions. After arrest, the police may take such measures for identification purposes. The courts take the position that the Fifth Amendment (regarding self-incrimination) does not apply because these are not *testimonial* communications.

The arrested person usually has certain rights that he can assert: the right to counsel, the right to a medical examination, the right to make at least one telephone call from the police station, and other rights that he may or may not have, depending upon the particular state. In addition, in most cases he has what virtually amounts to the right to be set free on reasonable bail.

SETTING BAIL

"Bail" is the system by which a defendant puts up collateral in order to obtain his freedom pending trial. The basic purpose of bail is to guarantee the defendant's presence in court when his case is called. Up until the late 1960's, the courts took many things into account in setting bail: the type of offense, the circumstances surrounding its commission, the defendant's record, the likelihood of the defendant "skipping" or showing up at the trial, the defendant's family situation, and so on. There were virtually no restraints on the judge except that bail was supposed to be reasonable and not exorbitant; but the fact is that the judge had practically unlimited discretion and his decision was rarely overturned.

The practice of setting bail was greatly abused and reforms were instituted in the late 1960's. Most of the old criteria were abandoned and the single most important question became: Will the defendant show up at the trial? If the answer was probably affirmative, very low bail was set or he was released "on his own recognizance" (legalese meaning no bail is required; his personal guarantee to appear at the trial is enough). In determining the likelihood of the defendant's appearance, certain factors are very important: Is his home here? Does he have a steady job here? Does he have dependents here? Has he always shown up in other cases? If the answers to these and similar questions are in the affirmative, the judge is supposed to set very low bail or to require no bail at all.

If bail is required, there are various ways of obtaining it. The best and least expensive way is for the defendant's family or friends to put up a house, a bankbook or actual cash as collateral. If the bail is $5,000, for example, that much cash or a bankbook with that amount is turned over to the court. When the case is over, the cash or bankbook is returned. It has not cost the owner of the bankbook anything because, of course, it continues to draw interest while it is held.

If bail is in the form of property, usually a house, the property is usually considered to be worth the difference between its fair market value and the mortgage on it. If the house would sell at $30,000 and there is a $20,000 mortgage, then the bail value of the house is $10,000. (Some courts distinguish between cash bail and property bail; such courts might require double the amount if the collateral is property instead of cash). The owners of the house merely bring their deed to court and deposit it there until the case is over. The deed is then returned to them.

The person who puts up bail gets it back when the case is concluded, regardless of its outcome. In addition, he has the right to withdraw his bail at any time before or during the trial. All he has to do is surrender the defendant to the court and say he no longer wants to go bail for him.

What if the person on bail skips? Theoretically, whatever has been put up as bail is forfeited to the state (to the extent of the bail). While forfeiture is always a possibility, of course, the fact is that the courts rarely impose such penalties. When the defendant is finally caught and in custody again, the person who put up bail can usually get it back minus something deducted for the time and trouble the state incurred in recapturing the defendant.

Professional bondsmen are available in most courts to bail out a defendant, for a price—usually either five or ten percent. If they put up $10,000 bail, they will get a fee of $500 or $1,000, depending upon the type of defendant and the bargaining powers of the people involved in the transaction. The bondsman's fee is paid in advance and he gets the whole fee regardless of the brevity of the case or its outcome.

The layman should understand bail enough to be alert to the possibility of double charges where the professional bondsman is concerned. Many cases which begin in a lower court may eventually be appealed or transferred or bound over to a higher court, and each court sets bail when the case is there. The professional bondsman may try to get a fee for putting up bail in each court, unless there is a clear understanding that the bail is for the duration of the case in both (or all) courts, and that there is to be just one fee.

A person who is incarcerated because of inability to obtain bail is entitled to a "speedy trial"—his case must be heard before those of defendants who are not confined.

"PREVENTIVE DETENTION"

The question of bail also comes up when we discuss "preventive detention," which refers to the prevention of crime by detaining a person in custody. The theory of preventive detention is that the court has good reason to believe a particular defendant is apt to commit additional crimes if allowed to be at large, so bail is set in an amount high enough to keep him confined. Experience has shown that certain defendants, notably drug pushers and robbers, accelerate their criminal activities once they have been bailed; thus, "law and order" adherents advocate preventive detention for them. The very idea is abhorrent to those civil libertarians who condemn confinement before there has been a conviction. At the present time, there seems to be no possible reconciliation of the two conflicting viewpoints.

THE RIGHT TO COUNSEL

Another question that often comes up before the trial is the right to counsel, guaranteed by the Sixth Amendment of the Constitution. The courts differ as to whether this amendment refers only to serious crimes and not to offenses that do not carry at least the possibility of a jail sentence. What happens if the defendant cannot afford counsel? In such a situation, the court will appoint an attorney

49

to represent a defendant who is "indigent." Such an attorney may be a member of some voluntary or official group such as the Defenders Committee or the Voluntary Defenders that are available in many states, or he may be a private lawyer appointed by the court to serve either with compensation (usually paid by the county) or without compensation, as a public duty.

Judges differ as to what constitutes "indigency." If the defendant has no money and no job, obviously he is indigent. If he is single and making good pay, obviously he is not indigent. An example of an indefinite area is one where the defendant has a family and a job that pays barely enough to sustain them. While it is not the only factor considered, most criminal lawyers and judges seem to believe that a defendant who can pay a professional bondsman for bail is not indigent, whether he has a job or not.

An arrested person is supposed to be advised of his various rights: to counsel, to a medical examination, to a telephone call, and so on. But what happens if the police do not advise the arrested person of these rights? Generally, the courts penalize the prosecution in some way for such failure of the police. That does not mean the case will always be thrown out; but it may mean the exclusion of any evidence that was obtained because of the failure to advise of these rights. Some courts simply dismiss the case, taking the position that the only practical way of ensuring such rights is by imposing a severe sanction against a police department that has violated them.

There are countless other rights that any accused person has as soon as he has been arrested; we have merely touched on a few of them. For example, the police line-up has been the subject of scores of cases. While the pendulum has swung back and forth between liberal and conservative courts, the basic test is always that a line-up must be "fair." If it is not, any evidence based on it will be excluded at the trial.

After a complaint or indictment has been issued against a defendant, the matter eventually winds up in the courts. Let's take a look at them.

LINEUPS MUST BE FAIR.

7
The Courts

THERE ARE TWO SOVEREIGN governments, federal and state, and each has a court system. By statute, each court is given jurisdiction, the power to hear and to decide, over certain cases. Jurisdiction may refer to geographic area or to the type of case that is to be heard. The court can redress every grievance, but you must be heard in the right court. To phrase it legalistically, you must go to a court that has jurisdiction over the particular matter. If someone has hit you over the head, you cannot get justice by going to the divorce courts. If you want a will probated, you do not go to the criminal courts; and if you are injured by the negligence of an automobile driver, you do not bring an action against him in the bankruptcy court. Each of these courts handles only cases within its own jurisdiction.

The federal and state legislatures have decided what cases will be heard by which courts, usually determined by criteria based on geography, the amount involved, the type of claim, the severity of the crime, or a combination of such factors. Jurisdiction may be original or exclusive or concurrent. If a court has original jurisdiction, it means that a particular type of case originates or begins in such place. If the jurisdiction is exclusive, it means that only that particular court may get a certain matter. Concurrent means that more than one court may have jurisdiction.

THE FEDERAL COURTS

Federal courts have jurisdiction over those cases where there is a federal question or diversity of citizenship. A federal question is involved when either a federal statute or the Constitution is concerned. There is diversity of citizenship when different states or residents of different states are parties.

The top federal court is the United States Supreme Court, consisting of nine Justices appointed for life by the President of the United States. It hears only those cases that it wants to hear. The only way a case comes before the United States Supreme Court is through a petition in which the appellant asks to have his case brought before it. If the Supreme Court decides to hear a case, it issues a Writ of Certiorari, a paper which orders the lower court to send the record up for review. The Supreme Court hears only cases of constitutional importance. The fact that the case involves millions of dollars does not mean that it qualifies; on the other hand, the fact that on its face it would seem to affect only one person does not mean it won't be heard. For example, what would seem to be a civil rights case concerning only one individual might actually result in a decision that would affect millions of persons. The Supreme Court would hear such an "unimportant" case where it might have denied certiorari in a case involving hundreds of millions of dollars. Out of 5,000 petitions for certiorari in a given year, the Supreme Court will grant less than two hundred.

The lowest court in the federal system is the United States District Court. There are some ninety-four District Courts with about four hundred judges. Do not be misled by the word "lowest" in any judicial system: often the so-called lowest court is actually the most important one in the entire system so far as the average person is concerned. The United States District Court is the federal trial court; its justices hear cases with or without a jury. Appeals from it go to the federal Court of Appeals, formerly called the Circuit Court of Appeals. These courts sit in eleven judicial districts to review cases solely on the record as they come up from the District Court. When there is reference made to any case being heard "solely on the record" it means that the Appellate Court does not hear witnesses or take other evidence, but simply decides whether the lower court was right in its decision on the testimony and evidence before it.

Those three courts—the District, the Court of Appeals, and the Supreme Court—are the backbone of the federal court system. Other federal courts are the Court of Claims (which decides cases against the government), the Court of Military Appeals, the Court of Customs, and such services or divisions in a court as the Bankruptcy Court.

Semi-judicial bodies include the Federal Trade Commission, the Federal Communications Commission, the Interstate Commerce Commission, the Securities and Exchange Commission, and similar boards and agencies.

THE STATE COURTS

The state courts are all very similar to the federal courts. The District Court usually has a limited geographic jurisdiction, handling the cases of a fairly small territorial area. In many states it is called by different titles: police court, municipal court, traffic court, and so on. In some areas it may be referred to as "low court" while the Superior Court is called "high court."

One of the best-known functions of the courts is the administration of justice in criminal cases—the trial of persons accused of having committed felonies or misdemeanors. District courts generally handle minor civil matters and criminal misdemeanors or lesser crimes. If a person is charged with assault and battery, speeding, reckless driving, driving under the influence of liquor, or other motor vehicle offenses, his case is probably going to be decided by a district court judge who sits without a jury. If the accused wants a jury, he can ask for it before the district court trial or (in some jurisdictions) appeal to a higher court where he gets a jury trial as a matter of right. The procedure differs in the different states.

The district court is generally regarded as the "people's court": it is here that the average citizen first comes in contact with the law, and first learns respect or contempt for our system of justice. It is a very important court for this reason.

The great trial court in most states is called the Superior Court, the Court of Common Pleas, or the County Court (because it usually has both civil and criminal jurisdiction of cases in an entire county or in a large geographical area in the state). It will usually be the appellate court for several district courts within its geographic area. It is in the superior court that the accused is guaranteed a jury trial; and it is here that the more serious crimes, the felonies, are tried, and the more important civil cases involving money or property.

EQUITY COURTS

Perhaps something should be inserted here about the "equity powers" of some courts, or judicial bodies, that are sometimes called Equity Courts or Courts of Chancery. This becomes a little

54

technical but, oversimplifying for the sake of better understanding, the terms refer to courts of "fairness" to prevent a situation where a strict administration of the exact rules and doctrines of law would somehow result in a conclusion that we would all regard as unfair.

In ancient days, England established Courts of Chancery to which a person could turn (in non-criminal cases) if the law did not seem to give him the chance of an adequate remedy with its available solutions. Eventually, in the evolution of the law, it was thought to be desirable to let "regular" courts do the same thing that Courts of Chancery were doing—that is, achieving fair and equitable results by new remedies when there was no specific doctrine or practice that gave "an adequate remedy at law." And so the higher courts were given "powers of equity."

For example, if A agreed to sell his land (or a unique painting) to B, but then reneged, all that B could do was sue for money damages. This really might not be "adequate" because he wanted the specific parcel of land (or the unique painting) not the money. But the courts did not have power to do any more than award money damages. Then along came the principle of equity: by court order, A could be made to transfer the specific land or item to B, because he had promised to do so, and money damages were really not an adequate remedy.

Or, your neighbor is constantly creating a nuisance that makes your life unbearable—dumping garbage on your property, running his record-player at an earsplitting level in the middle of the night, conducting all-night drunken parties in his backyard, and other such endearing conduct. His answer to your objections is: "So sue me!" He not only has no money or assets of any kind but, in addition, his conduct would require you to file so many lawsuits that you would have to spend virtually the rest of your life in court—to say nothing of your legal fees, because no lawyer would take such cases on a contingency fee basis. You really have no "adequate remedy at law," but you do have in equity. Today a court will exercise its equity powers and enjoin (order stopped) your neighbor's conduct. Translating the injunction into everyday language, the court is saying to your neighbor: "You are ordered to stop such conduct. If you disobey, you are in contempt of court. For such contempt, you will go to jail." Technically, the court is not jailing your neighbor for committing the nuisances. He will be jailed for the contempt of court he shows by disobeying the court's order.

55

While the distinction between law and equity has been largely obliterated in many jurisdictions by new rules of civil procedure, in most states only the higher courts, the superior and supreme courts, have equity powers. Before any court will invoke its powers of equity it follows a great many well-established principles called "maxims of equity," all well-founded in logic and experience. One common one is: "The petitioner must have clean hands"—he must not have been shady or underhanded in his own conduct in the particular matter. Another is: "The petitioner must not have been guilty of laches"—he must have been diligent in asserting his rights and not have "slept" on them. An essential one is: "The petitioner does not have an adequate remedy at law"—the award of only money would not really have been a remedy.

There are countless other "maxims of equity" but they are all based on fundamental principles of fairness and justice.

Over the Superior Court, and all state courts in fact, is the State Supreme Court (it may be called the Supreme Judicial Court, the Supreme Court of Errors or something similar). These courts do not generally utilize witnesses or juries; they simply decide whether the lower court committed an error of some kind.

The other state courts include the Probate Court (sometimes called the Surrogate Court, Family Court or something similar), which has jurisdiction of estates, divorces, domestic relations, and so on; the Land Court; the Juvenile Court; the Housing Court; and a flock of administrative boards such as a Commission against Discrimination, a Tax Board, a Civil Service Commission, a Public Utilities Commission, an Industrial Accident Board, and countless others. The administrative boards usually follow their own rules of procedure.

Many of the courts also have divisions or sessions or proceedings within them that have great importance; for example, the Small Claims Division, the Poor Debtor's Court, and so on. The Small Claims Court usually consists of the judges of the local court, hearing both parties without strict rules of evidence or any other formalities. There is a jurisdictional limit to the claim — something in the neighborhood of $300 or $500 or $750, depending on the particular state. While lawyers are not barred from practicing in the Small Claims Court, their appearance is frowned upon because one of the reasons for the creation of this court was to avoid legal expenses in minor matters. (But don't be surprised if a lawyer appears for your opponent.)

The Small Claims Court is intended to provide an informal hearing quickly and at little expense to the parties. All the plaintiff (the claimant, the one bringing the action) must do — in most states—is to tell his story to the Clerk, pay a small fee (less than $5 in most places), and appear at the actual hearing within a couple of weeks (unless there is a continuance, which is not unusual). The plaintiff states his case, the defendant responds, and the Judge decides—sometimes immediately and invariably within a few days—and the decision is not appealable. If you have a comparatively small claim against someone who ignores you, call up the District Court of your community and ask the Clerk about what you have to do to get action in the Small Claims Court. It is there for your convenience.

The judges of these courts are very important—and they are influenced by various legal factors, such as "the citation of authority," which we will discuss in the next chapter, and the "appointing authority," whether that is an appointive or an elective authority.

YOU DON'T NEED A LAWYER FOR EVERY CLAIM.

8
Citing Authority

CITATIONS! IN COURT, WHEN a lawyer asks the judge to rule in some way on a given point of law, the judge usually says: "Can you cite some authority to me?" What that means, in most instances, is: Can the lawyer refer to some statute passed by the legislature, or a decision made by some court, on the question? If the lawyer can, the judge probably will rule in his favor, following the sacred doctrine of *stare decisis* (to stand by decisions). So the successful lawyer anticipates questions that may bother the judge and, more important, their answers. That means he has to look up the law.

The attorney's sources are hundreds of books containing answers to legal questions: legislative enactments, judicial decisions, law journals, textbooks, treatises, and so forth. Judges are not particularly impressed by the mental processes of even the most famous lawyer. Judges want "authority"—and authority usually means something in print in some law book. So the lawyer must be intimately familiar with the lawbooks, and the layman should have at least a speaking acquaintance with the ordinary sources of authority.

What do you do if you have a legal question? Suppose, for example, that your question is: Is a parent liable for the wrongful acts of his child? Where would you find the answer in either the statutes of the legislature or in cases decided by the court? (Both of these sources are either controlling or very persuasive to any court.)

Most states have lawbooks with the answer. The statutes are collected in volumes; and so are the decisions of the courts. So you will go to such volumes, probably beginning with the index to each. But if you are going to use an index, you must have a key word.

"Is a parent liable for the wrongful acts of his child?" Well, certainly "parent" is a possible word; so is "child" or "children." It could be "liable" or "liability" or "responsibility." "Wrongful acts" might be the legal word, or "torts," which means the same thing.

So you make up a list of key words as a starting point. Turn to the index and look under each; and perhaps under one or more you may find a reference to a particular statute.

You can follow the same procedure with the law books, most of which are indexed. For example, the Commonwealth of Massachusetts has a Digest that includes references to all its judicial decisions. Its counterpart, nationally, is a set of volumes called *Annotated Law Reports*, another called *Law Reports Annotated*, and still another called *Corpus Juris*. Whatever has been decided by the highest court of any state in the United States is someplace in one or more of those volumes.

Let's take another example involving the offense of driving under the influence of liquor. What are the key words? Several come to mind: driving might be under "operating" or "motor vehicle" and liquor might be "alcohol." We could look under "crimes"—because it is a crime. What about "influence"? And so it goes—you know or guess at key words, look them up, and hope you find a reference to some decision that will be regarded as either authoritative or persuasive.

If you go to a law library, you will find hundreds of volumes of reported legal cases. The decisions of the highest court of every state are printed, bound in volumes, and sold by commercial publishing houses. A company may choose to print the cases of only one state. Such law books will refer to a case by its title—*State v. Jones*, *The People v. Jones*, or a similar heading in a criminal case, and *Smith v. Green* in a civil case—and then follows the volume and page where it may be found. For example, *State v. Jones*, 90 Vt. 26, means that the Jones case will be found in Volume 90 of the Vermont Supreme Court reports at page 26. *Smith v. Green*, 100 Ky. 93, is found at page 93 of Volume 100 of the Supreme Court reports of Kentucky.

Other commercial companies may publish reports of several states in one volume. The *Northeastern Reporter*, for example, collects the cases decided in the Supreme Courts of several northeastern states. The case cited above of *State v. Jones*, 90 Vt. 26, may also be found in 160 NE 287—which means the identical words that appear in 90 Vt. 26 will also be found in Volume 160 of the *Northeastern Reporter* at page 287. There are other publishing companies that publish cases of the southwestern states (abbreviated as SW), the western coast (abbreviated as P for Pacific), and so on.

Every state also has "Advance Sheets" composed of decisions so recent that they have not yet been published in a bound volume. The library usually will have a loose-leaf book with the "Advance Sheets" of such cases. They will be cited by year and page—for example, 1974 AS 852 will be found at page 852 of the Advance Sheets for 1974 in the particular state. Several months later those Advance Sheets will be reported in a bound volume, of course; and then the new "Advance Sheets" will be for the new year.

In a law library, you will find the cases and statutes of the entire nation separated by states. Along one wall will be some 370 volumes of Massachusetts cases, together with other books that have every statute passed by the Massachusetts Legislature. Another will have all the Kansas volumes of cases, together with the statutes passed by the Kansas Legislature. Other walls will have all the other states (in a large library; the smaller libraries will only have those of the state in which the library is located).

Another section of the library may have cases decided by the United States Supreme Court. There are several companies that publish federal reports. One lists its cases, for example, *Thomas v. Collins*. 323 U.S. 516—which of course means that case will be found at page 516 of Volume 323 of the reports of the United States Supreme Court. That same case may be found in 65 S. Ct. 315, which is the *Supreme Court Reporter*. Cases in the lower federal courts may be found in volumes reported in the *Federal Reporter*— 210 F 975.

The federal statutes, laws passed by Congress, will be found in many thick volumes called the *United States Code* (USC) or the *United States Code Annotated* (USCA), which has citations of federal cases construing or interpreting each statute.

The library will also have scores of other authorities in law: textbooks that spell out the general principles and rules of law; books that report specific points of law raised in cases in every state, giving the majority and minority viewpoints where the jurisdictions have split; law journals that clarify or criticize; books on Evidence or other specific fields of law; dictionaries; digests; treatises; articles; and so on. The layman should know that there are libraries where books are available to help him (or to further confuse him). He should know how to look up law in the legislative statutes and (if his state has a Digest) how to find cases in his state's Digest on a particular point—the Digests are well-indexed by key words. He can also read a textbook on any subject that catches his fancy although (as when reading anything in law) the layman is advised to skip philosophical discussions that wander off into hair-splitting technicalities—they are more likely to confuse than to clarify. Law dictionaries, on the other hand, are almost always helpful, and the method of using a law dictionary is the same as with any other.

"BRIEFING A CASE"

While we are on bibliography, perhaps this would be as good a place as any to discuss "briefing a case." The word "brief" has many meanings in law, as both a verb and a noun. When a lawyer appeals a case to the Supreme Court, for example, he must prepare a printed document that fully summarizes the facts of the case, the points in dispute, and the citations of authority that substantiate his position on the issues. This is one legal meaning of the word "brief" when it is used as a noun.

When lawyers use the word as a verb, in the phrase "to brief a case," they refer to the practice of explaining briefly the facts and law of a particular case. If the lawyer cites a case as his authority, the judge almost certainly will ask: "What does that case hold?" The judge wants to know what the decision was on the particular point in question, not simply that the plaintiff won or the defendant was convicted. For example, if the question is whether certain evidence is admissible or not, or if some motion should have been allowed, or whether some statement is hearsay, or any other kind of question that might arise in a trial, the lawyer should be prepared with authority to sustain his position. He will usually refer to some case in which the supreme court of his state ruled on the point. The only way the judge can know if the matter at issue is identical with that decided in the case cited is by knowing what the facts were and how the law applied to those facts in the authoritative decision. Some cases are two or three pages in length, a few fifty or more; most probably are between five and fifteen pages long. Of course the judge could read the entire case, but that is not practical: it is not only too time-consuming but, in addition, every case usually has many facets and his present interest is only in the one point at issue. So the lawyer will have "briefed" the case—that is, he will have reduced the facts to those that are meaningful for the salient point to be decided.

The usual way of briefing a case is to do it in four parts: the facts, the question or issue to be decided, the actual ruling on the point, and the reasons for the decision. Most of the time the judge will not be interested in the reasons or philosophy given in the decided case but, if he does want them, the lawyer will be prepared to answer. By "briefing" the case he can tell the judge in a minute or two whatever is necessary to understand the point decided by a case that might not be read in less than fifteen or twenty minutes.

When citing authority, the lawyer is supposed to stick to decisions of his own state supreme court or (if there is a federal question) the United States Supreme Court. Such decisions are controlling under the legal doctrine of *stare decisis*—to stand by decisions. Sometimes the particular point will not have been raised in his state and the lawyer will then look to other jurisdictions for guidance. Decisions from other jurisdictions are said to be "persuasive" but not "binding" or "controlling" because a court has to follow only decisions of its own supreme court on state issues (or the United States Supreme Court on federal issues). The effect of "foreign" decisions (those of another jurisdiction) is often determined by the nature of the states involved: so-called "liberal" or "conservative" states tend to follow their judicial counterparts.

There are books other than the statutes and digests or judicial decisions, of course; but these are the ones you begin with. Some states have statutes that are "annotated," which means that cases construing the statute are listed. This greatly simplifies your task because all the necessary information is in the same book. Massachusetts, for example, has some forty-eight volumes of annotated laws. Find the statute and, following it, you will find paragraphs giving the substance of every decision construing various sections of the particular statute.

Knowing the law is one thing; knowing the judges who will interpret it is another. The layman should know something about judges, who they are, how they ascended to the bench, and what they are like. Read on.

IT'S IN ONE OF THOSE BOOKS. ALL YA GOTTA DO IS FIND IT!

9
Know Your Judge

KNOWING THE JUDGE IS an important part of law. Sometimes this means knowing him personally. Usually it merely refers to some general knowledge of what he is like; for example, whether he is liberal or conservative, lenient or severe, or easy on some crimes and tough on others.

THE SELECTION PROCESS

Judges are selected in different ways. About eighty percent of the judges in America are elected; the remaining twenty percent are appointed. In states that appoint judges, the appointment is made by the governor with the advice and consent of an elective body, such as the state senate or (as in Massachusetts) the Executive Council. Federal judges are appointed by the President and confirmed by the Senate. As a practical matter, except for United States Supreme Court Justices, other federal judges are selected by the United States Attorney General and the United States Senator from the judge's state who is of the same political party as the President. Parenthetically, with reference to what a Supreme Court Justice's qualifications should be, the former United States Supreme Court Justice Felix Frankfurter said, "The essential qualities of a Supreme Court Justice are but three: those of the philosopher, historian, and prophet." To which Justice Brennan added, "And inordinate patience."

Actually, the qualifications of any judge differ as the court in which he sits will differ. For some courts, the personal characteristics of temperament, disposition, and general fairness can be more important than a giant intellect.

A few states, notably California and Missouri, have systems that involve a combination of appointive and elective features. California has the so-called "sitting judge" principle. A Commission on Qualifications is established, composed of a state Supreme Court Justice, the Attorney General, and the presiding judge of the court to which an appointment is to be made. The governor submits his nominee to it. If the Commission accepts, he is appointed for one year and then he may be elected for a twelve-year term. In the election, the judge's name is the only one on the ballot and is followed by a question: "Shall (name of judge) be elected?" The people decide and, theoretically, the decision is based on what kind of a judge he has been during his one-year term.

In Missouri there is a commission with a membership that differs from time to time. It might be composed of a Chief Justice, three lawyers selected by the Bar, and three citizens appointed by the governor. A procedure similar to California's is followed.

These mixed systems (appointive-elective) seem to be popular and have been successful wherever they have been tried. Experience shows that the "sitting judge" is invariably elected. In Missouri, in the thirty years between 1940 and 1970, there were 179 judicial contests and only one "sitting judge" was rejected by the voters. That particular sitting judge was narrowly defeated after he had been prominently identified with the then discredited Pendergast political machine.

The state appointing authority usually has potential nominees screened by some qualified body before officially submitting a person for confirmation as a judge. The screening body is usually a committee of the bench or officials of the Bar Association.

Federally, the practice has been to have the American Bar Association rate nominees as exceptionally well-qualified, well-qualified, qualified, or not qualified.

There are advantages and disadvantages to both the elective and the nominative systems of selecting judges. The obvious advantage of a system where judges are nominated is that they serve for life and this makes for an independent judiciary: no one can throw the judge out of office except by impeachment, a virtual impossibility. The independence of the appointed judiciary is generally recognized by everyone familiar with the courts. President Truman once said, "Packing the Supreme Court cannot be done. I've tried it and it won't work. Whenever you put a person on the Supreme Court, he ceases to be your friend." Most governors are familiar with another maxim: every time a governor appoints a judge, he makes nine enemies and one ingrate.

Having an independent judiciary is a very good thing, in general. On the other hand, if you have a "bad" judge, one who is abnormally impatient, irritable, abusive, or stupid, how do you get rid of him? Another advantage, theoretically at least, is that the person selecting the judge knows what qualifications are necessary and makes sure that any judge named or confirmed is well-qualified.

The obvious advantage of elective judges is that if you have a poor judge, the people can throw him out of office (with or without a good reason). Of course they can do the same to a "good" judge. The obvious disadvantage is that a completely unqualified person may become a judge under strictly political considerations. One criticism of elective judges was made by California's Chief Justice Traynor: "The greatest single improvement of the administration of justice would be to get rid of popular elections of judges."

MANEUVERING TO GET A "FAVORABLE" JUDGE

The layman should understand that trial lawyers (those who go to court—most lawyers do not) try very hard to see that their clients have a "fair" judge. To the lawyer and his client, that means the judge who is most likely to see things their way or to be lenient in sentencing. For example, the cautious lawyer knows that Judge A is easy on forgery cases but very rough on rapists; that Judge B is a soft touch for a woman who cries but is hard on a juvenile who stabs someone; that Judge C is a stickler for making the prosecution prove every single item but hands out severe sentences; whereas Judge D allows everything in evidence but is compassionate in sentencing. Such knowledge is often the reason why lawyers seek continuances, trying to avoid one judge or hoping to get another.

This knowledge of judges applies in offering a plea of guilty as well as in determining when to go to trial. Maneuvering to get a favorable judge is generally accepted by both bench and bar as one of the arts in the kit of an able defense attorney. "Favorable" judge does not mean anything sinister: lawyers use the term to refer to an honest judge who has general leanings one way or the other, without regard to who the lawyers or parties may be. As we pointed out earlier, judges are human. A good lawyer not only knows the law; he also knows some of the characteristics of the human beings who administer the law. And the layman will not understand the law unless he, too, is aware of them.

66

There are other important people around the judge who may play very important parts in whatever sentence the judge decides to give a defendant. The judge may consult with the probation officer; he may also want to have the recommendation of the District Attorney or even some member of the police department who was in charge of the case. In informal bench conferences, the clerk of the court may also give his advice. In addition, even the attitude of the court officers and stenographer may come to the judge's attention. A capable defense attorney always tries to get the probation officer on his side, and he does well if he manages to give the clerk a favorable attitude, too. It may not do any good, but it certainly doesn't do any harm.

We've been discussing judges in relation to criminal cases; they also sit in civil matters, of course. Let's look at a civil suit.

THE LAW IS WHAT HE SEZ IT IS.

10
The Drama Begins:
The Civil Suit

A COMMON QUESTION ON any set of facts is: Can a person sue for that? We must remember that a person can sue for *anything*. The question should be, will a person probably win in a suit for that?

The layman should know that there are specialists in law just as there are in medicine or any other profession. He should find out in what field, if any, a lawyer specializes, and choose one who is best suited to his needs.

There is a great deal more to a legal claim, case or law suit than we learn from television or the movies. We've all seen Perry Mason investigate his cases and then win them during the preliminary hearing when the real criminal confesses in open court. Perry Mason is investigator, father figure, and romantic interest—the average lawyer is very seldom any of those things. Practically no lawyer investigates his own cases. Usually there is no investigation, but a private investigating firm may be hired for the most important cases promising large fees. We know about the trial itself, but the trial often comes months or even years after the events that caused it. What goes on in the meantime?

In the meantime is when the lawyer does most of his work. The facts that eventually give rise to a trial: the crime itself, the accident, the breach of contract, whatever is the reason for the parties to be in a courtroom—this "happening" and the trial itself are separated by months during which the lawyer puts in countless hours on various matters in which the client plays almost no role.

SETTLING OUT OF COURT

There usually is some form of communication—correspondence, telephone calls, personal meetings—between your side and the other side. Lawyers don't just begin lawsuits. They discuss, negotiate, write, and talk about all the possibilities of settling out of court. Talk is the lawyer's stock in trade.

Next, lawyers procrastinate. They may not all excel in oratory or legal knowledge, but every single one of them excels in the art of procrastination. And, no joke intended, procrastination itself takes time. Lawyers spend a great many hours explaining why they are busy, why they have not called or written, and why they will call you next week with some news about the case.

Lawyers also investigate—but not like the real investigator or private eye. They collect information or facts that will have a bearing on the outcome of the case. For example, in an automobile accident case a lawyer will usually look at the police report of the collision, get names of witnesses, and talk to those witnesses. He will also try to get a letter from the doctor spelling out the specific injuries and the type and length of incapacity of the patient. With many doctors, the lawyer will spend quite a lot of time just trying to get a detailed report that will be helpful in talking about a possible settlement. Most doctors eventually cooperate and most lawyers protect the doctor's fee by paying it out of the settlement before the patient-client gets his money.

Incidentally, most doctors prefer or even insist on the lawyer's protection of their fee in cases where there is not full insurance coverage. Otherwise they often would not be paid or would be bargained down by the patient. Also, some unethical doctors build up a case, which usually meets with the patient's approval—the more serious the injury appears, and the bigger the doctor's bill, the bigger the settlement. However, after the settlement, the patient often wants to pay the doctor only for actual visits—say three, instead of the fifteen that were presented to the insurance company. Doctors who engage in such illegal practices usually think it is highly unethical for patients to quibble about paying for fictitious visits. The lawyer has fee problems only in criminal cases. He either gets paid on the line before the case or he doesn't get paid. There are exceptions, of course, but the usual criminal who is willing to rob or cheat anyone does not make an exception of his lawyer.

69

In any case, lawyers do some investigating of the facts, even though often they are the least important part of the case. The lawyer must also check out the law to see how it applies to those facts. The statutes, the Supreme Court decisions, court rules, dictionaries, *Corpus Juris* and other digests, law journals, and all the rest that we discussed in Chapter 8 come into the action here. Usually there is some point of law that the attorney must ascertain. Possibly the lawyer has to spend a good deal of time looking up the law. If it is an important case, he wants to; if the case is not important, he may have to anyway—he has both his pride and a possibly angry client to contend with.

If the case is settled fairly quickly, the lawyer probably has not made much more than a scanty investigation: a few telephone calls, and maybe a couple of personal conferences. But suppose the case is going to court? Now the details begin—and these are details of which the client has virtually no knowledge at all.

"WE'LL SUE"

For example, let us look at a civil case—one in which the client is suing someone for money damages. Someone struck you with an automobile, or damaged your property by trespass, or broke a contract with you, or refuses to repay a loan. The lawyer has investigated, talked, procrastinated, and done all the things a lawyer does before he formally begins a lawsuit, but your stubborn and unreasonable opponent won't give in to your determined and reasonable efforts to achieve justice. The lawyer says to you: "We'll sue." What happens next? You wait. You telephone the lawyer, and wait ... and stop in at the lawyer's office and wait some more. While you are waiting, the lawyer is preparing something called a writ—a formal document that is the authorization by the court to begin suit, and which gives notification of the fact of suit. The writ is given to an impartial person to serve on the defendant (the person sued). The server is usually an officer of the court called a sheriff or constable. When he has handed it to the other party or left it at his usual place of residence, he signs a writ attesting to the fact that it has been properly served. The point is to make sure the defendant is aware of the fact that he is being sued, in what court, for what reason, and how much time he has to get a lawyer to answer the suit or take whatever action he wishes.

Your lawyer now prepares a legal pleading. A pleading is any paper filed in court in a given matter. The first pleading is usually called a declaration, complaint or petition that spells out in great detail the exact reason for the writ. It may take several paragraphs to say what might be boiled down to something like this: Whereas the plaintiff was carefully walking where he had a right to be, the defendant carelessly ran over him, causing the plaintiff injury and expense—Wherefore the plaintiff wants the defendant to pay him for it. But of course no legal document can be so oversimplified. Not because lawyers prefer five-syllable words and lengthy sentences (which they may) but because the law requires that the defendant be told exactly and specifically with what he is charged so that he may properly defend himself. The writ and the declaration (petition, complaint) must be filed in the proper court—that is, the court having jurisdiction over the matter to be decided.

The defendant may answer by denying everything, or by admitting something but explaining, or by admitting everything but saying the writ was brought too late or in the wrong court or does not properly charge him with anything. Or he may counter-claim that the plaintiff has wronged the defendant in some way, or say both parties were at fault.

There can be interrogatories filed by either party asking for more details about the cause of action: "When did you first see the defendant's automobile?" "Where was it?" "What did you do when it was fifty feet away?" "What did you do just before the impact?"

In addition, there usually are Bills of Particulars or Motions for Specifications, which ask the parties to describe or specify exactly what took place. There may be various requests by both parties asking the court to extend the time for doing certain things. And there are often Affidavits—sworn written statements—that by rules of court have to accompany many of the documents. For example, the lawyer may have to swear to the fact that he did actually perform some act he has referred to in some paper he filed in court.

There can be literally scores of legal papers filed by either side—and every paper filed usually calls for an answering paper from the other side. The entry of a lawsuit brings forth a veritable snowstorm of legal documents. And some of those filings are followed by hearings before the judge on whether or not certain motions will be allowed or denied.

The client himself knows little about the work the lawyer does on "discovery"—which is the name for the overall legal procedure by which each side finds out something of the merits of the other side's case. In addition to the various pleadings, there may be depositions

71

taken: witnesses are called into the office, put under oath, interrogated before a stenographer, and their testimony transcribed. They have been deposed, in legal terminology, and these depositions may or may not be admissible in the court hearing at some future date. All these activities are part of the "representation" that the client is getting for the fee his lawyer eventually receives. The client should remember that in all contingency cases (and in many other cases, too) the lawyer may put in time and effort without payment if the case is lost.

So between the beginning of the lawsuit and the actual trial itself, the lawyer works, doing the things that need to be done to earn his fee. There may be times when he gets well paid for doing very little (like a real estate agent who sells a $50,000 home with one telephone call) but they are the exceptions—most of the time he earns whatever he receives.

LAWYERS' FEES

What do lawyers charge for their services? The charge might go all the way from nothing to thousands of dollars, depending upon the type of case and the lawyer. But lawyers who handle the same kind of business are apt to charge about the same fee. The lawyer needed by the average layman—not a businessman or a corporation executive—is apt to be someone handling a case involving divorce, an automobile accident, or a minor criminal offense (for example, drunken driving, assault and battery or shoplifting). Bar Associations usually have minimum fee schedules (which may have been outlawed by the time you read this) or a general pattern of fees followed by their membership. If it's a case where you are probably going to recover something but the amount is uncertain (the usual situation in an automobile accident or Workmen's Compensation case), the lawyer is probably going to be working on a contingency basis: he gets a percentage of the recovery if you win and nothing if you lose. The fee in such negligence cases will almost certainly be no lower than twenty-five percent or higher than fifty percent, and probably will be between thirty and forty percent, depending on whether it is settled out of court or actually tried. In an industrial accident case, the fee will be about fifteen or twenty percent and probably will be subject to the approval of an Industrial Accident Board (or whatever the agency may be called). These percentages may seem high but, in most cases, the lawyer is worth it because he is able to get you a better settlement than you could get yourself. Laymen should guess at this fact if insurance adjustors advise them to handle a case without a lawyer. Their reason is that a lawyer can make the insurance company pay more.

The simple, uncontested divorce case, probably runs from $150 to $500. If it really is simple and uncontested, any lawyer will do. If it is a contested case, or if much property is involved, of course the fees are higher—and it is important that you have a *good* lawyer.

Criminal cases are usually handled by "criminal lawyers"—and they are accustomed to being paid in advance. The lawyers practicing criminal law may either overcharge or undercharge. It is more important to select a criminal lawyer who knows the judge than one who knows the law. Knowing the judge usually means only that the judge has a friendly feeling towards your lawyer. Traffic courts are apt to be places where personal bias plays a strong part. If a case is going to an appellate court, it's a different story: it is usually more important to have a lawyer who has genuine ability.

In general, lawyers are men and women of honor and integrity. The layman can rely on those qualities in the average lawyer. There are exceptions, of course—but that's also true of bankers, plumbers, contractors, carpenters, doctors, or any other profession or occupation. If you are not satisfied with your lawyer's performance, discuss it with him frankly. If you are really being swindled or overcharged in some way, he probably will adjust it; if you are still not satisfied, you can always go to the grievance committee of the Bar Association.

The layman should have some general idea of the fees lawyers charge and what they do to earn those fees. You don't have to know everything your lawyer is doing, but you should at least be aware of some of the things he *may* be doing between the time he gets the case and the time it is decided. Such knowledge is helpful to both the lawyer and his client.

Incidentally, many laymen are afraid to ask a lawyer for advice for fear that merely talking to one may be overly expensive. Such fears are usually groundless, but it is not difficult to investigate. Pick a name out of the yellow pages (under "attorney"), telephone the lawyer, and say: "I don't know if I have a matter where I need a lawyer or not. Will I have to pay you a fee merely for outlining the facts to see if you believe I do have a possible claim?"

One caveat: you probably should not bother a large law firm with such a request. They have to be fairly impersonal, and you might not get past a secretary.

"SUBSTANTIVE" V. "PROCEDURAL" LAW

In discussions of either civil or criminal law we sometimes hear about "substantive law" and "procedural law." What do those terms mean? In general, substantive law is the doctrine or goal, and procedural law is the means or methods by which we enforce that doctrine or arrive at that goal.

Procedural law refers to the method of enforcing rights; it is the machinery for carrying on a lawsuit; it is the procedure by which a legal right is enforced. The substantive law gives a right, and the procedure puts it into effect.

Substantive law is that part of law that creates and defines rights. For example, the Fourth Amendment has substantive law which creates your right of privacy or freedom from illegal search. The procedure by which you enforce that right is the filing of a Motion to Suppress (prevent the use) of any evidence taken in violation of that right.

The papers filed in court (the pleadings) and the steps a litigant takes (appeals, objections, exceptions, etc.) are examples of procedural steps.

Lawyers practice criminal law as well as civil law. Civil practice usually pays the most—but criminal law is the form you see portrayed on television. It's dramatic and filled with human interest, and is the subject of the next chapter.

I WAS MY OWN LAWYER!

11
Criminal Law

THERE ARE MANY DEFINITIONS of a crime but they all
indicate that it is an act which injures the public, or injures an individual and so ultimately the public. Some authorities describe it
as a social harm defined by law and punishable. Crimes are acts
that are *malum in se*—bad in themselves, such as rape or burglary
or murder—or *malum prohibitum*—bad only because some legislative body has so declared it, such as jaywalking or selling liquor
after hours. Crimes are also distinguished as misdemeanors (minor
infractions) and felonies (serious offenses).

Most states treat the same acts as crimes and the penalties prescribed by legislation are comparable. To be an unlawful act the
prosecution must usually prove the defendant had a general
criminal intent. While this is not true of every crime, it is the
general rule that the accused must have intended the wrongful act.
There are also some cases where what is known as a *specific* intent
must be proven: these are usually cases where the statute defining
the crime says it must have been done willfully or with intent to
defraud or some other specific intent.

Every crime except (in most states) murder is subject to a Statute
of Limitations, which means that if the person who committed the
crime is not charged with it before a certain time he cannot be
prosecuted. The usual time limits are ten years for serious offenses
and something less than that for minor ones. The time that an accused is out of state is excluded in counting the years.

The procedure by which the accused is "brought to bar"
(brought into court) differs in different states and, in the same
state, differs according to the seriousness of the offense. In minor
crimes, the case is usually begun by complaining to the clerk of

75

court. In serious crimes, it is begun by an indictment by the Grand Jury in those states (mostly eastern) that have the Grand Jury system; while other states may have the system of the prosecutor filing an information before a judge.

THE GRAND JURY

The Grand Jury meets in secret and its deliberations cannot be revealed. The only evidence heard is that presented by the prosecution. The defendant has no right to be present, to hear the evidence, or to examine the witnesses. As a practical matter, there are no rules of evidence to prevent hearsay, opinion or anything that might be immaterial, irrelevant, and incompetent. If there are any questions the Grand Jury wants answered or interpreted, the members look to the prosecuting attorney for guidance.

The function of the Grand Jury is not to hear both sides of the case—that is reserved for the trial itself—but merely to decide whether the accused should be put on trial. For that reason, the Grand Jury hears only what the prosecution wants to present, and the person being accused has no rights of any kind. (The practice has been thus up to 1975; but the increased public knowledge generated by the indictment of former Vice President Spiro Agnew may bring some changes in the system.) If the majority of members of the Grand Jury believe the person should be tried, they return a "true bill"; if they feel otherwise, they return a "no bill."

There are both advantages and disadvantages to the Grand Jury system. The favorable arguments usually cited are its secrecy and the broad scope of investigations it can make. The unfavorable arguments usually are that it can be a rubber stamp for the prosecuting attorney and that it follows no rules of evidence to protect an accused. While it is true that the Grand Jury almost certainly will do whatever the prosecuting attorney wishes, the fact is that in ninety-five percent of the cases the prosecuting attorney does not really care whether the Grand Jury indicts or not. The prosecutor feels he has done his duty once he's presented the evidence to the Grand Jury—then it's up to the Grand Jurors.

Many of the "defects" in the Grand Jury system could be easily eliminated by the Grand Jurors themselves if they fully understood their own powers. Of their own motion, they have the right to call any witnesses they want to hear, they may insist that only legally admissible evidence be considered, and they may even order the prosecutor from the room or request a new prosecutor. In brief,

IT'S FAIR...EXCEPT YOU DON'T HAVE ANY RIGHTS OF COURSE!

they are really "the bosses"—within their legal authority, of course. Most Grand Jurors do not fully understand the tremendous powers they enjoy—and you may be sure that very few prosecutors remind them of those powers. If you ever serve as a Grand Juror, you should be aware of the authority given you by the law: you may not want to use all these powers but you should at least know of them.

Before the trial the defendant is called on to plead. Besides the usual pleas of guilty or not guilty, there is another one sometimes available called *nolo* or *nolo contendere*. These are Latin words that mean "I do not wish to contest." Such a plea is usually interpreted as an implied confession of guilt although it does not create the type of criminal record that can be used against the person in most instances. It is discretionary with the judge to accept or refuse a plea of nolo—and judges customarily do not accept it if the defendant has a previous record or if the charge is a serious one.

Some courts have the practice of continuing a case "without a finding" if the defendant has no record and the case is a minor one. Again, this is discretionary with the court. It has all the deterrent effects of a sentence of probation or suspended sentence but still saves the defendant from having a criminal conviction on his record. The judge merely says that the case will be continued without a finding for six months or a year and, if at the end of that time the defendant has not been in any trouble, the case is then dismissed.

PLEA BARGAINING

The subject of plea bargaining comes up whenever the matter of pleas by a criminal defendant is discussed. Plea bargaining is part of virtually every criminal case. There are two general types: one, where defense counsel and the prosecuting attorney merely decide on the length of sentence the prosecuting attorney will recommend if the defendant pleads guilty to the charge; the other, where the defendant agrees to plead guilty to a lesser crime. In this latter type, someone accused of possession of drugs with intent to sell (a felony) may agree to plead guilty to simple possession (a misdemeanor). Or someone charged with assault with a dangerous weapon (a felony) might agree to plead guilty to a simple assault (a misdemeanor).

Although there are many arguments for and against the practice, plea bargaining is engaged in either officially or unofficially in every court in the nation. It unquestionably eases congestion in the courts; and, equally unquestionably, it sometimes leads defendants to plead guilty to offenses they have not committed.

GRANTING IMMUNITY

Plea bargaining often involves something called "immunity," which dictionaries define as "freedom or exemption from some charge or duty." In law, the granting of immunity is a practice engaged in by practically every prosecuting attorney in the country, sometimes under the authority of a statute and sometimes not. Immunity may be offered formally or informally. In the informal type, the prosecutor either tells the defendant (or his attorney) that he will not prosecute or else broadly hints that he will not. In the formal type, the prosecutor has a grant of immunity approved by the court through whatever procedures are provided by the law of the particular jurisdiction.

The usual reason for granting immunity is to obtain something that the prosecution wants. It may be one element of plea bargaining and concern only the defendant himself. More often, it is to obtain testimony against another defendant.

Those who favor the use of immunity as a tool in the prosecutor's kit point out that often convictions could not be obtained without it. They also stress the fact that some jurisdictions apply various safeguards to prevent its misuse or limit it to cases involving organized crime.

Opponents of the practice of granting immunity say that when it is exchanged for testimony, the transaction looks very much like a form of legal bribery: the defendant is given years off a possible sentence in return for testifying in support of the prosecution's case against some other person. They reason that if a defense attorney offered the person $5,000 in return for favorable testimony, it would be a crime that would subject the lawyer to both disbarment and a prison sentence. But if a prosecuting attorney offers the person freedom instead of five years in prison (certainly a far greater inducement than $5,000) it is perfectly proper and is not considered either illegal or unethical. In fact, the granting of immunity is accepted by the public as a normal and customary part of the judicial scene.

Of course we must remember that the person who testifies has no "immunity" against a charge of perjury if he testified falsely—and the witness's knowledge of that risk is supposedly a safeguard against perjured testimony. But how much of a safeguard is it?

79

Realistically, the witness knows that the testimony being given is that desired by the prosecutor; and, practically speaking, the prosecutor is the one who decides whether or not it is perjury. The possibility of a perjury charge doesn't seem like an infallible safeguard of truth.

Opponents of immunity also say it may result in unjust convictions through perjury. They argue that, obviously, the prosecution is not going to grant immunity unless the testimony to be given is favorable to the prosecution's viewpoint. When the stakes are years in prison or freedom, the person being given immunity is certainly under tremendous temptation to testify to whatever the prosecution wants. Certainly the defense is in no position to even attempt to match the prosecution's offer. Obviously, the person being offered immunity knows what the prosecution wants, and that there will be no immunity without the desired testimony.

The truly basic argument against the practice of granting immunity is that it really erodes or circumvents the Fifth Amendment. It is in derogation of the right against self-incrimination because it compels a person to testify even if he does not want to. It can force him to admit to the commission of a crime, or complicity in it, even if he wants to avail himself of the Fifth Amendment's guarantee that he does not have to incriminate himself. True, he may not be prosecuted for it; but it is equally true that his admissions may degrade him in the eyes of his neighbors, brand him a criminal or scoundrel, cost him his job or hurt him economically, and subject him to ridicule, scorn, ostracism or other forms of social punishment. The law's punishment is often not nearly so severe as the sanctions that can be imposed by society itself. And there can be no grant of immunity from such a judgment.

Whatever be the merits of a position for or against immunity, one thing is certain: it is both a dangerous and a powerful weapon in the prosecutor's arsenal.

Before the trial itself, there may be motions filed by the defendant in which he asks for further information, asks to examine some of the prosecution's proof or to suppress evidence that he alleges was illegally obtained, questions the validity of the indictment, or seeks other relief that he believes will be helpful to him. There can be countless motions and often there are. Only after they have been disposed of, does the trial begin. (We will look at trial procedure in the next chapter.)

POSSIBLE DEFENSES

There are many possible defenses in any criminal case, but as a practical matter the most common one is the question of identification: Is the defendant the person who held up the bank, raped the girl, burglarized the house, sold the drugs or committed the murder? The question of identification is the major one in a trial where there is no doubt that a crime was committed and the only question is by whom.

Other crimes may not involve the question of identification, but the defense may be simply that no offense was committed. The defendant was driving the car but was not under the influence of liquor; the defendant did not commit rape because the girl consented; the defendant was operating the motor vehicle but did not drive recklessly; the defendant published the book but it was not pornographic; and so on. In other words, there was no crime committed.

Sometimes there are specific defenses: self-defense; temporary insanity, where the defendant did commit the act but was not sane at the time; entrapment, where the defendant did sell the illegal drug but was persuaded to do so by the policeman; consent, where the defendant did have intercourse with the girl but she was of legal age and was willing; license, where the defendant was carrying a gun but had a permit to do so; double jeopardy, where the defendant did commit the crime but had been tried for it once before; alibi, where the defendant does not contest the fact that a crime was committed but claims he was someplace else at the time; and so on. There are many defenses and one or more may be presented at the trial.

The layman should understand that the law gives the accused person both advantages and disadvantages. He is given the protective shield of the presumption of innocence—but the prosecution is given the sword of the legal maxim that ignorance of the law is no defense. Everyone is presumed to know the law. The prosecution must prove its case beyond a reasonable doubt (as compared to a mere preponderance of the evidence in a civil case)—but the defendant acts at his peril when he refuses to answer a *prima facie* case against him. The individual feels secure in the assurance that the language of criminal statutes must be clear and understandable, they are to be interpreted favorably to the accused whenever there is a question of meaning, and the defendant does not have to incriminate himself or testify in court—but, practically speaking, statutes almost invariably are clear and certain, there are few accusations without proof, and juries look with cynical skepticism on a defendant who refuses to take the witness stand.

The layman should realize that, with all the hedges and constitutional rights that protect the defendant from punishment, the basic aim of the law is to protect *all* of society, not just the transgressor. While it is all right for anyone to rely on the law for his protection, he had better assume that society can also rely on the law for its own protection. The layman who really understands the law will also understand that whoever violates it is very likely to be caught, convicted, and punished. We all hear about the fellow who "gets away with it"—but such a lucky person is almost invariably "the other fellow."

The average person does not get accused of murder, rape, robbery, and such serious offenses, so there is no need for him to prepare for such accusations. But he may flirt with the possibility of legal charges involving his automobile in complaints of illegal parking, drunken driving, and other traffic violations.

TRAFFIC VIOLATIONS

The owner of an automobile is usually faced with a statute that says the owner is presumed to be the driver or person in control of it. How else could authorities hold a person responsible for damage done by a motor vehicle which disappeared after an accident? So state legislatures always pass statutes that say the owner is presumed to have been the driver unless he can prove the contrary.

In parking ticket situations, the police do not know who actually parked a car near a hydrant. Again, most states have a statute that calls for the owner to pay the parking ticket, on the presumption that the owner was the violator unless he can prove the contrary. The point to the car owner who loans his vehicle to a friend is, if his friend parks it in the wrong place, the owner gets the ticket unless his friend comes into court, accepts the blame, and pays the fine himself.

DRUNKEN DRIVING

Driving under the influence of liquor is a common hazard. Proving the offense is not particularly difficult and the evidence does not need to be nearly as great or as clear as the layman might imagine. In most states, the only proof required is that the driver was "under the influence" of alcohol, not that he was drunk or even tipsy. And the driving must have been on a "public way" or a place to which the public has a "right of access." Usually there's an agreement by counsel that the street or place was of this nature, or there is testimony of its use or character. That phase of the proof essential to a conviction is not too difficult.

On the question of sobriety, over the years judges have said such things as: "Imbibing any amount of alcohol is sufficient for conviction *if it affected his driving* to even the slightest degree." One drink (or even less) might conceivably cause the driver's downfall. The test was whether the person's driving had been affected by the imbibing of *any* amount of alcohol. If so, even though the effect was slight, then he was driving "under the influence" of alcohol.

Before the days of scientific analysis by breathalyzers and similar inventions, the usual testimony was merely the observations of a police officer that the driver staggered, was not coherent in speech, had glassy eyes, or an odor of alcohol, along with the officer's opinion that from those observations he had concluded that the accused was "under the influence." The officer could freely admit that the accused was not "drunk"—the conviction would be had for merely being "under the influence."

Didn't this mean that the accused was often convicted on such flimsy evidence as mere opinion? Certainly, and that was often the case. It is still the situation even after the arrival of the breathalyzer and its brethren.

Today some scientific gadget is the main witness in most states. The statutes differ as to the degree of alcoholic content it must show in the blood or lungs, or other physical evidence, but they all have some standard below which it is presumed the person is sober and above which it is presumed he is under the influence of alcohol. Such scientific inventions as the breathalyzer may thus be either helpful or harmful to an accused person. Another point that is often not understood is that the very existence of such scientific instruments also has a bearing. Most state statutes will provide, for example, that the mere refusal to take a breathalyzer test is justification for suspending the driver's license. The Supreme Judicial Court of Massachusetts ruled that such a statute is constitutional and does not constitute coercion or involuntary self-incrimination.

The layman should understand that driving under the influence of liquor is not too difficult for the police to prove in court. And even if the proof fails, the Registry of Motor Vehicles usually has "discretion" to suspend or revoke a driver's license on nothing more than the accusation. True, that usually is not done—but it can be in most states. Practically speaking, once something is within the realm of "discretion," the courts usually will not overrule the action taken. If there is a conviction in court, most states have laws making it mandatory to suspend all driving privileges for a long period of time. Don't be misled by stories that some influential politician can "take care" of it—you will hear such rumors but you will never find any driver who succeeded in finding such a person.

The layman should also remember that many states have laws, rules and regulations written by a department supervising the operation of motor vehicles which prohibit driving after drinking. That means that the person does not even have to be under the influence of alcohol: if he had any liquor and then drove his car, it's driving after drinking. The laws are harsh, but not as harsh as the statistics showing there are over 55,000 deaths a year caused by drunken driving.

There is a much more recent offense, usually called "driving under the influence of narcotics." The law on these cases has not been interpreted or ruled on to the same extent as driving under the influence of alcohol (which is also a drug but usually considered in a different category than all other drugs). The laws on driving under the influence of a narcotic drug are in the process of being enacted, evaluated, and amended—but, in the final analysis, they will be treated virtually identically with alcohol. Today the method of proof differs. We can't "smell" many drugs, there's no practical "narcotics breathalyzer," and courts don't accept a layman's opinion as they do regarding sobriety. However, it will not be long before simple methods of proof will have been devised. In the meantime, the layman should understand that driving under the influence of alcohol or any other drug is a risk to be avoided at all costs if he wants to keep his driver's license. Taking a cab is expensive, but losing a driver's license is costlier and he positively cannot afford that.

ASSAULT AND BATTERY

Another crime that may confront many laymen is assault and battery, often designated as assault. Assault is the unlawful threat to use force against another, or the actual unlawful striking of another. (The definition and the examples given here are oversimplified in the interests of clarification but they will illustrate the type of case that may involve the average person.) Assault can be, for example, "taking a poke" at someone who has insulted you or your girl or wife. The law says that no one can strike another except in self-defense. That means that the other person must swing at you first; and even then you can only retaliate to the extent necessary to defend or protect yourself.

Imagine that you are walking with your best girl, who is a respectable young lady. As you pass the corner where some fellows are standing, one says: "Hey, how come you take out a prostitute like her? Everybody's slept with her!" The insult is surely sufficient provocation to punch him in the nose, you feel, and you do just that. In legal language, you have committed an assault and battery upon the person of another.

Probably most of us would agree that the application of force by you in the form of a fist is not only reasonable and justifiable but is salutary in general. Yes, probably as human beings we will so agree—but the law does not. The law says, "Mere words, no matter how insulting or provoking, do not justify the use of force." Let me hasten to add that, while your punching the corner scoundrel constitutes assault and battery legally and technically, the average jury probably would not convict a defendant so accused. Jurors usually follow the law as given to them in instructions by the judge, but they also often follow the dictates of common sense, decency and even gallantry. You should understand that there is virtually never any excuse for the use of physical force except in self-defense; and that mere words, however vile or abusive, do not constitute justification. That is the law *technically*, even though it may not always be followed as a practical matter.

DISTURBING THE PEACE

Another common crime is "disturbing the peace." This consists of behavior that disturbs or annoys other law-abiding citizens. It includes unruly behavior, public drunkenness accompanied by noise, fighting or brawling that causes a disturbance, committing a nuisance, awakening people by shouting in the middle of the night, and similar conduct that interferes with the tranquility of the public.

Charges of "assault and battery" or "disturbing the peace" may also confront the person who does not move along when a policeman tells him to. The corner loafer who "insults" a minion of the law may find in court that his whispered word "pig" has been

85

transformed into shouted obscenities. The man in blue knows the law and he knows what charges are technically accurate. Usually he is not going to take insults or abuse simply because there is no statute that forbids such conduct, and so technical charges of assault and battery or disturbing the peace may be brought even though the actual incident did not constitute either. It is well to know more than the technical definitions of certain crimes that can be hauled out of the policeman's arrest bag. Refusal to move along may not be a crime, but assault and battery or disturbing the peace are. The moral to the layman is: don't press your luck. If a policeman tells you to move, don't quote the lawbooks. They may be right and the policeman wrong but your lawbooks don't testify in court.

RECEIVING STOLEN PROPERTY

A crime that has become more common (as shoplifting becomes more prevalent) is receiving stolen property. The gist of this offense is that the accused received property with knowledge that it was stolen. It's easy to prove the item was stolen—but how does the prosecution establish that the recipient knew it was stolen? It's really not all that difficult: it's done by inference. All the prosecution must do is to show facts from which it can reasonably be inferred that the receiver must have known the article was stolen.

If you buy a $200 television set for $50, you're on thin ice. Why should a truck driver sell you a brand new refrigerator for twenty-five percent of its cost in any store? Shouldn't you be suspicious of the youngster who wants to sell you for $35 a brand new record-player that costs over $150 in any store? If you buy an item you suspect is "hot," you're flirting with a charge of knowingly receiving stolen property—the "knowingly" being inferred from the circumstances.

TRESPASS

Another crime that has often confronted college students in recent times is trespass: being on someone else's property without permission. The mere fact that the person has a right to be on college property does not mean he has a right to be everyplace within the campus boundaries. There is not much question of his right to be in assigned classes at scheduled times, in the library when it's open, in the dormitories, on the grounds of the campus itself, and similar places that all of us would probably assume were within the lawful rights of any student of the institution. The same would be

86

true of his right to visit the office of faculty or administrative officials during business hours. But it would be unreasonable to think that the student could go into the president's office or official bathroom whenever he wanted to simply because it was part of the educational institution in which he was a duly authorized and accredited student. The right to be someplace on the campus is qualified by the rights of others, as is true in every other legal situation. If a student insists on entering some educational office without permission, or at a time other than during regular hours, or in violation of some other reasonable restriction, it is trespass. And of course, "occupying" by force is invariably so interpreted, too.

Trespass is not ordinarily a serious crime, but it can be both a crime and a civil wrong. A "trespasser" never has as much protection in the law as a person who is not violating some rule or custom. Most states have laws or decisions that distinguish between trespassers and non-trespassers. The latter may be classified as invitees, social guests, and licensees. These distinctions can become extremely technical. Perhaps a sufficient rule of thumb, so far as legal rights are concerned, is that the trespasser is at the bottom of the totem pole, the invitee at the top, and the social guest, licensee, or business invitee somewhere in between. The owner of the premises owes a different duty to each (in most states) depending upon the category into which the person falls; and there are shadings and distinctions even within the category itself. The best we can do is to understand that there are such differences and to examine the circumstances of the particular case and explore the possible liability of the owner under each—but keeping in mind that the law is in the process of change in this whole area.

The definitions of these terms are not uniform and the degree of care to be exercised by the owner of the premises may vary in different jurisdictions. A "trespasser" is someone who is on the premises without consent or authorization of any kind. (That statement gets watered down when we acknowledge that the trend of the law is to hold that a person who makes an unintentional and non-negligent entry on the land of another is not a trespasser.) Certainly a tramp and a burglar are both trespassers, and *maybe* a youngster playing on the premises is, too. In any event, the owner of the premises is usually responsible to a "trespasser" only for willful, wanton or reckless conduct.

A "guest" is there for social purposes, and the host or owner is responsible for "gross" negligence. We think of gross negligence as

87

some lack of care between ordinary negligence and willful, wanton or reckless conduct. The golfing partner and the friend who drops in are usually social guests.

A "licensee" is someone who was not invited to enter the premises, but neither was he forbidden. He is there in the hope of doing business, probably for his own benefit. The owner's responsibility to a licensee is somewhere between the duty owed to a trespasser and that owed to a social guest or business invitee. The Fuller Brush Man is a licensee.

An "invitee" is someone who is invited on the premises for business rather than social purposes. The business may be for the mutual benefit of the parties or solely for the benefit of the owner of the premises. The owner is probably liable for ordinary negligence. Whether a person qualifies as an invitee depends upon the extension of such an invitation, either expressly or impliedly.

Puzzlers can arise when injuries are sustained by firemen, policemen, mailmen, or deliverymen. The cases, and subtle distinctions, are confusing to lawyers as well as laymen. While not exact, the following "rule of thumb" may help: an "invitee" is on your property for your benefit and by your invitation; a "licensee" is there without objection by you, and probably primarily for his own benefit; a "social guest" is there by mutual consent and for no one's particular benefit; and a "trespasser" (the low man on the totem pole) is there without the consent or authorization of anyone. The degree of care owed by the property owner decreases as we descend from invitee to licensee to social guest to trespasser. (This statement is not intended to be technically exact and accurate for *any* jurisdiction—it is oversimplified to help you understand the general concept of the varying degrees of care owed by the property owner to different classes of persons.) But to what degree does the responsibility of the property owner differ for each? No rule of thumb is possible because the states have different standards and, even within a given jurisdiction, the law may be changing. For example, Massachusetts reversed its law in 1973 and decided that there should be no distinction between the degree of care owed to licensees and invitees; and in a landmark decision also ruled that the landowner must refrain from negligently injuring even a trespasser.

There are many ways of determining the different duties owed to invitees, licensees, social guests, and trespassers, but the technical distinctions are for lawyers. In fact, it would not be exaggerating to

88

say that some of the differences are so indistinct that they can be seen only by the most exacting of "Philadelphia lawyers."

COMPENSATION FOR VICTIMS OF CRIME—AN IDEA WHOSE TIME HAS COME

Compensation for victims of crime—the policy of paying money to those the state has failed to protect—is generally regarded as a new idea but it has antecedents in the dim centuries of long ago. The first recorded instances are found in the first English code of law written in the seventh century. One phase of what was known as "Kentish Law" was that any money or property extracted from a criminal in punishment of his offense went to the victim of the crime, not the sovereign or government. If the crime was homicide, it went to the family of the victim. The philosophy was that it was the victim or his family who had been most seriously and directly injured by the violation of the criminal law, so it was the victim who should get the benefit derived from the punishment rather than society in general. (The personal crime often became very personal in other ways, too. For example, in serious cases a criminal might be declared to be beyond the pale or outside the peace—which meant that anyone could destroy his property or hunt him down like an animal.)

Today when we talk of compensation for the victims of crime, the idea is regarded as a modification of our belief that crime is directed against society as a whole rather than simply the individual who has been directly affected. If the punishment is a fine, in modern times the money goes into the county treasury instead of the victim's pocket. The criminal goes to jail to serve his time, not to the victim's farm to plow his fields in some form of servitude.

The new form of compensation for victims of crime has been pioneered in a few states, notably California and Massachusetts, with the compensation being restricted (at least in the beginning) to victims of *violent* crime. A limit on the amount of compensation is set in the statute. The maximum in Massachusetts in 1973, for example, was $10,000. In practice, if A lost $5,000 to a robber who struck him on the head with a weapon, and B lost $5,000 to a thief who quietly picked his pocket without B even being aware of it, A could be compensated by the state but B could not: A was the victim of a *violent* crime, B was not. Both lost the same amount of money and (assuming A's injury was merely a slight bump or

89

bruise) neither suffered great physical injury but the philosophy of the statute is to compensate only victims of violent crime.

The reason for the limitation of both the type of crime and the amount of recovery is that, without restrictions of some sort, the doors would be open to so many claims that a state might not be able to afford the program. So other strict limitations are usually imposed: the crime must have been reported to the police immediately, the proof of what happened must be clear and convincing, and so on.

In 1974 California amended its eligibility list to include victims of some automobile cases—driving under the influence of alcohol or other drug, and hit and run. In the first year of California's experience, some $2,092,810 was paid out to satisfy 1,128 claims that had been allowed out of 2,394 claims made. The maximum allowed was changed in 1974 from $5,000 to $23,000. The injured person does not have to be a welfare case: the rule of thumb adopted is that you can be compensated if you really cannot afford the loss occasioned by the violent crime.

The experience in Massachusetts in 1973 was limited to 146 awards made after 147 hearings (one claim was denied). A total of $690,000 was paid out to victims of violent crime and, as of this writing, 204 claims were still pending. Compensation for victims of crime will be discussed more and more in all the states as crime increases.

"VICTIMLESS" CRIMES

In recent years we have heard a great deal about "victimless" crimes. This refers to offenses in which some authorities argue that the only one really hurt is the person who commits the crime. The usual example is drug abuse (not selling drugs but simply using them illegally). Other common illustrations are homosexuality, prostitution, and "crime between consenting adults in the privacy of the bedroom." Many authorities distinguish "victimless" crimes from those where someone is hurt other than the person committing the crime—for example, the victims of rape, robbery, or murder. They argue that "victimless" crimes should be treated as social problems rather than as something for the criminal courts.

Those who maintain there is no such thing as a "victimless" crime take the traditional view that every individual, including the person hurting only himself, is a part of society—and a crime is committed whenever a member of society is hurt by some offense, even if it is merely a crime committed on himself. In a drug abuse case, it is argued that the drug addict becomes a burden to the rest of society in many obvious ways such as failing to support himself or family, and often by committing larceny and other crimes that victimize others. The theory of "victimless" crime has become popular with young people (because of the drug abuse phenomenon) but most legal authorities still hold to the position that any crime should carry a penalty.

Incidentally, suicide is a crime. It is, ironically, the only crime where someone who fails in the crime could theoretically be brought to trial whereas someone who succeeds is never prosecuted.

Of course, not everyone who commits a crime is brought to trial. But the trial is to law what critical surgery is to medicine, and what the "moment of truth" is to the toreador in the bull ring: it is life or death. The trial is the ultimate in law.

WHO'S THE VICTIM?

12
The Ultimate
Test of the Law:The Trial

THE TRIAL IS THE ultimate test of the law. Without the trial, everything is as nothing: the law, the judges, the lawyers. The movies and plays you may have seen probably did not bear much resemblance to an actual trial. The movies are more entertaining. In them, the hero always solves the case and achieves justice—a real trial is not so clear-cut.

The first thing a layman should understand is that a trial is not a search for truth: it is a battle for victory conducted by merciless adversaries. The law books refer to it as an "adversary proceeding." Each party and his lawyer are trying to win, and they are advancing only those facts that may result in victory. Theoretically and ethically, the lawyer offers whatever is helpful to establishing the truth of what actually happened, but almost no lawyer sees or knows or remembers anything that is adverse to his position. The only exception is the occasional (and unusual) practice of some prosecutor who may volunteer something that is helpful to the accused. (This is not to be confused with the daily situation where the prosecutor *has* to disclose something to the defense or risk the granting of a new trial because he did not.)

Before you contest this position, let me ask your reactions to a couple of situations. First, you are being tried for holding up a bank. The prosecution has ended its case with very doubtful identification of you. During the recess before you begin your defense, your lawyer informs you that he has just talked to a spectator who says he was in the bank and positively identifies you as the bandit. The prosecution does not know of that witness. Would you tell your lawyer to put that witness on the stand? I cited such a situation to a student and his answer was that it would be immaterial if the witness testified under such circumstances: the defendant would have to be let go for insanity.

Another illustration is a civil case in which you were badly injured in an automobile accident. The only question is on which part of the road did the accident happen? The only witnesses are you and the other driver and you each claim the other was over the center line. Before the case ends, a courtroom spectator tells your lawyer that he saw the accident and you were positively on your wrong side of the road. The other side does not know of this witness. Do you tell your lawyer to put that spectator on the stand? In both illustrations, if the trial were really a search for truth, you would put the witness on. But since it is an adversary proceeding, the average party and the average lawyer almost certainly would not.

We are not discussing the merits or ethics or morality of such a decision: we are merely exploring the situation as it is so that the layman can understand the trial as it *is* and not as it *should be.*

Let's take a look at a jury trial of a criminal case. We all know what the courtroom looks like: Perry Mason and the movies are all accurate on that point, at least. The judge sits on a raised bench and just below him is the clerk at his desk. Between the judge and the jury box is the witness stand, usually with the stenographer seated in front of it. The opposing lawyers are at desks, and a few feet behind them are spectators. Near the jury box is usually a raised seat or box for a court officer or a uniformed guard.

JURY SELECTION

The case begins with the clerk reading the indictment—the accusation that is made by the prosecution against the defendant. Then the jury is selected from a panel of fifty or one hundred citizens from the county or area of the court's jurisdiction. There are certain cases, usually minor misdemeanors, in which the law may allow a jury of six; and there are occasions when a case is going to be so lengthy that two or four alternate jurors will also be named, in case of illness or other incapacity of a juror during trial. But usually, as we all know, the jurors number twelve.

The prospective jurors are called one at a time. Counsel will usually know at least the residence and occupation of each and, depending on the investigation he has made, may even know what clubs the prospective juror belongs to, what his political affiliation is, and what kind of person he is. In most states, counsel is allowed to question each prospective juror at considerable length; in other states only the judge can ask questions, and then only a very few intended to elicit whether the prospective juror has any prejudices or is unable to render a fair verdict. It is the rare (almost nonexistent) juror who ever acknowledges that he is biased or could possibly be unfair, but some judges seem to be unaware that jurors are reluctant to admit such frailties.

A prospective juror may be challenged (forbidden to sit) "for cause": he has shown some bias or prejudice, he knows one of the parties, he has read about the case and formed an opinion, or another reason that makes it apparent that he should not serve. There is no limit to the number of challenges a party has "for cause." In addition, there are a number of "peremptory" challenges—the party simply says he does not want such and such a juror, without having to assign a reason. The party is limited in the number of peremptory challenges he has, the number usually varying from three to twelve. It depends upon the state and also upon the number of indictments or counts that are being tried.

Incidentally, the exercise of a peremptory challenge does not necessarily mean the party does not want that particular juror; it may simply mean that he is hoping that another member of the panel will be called. Jurors usually serve for a period of a month or more, and word gets around among lawyers that so-and-so is generous, or compassionate, or whatever. A lawyer may or may not want such a juror, depending upon which side he is representing. During the selection of the jury, counsel may often be seen conferring with the client to be certain that he is satisfied with acceptance of the jury.

The final selection of the jury may well be the most important step in the trial because these are the people who will decide whether or not the prosecution (or the plaintiff in a civil matter) has proven its case. Their decision may be based on the evidence, on prejudice or on who knows what? Probably most juries base their decisions on an impartial analysis of the evidence—studies that have been made indicate this very emphatically—but many believe the cynical admonition of author Honore de Balzac: "A jury is twelve men chosen to decide which side has the better lawyer."

THE PROSECUTION AND THE DEFENSE

Once the jury has been seated, the prosecution (or the plaintiff in a civil case) makes its opening statement. This is merely a general statement of what the prosecution expects to prove, what the various witnesses will testify to, and some general understanding of the prosecution's case so that the jury will be better able to follow it. The opening statement is not supposed to be an argument but is merely supposed to disclose the facts that the prosecution expects to offer. Following that, the prosecution calls its witnesses for what is known as direct examination. When the prosecution finishes with a witness, the defense is entitled to cross-examine that witness. Following the cross-examination, the prosecution is allowed "redirect" examination, which is not supposed to go over the entire case but is merely intended to clear up anything the cross-examination has brought out. The defense is then entitled to re-cross, and so it goes. Of course this does not continue indefinitely and usually there is only direct examination, cross-examination, and a very brief redirect.

When the prosecution has completed its case through the testimony of witnesses or the presentation of other evidence, the prosecution rests. It is then the turn of the defense. The defendant has the right to make an opening statement in which the defense discloses what its case will be. Following that, the defense calls its own witnesses and the process of direct examination followed by cross-examination and redirect goes on. When the defense has concluded its case, the defense rests. At that time the prosecution will determine whether it has something to offer in rebuttal. The rebuttal is not supposed to be the kind of evidence that the prosecution should have offered in its direct case, but is intended to be limited to evidence that is called for because of something brought out by the defense in its case. As a practical matter, the courts often are lenient in allowing either side to put in some evidence that it simply had forgotten to present.

Courts insist that the "best evidence" be introduced. If there is more than one kind of evidence available to establish a point in controversy, the law will insist on the best evidence. The letter itself is the best evidence, not a witness testifying to what was in it; the gun itself rather than the description of it; and so on. Usually, by statute, certified copies of such documents as deeds will be permitted.

Statutes play an important role in many cases. Courts invariably take the position that a statute means what it says and not what the legislature might have intended it to say.

Words are given their usual and ordinary meaning. Where there are possible different meanings, the interpretation to be made is that which is most consistent within the context of the general conversation or agreement in which the word appears.

(Occasionally in a trial a judge will say he's taking "judicial notice." That means the judge is saying a fact or event is so well known there is no need to produce evidence to prove it. A judge might take judicial notice that Christmas comes on December 25th, that Niagara Falls is located on the American-Canadian border, that Abraham Lincoln was President, and so on.)

When a person is brought to trial for having committed a crime, the prosecution must prove beyond a reasonable doubt every essential element of the offense. We have already discussed some of the constitutional rights that protect an accused; some other important ones that come into play at the trial are the presumption of innocence and the right of the defendant not to testify.

Every person is presumed to be innocent, which means that the prosecution has the burden of proving his guilt. Every court in America follows this precept.

YOUR RIGHT NOT TO TESTIFY

The right not to testify is a very important one—and if the defendant does not take the stand in a criminal case, the jury is instructed that it cannot draw any inference against him because of such failure (the rule in a civil case is different). The question of whether or not the defendant should testify is perhaps the most difficult one that a defense lawyer has to decide. His criminal record becomes admissible if he testifies, and he is also subject to cross-examination. But if he does not take the stand, the jury is quite apt to infer guilt, regardless of any instructions by the judge. There is no satisfactory answer to this dilemma.

The concept of "privilege" is important in various relationships: for example, neither spouse can be compelled to testify against the other. In a criminal case where the wife has the privilege of not testifying against her husband, it is her privilege, not the husband's. She can testify if she wants to. There is a lawyer-client relationship that is privileged in the sense that the lawyer cannot reveal any confidences by the client without the client's waiver of the privilege. The doctor-patient relationship is not so clear. Some states say the relationship is privileged, others do not. The same is true of a religious adviser-parishioner relationship. Most teachers and students think there is a confidential relationship that makes disclosures by the student privileged. In many states there is no such privilege protecting the student's conversations with the teacher or with a guidance counselor. Conversations between husband and wife are usually privileged unless they are overheard by a third person or are abusive words rather than conversations.

"IMPEACHING" A WITNESS

A topic that touches on the success or failure of the outcome of any legal matter is the credibility of witnesses. When a case is being tried in court, this is vital. A party will usually try to show that the opposition's witnesses are not worthy of belief—as the law books express it, one side will try to "impeach" the other's witnesses. Impeaching a witness means to discredit him by showing bad character or to contradict him by showing inconsistent statements, for example.

Telephone conversations can cause problems of admissibility in evidence. If the witness is the person who was called, he cannot testify to the conversation unless he can identify the voice on the other end of the line. If the witness is the caller, and he can testify that he looked up the telephone number and asked for A, he probably then may testify to what A said even if he is unable to identify the voice as A's. Or there may be other circumstances such that the court is reasonably sure of the identification of the person at the other end of the line.

When both defense and prosecution have rested, it is then time for argument or summation by each side to the jury. Customarily, the defendant argues first. followed by the prosecution. As a practical matter, this means the prosecution has opened the case at the very beginning and closes the case at the very end. The procedure may vary in the different states, and some states will have the prosecution argue first or may allow rebuttal.

THE VERDICT

After both arguments have been concluded, the judge then "charges" the jury. This means that he instructs the jury as to what law is applicable to the facts of the particular case. When he has concluded, the jury goes out to deliberate and returns when it has arrived at a verdict. In jury trials, the jury is the sole judge of what the facts are and it determines those facts; the judge decides what the law is with reference to such facts. If there were any facts that could be found by reasonable men, an appellate court will not ordinarily disturb the verdict of the jury even if the appellate court itself might have found the facts to be otherwise.

If the defendant has been found not guilty, the case ends at that point. If the defendant has been found guilty, then the time comes for sentencing the defendant.

Before sentencing the defendant, the judge usually will look closely at the defendant's past record. He will discuss the matter with the probation officer or, in some jurisdictions, may even refer to a panel composed of psychiatrists, social workers, and others for their recommendation. The prosecution usually will have a recommendation to make and the defense counsel will always have something to say in mitigation of any sentence to be given by the judge.

"I OBJECT, YOUR HONOR"

At various times during the trial, one or the other of the attorneys will object and, if his position is not sustained, take an exception. All this means is that the attorney who is excepting is preparing the record for appeal to a higher court on the ground that the judge has made some error in the point raised.

The trial of a civil case is pretty much the same as a criminal case, so far as form and procedure are concerned. In a civil case, however, the degree of proof necessary is different from that in a criminal case. In a criminal case, the court will instruct the jury that the essential elements of the crime must be proven "beyond a reasonable doubt" by the prosecution. In a civil case, the plaintiff (the one bringing the suit to trial) usually has to prove his case by merely a "preponderance of the evidence."

In the trial of either a civil or a criminal case, the two most common objections are that a statement offered is "hearsay" or that a statement offered is "immaterial, irrelevant, and incompetent."

What constitutes hearsay is a very technical subject and there are scores of exceptions to the so-called hearsay rule. In general, hearsay is most simply defined as a statement that is made out of court by someone who is not a witness. The statement can either be oral or written.

There are many definitions of what is immaterial or irrelevant; most seem to take the position that something is offered which either doesn't matter at all or is so remote that it should have no place in the trial. If something is incompetent, it means that it is not coming from a legally approved source—it is not coming from the right witness or it is not the right document, and so on.

Another objection that is frequently made in court is that the party is "leading" the witness. This means that the party who calls a witness to the stand is not supposed to put words in his mouth or lead him in the examination. Leading questions are not permitted on direct examination but they are permitted on cross-examination because the cross-examiner has not put the witness on the stand.

As we saw in Chapter 10, a great deal has taken place between lawyers on both sides before the case ever came to trial. Each side may have filed motions or sought discovery of evidence that the other has. In criminal cases, there has almost always been a motion to suppress, alleging that the prosecution made an illegal search or gained some evidence through a violation of the rights of the defendant and that, as a result, such evidence should not be allowed at the trial. Sometimes both sides have filed interrogatories to each other or have made agreements between themselves that eliminate the necessity of certain proof at the trial.

Legislatures (by statute) and courts (by decisions and rules) are constantly simplifying these legal procedures, instituting pre-trial discovery to prevent surprise, and experimenting with various innovations that will improve the administration of justice. As a result, both substantive and procedural law are usually in a state of flux until they "settle down" into an accepted practice. That is why it is impossible to state with complete finality the procedural steps that will be followed once a case is entered in court. What is true today may have been changed by tomorrow. In Massachusetts, for example, where once it was necessary to file various motions under technically proper titles, today it is sufficient if a motion is merely labeled one "for appropriate relief." The aim of every suggested improvement is to make it a little easier to arrive at justice in the trial itself.

A trial is admittedly not the ideal way of establishing truth—but the haunting question remains, "What is better?"

13
The Sentence

EVENTUALLY, THE TRIAL ENDS and the defendant is found guilty or is acquitted. Occasionally there is a "hung jury"—it cannot decide the case—and the prosecution then has to decide whether to try the case again or not.

If the defendant is acquitted, he is free to go. If convicted, he is sentenced.

The sentence may be anything that is permitted by the statute defining the crime and specifying the punishment. Minor crimes usually call for a fine or a short jail sentence of several months. More serious offenses are penalized by a sentence to state's prison, usually with a minimum and maximum period set: three to five years, seven to ten, one to ten, and so on. The judge who sentences usually figures out when the prisoner would be eligible for parole and sentences accordingly. For example, in states where the prisoner becomes eligible for parole after serving one-third of the sentence, a judge's mental arithmetic might go like this: "If I give him twelve to fifteen years he would become eligible after four years, but he gets off ten days of each month for good behavior and he gets more time off if he gives blood. He'll probably take a rehabilitation course, and that will give some more time off, so the twelve years only amounts to about three years. That's about right."

When a defendant has committed more than one crime, he will get a sentence for each one. For example, if the defendant shoots someone while holding up a bank, he may be charged with robbery, assault with intent to kill, and carrying a firearm. The vital question here is whether the judge will make the sentences "concurrent" or "on and after." Let's assume a defendant gets three to five years for each of the three crimes. If the sentences are ordered to be served "concurrently"—at the same time—the defendant actually has to serve only three to five years. But if the judge uses the dread words "on and after" it means that the defendant will serve the first three to five years sentence, then begin the second one and then, after completing the second sentence, begin the third. The "on and after" phrase means that his actual sentence could be nine to fifteen years. (This illustration has been over-simplified.)

The judge might give probation or a suspended sentence. In both, the defendant does not get confinement—and in both the defendant has the possibility of confinement hanging over his head if he violates the terms of the probation or the suspended sentence.

Or the judge might say, "Filed" or "Continued day to day," which theoretically means sentence is being postponed until some future time. As a practical matter, in 999 cases out of 1000, it means an end to the matter.

YOUR RECORD

Whatever has happened, there is an official record on file in the probation department of the court, and that record may or may not come back to haunt the defendant in many ways. The states differ in how these records may be used against the defendant. Sometimes it depends upon what the plea or sentence was; a plea of nolo or a plea of guilty followed by probation or suspended sentence may not be regarded as a "conviction" for certain purposes—to impeach a witness in court or on an application for employment, for example. The question becomes very technical but you should know that there may be different consequences depending upon exactly what the record was.

Whatever the record, the layman should also know that there may be ways of protecting himself from its consequences. It may be possible to obtain a governor's pardon; that is not as difficult as it might sound. The state may have statutes that permit the record's expungement or its sealing under certain circumstances. There may be laws that allow a person with a record to answer "no record" on certain applications for employment under certain conditions. For example, in Massachusetts, General Laws Chapter 276, Sections 100 A, B, and C provide for the sealing of certain records, or allow certain persons to deny the existence of such records, on employment applications under certain conditions.

The Commission against Discrimination (in those states that

have such an agency) also may take action against any prospective employer who improperly uses a person's criminal record as a basis for denying employment. This possibility is at least worth investigating.

REQUESTING A NEW TRIAL

There is also another step that is open to persons who have been convicted of a crime: they may file requests for a new trial. This actually does not offer too much hope because such requests are rarely granted. The main hope for a new trial lies in the discovery of new evidence that the defendant was unaware of and could not have discovered at the first trial even by the exercise of due diligence. Another ground that has become popular in recent years is to ask for a new trial on the ground that the defendant's lawyer was incompetent and did not adequately represent the defendant. Incidentally, it is the fear of this charge that leads many defense lawyers to file countless motions simply so the record will show that they have done everything within their power for the defendant. Sometimes the motions actually harm the defendant, but the defense counsel doesn't wish to run the risk of being accused of having overlooked any possible motion.

Before we leave the subjects of crime and punishments, we should not overlook the fact that some penalties are meted out by other agencies than the police and the courts. There are associations, boards, and commissions that may deter offenses or punish for infractions of rules or regulations or codes of ethics. Their action may be more severe in effect than anything the courts themselves do.

To cite just a few illustrations, the Registry of Motor Vehicles may suspend or revoke licenses to operate a motor vehicle; the Bar Association or the Medical Association may suspend, revoke or otherwise discipline the right to practice; and various associations of craftsmen might expel the person for some reason.

It is easy to see that penalties can be inflicted by more than the courts alone. Disciplinary action by organizations such as these, plus the tremendous force of public opinion, can have a deterrent effect on behavior that may be even greater than that of the law itself. In the following chapter we will take a look at these administrative agencies.

14

Administrative Boards and Regulatory Agencies Can Help You

ADMINISTRATIVE BOARDS, COMMISSIONS, AND agencies are semi-judicial bodies. While they are not courts, they do have judicial functions and they do determine basic rights of those who come before them. They are usually governed by established rules and procedures and they have all the qualities of a judicial hearing, in most instances. As little as they are known to many lawyers, they are even less well known to the layman—and yet they create more "law" and try more cases than all the courts and legislatures in the nation. They are tremendously important.

Administrative boards came into being gradually over a period of time because there was a need for them. When the United States was becoming an industrial nation, great power accrued to certain individuals and corporations. They often abused it and the average person was badly hurt by such abuse of power. The government had to do something to regulate practices of powerful corporations that were hurting the public. Merely passing laws was not enough because the laws were meaningless unless they were enforced. Legislatures did not have the time or knowledge to enforce regulations and laws that they had passed. The courts were in the same situation. Gradually, regulation began to be given to administrative officials. Of necessity these officials also had to be given great discretion because they were ruling on various matters during rapidly changing conditions. The net result was that functions that had previously been reserved to the courts and legislatures began to be handled by administrative officials.

Perhaps the first important semi-judicial agency was the Interstate Commerce Commission, established in 1887 to regulate railroads. At first the courts were hostile to it but they gradually came to recognize its powers and it grew in importance. It was then followed by the Federal Trade Commission, the Federal Power Commission, The Federal Communications Commission, and others.

The Securities and Exchange Commission and the National Labor Relations Board were two important federal agencies that came into being in the twentieth century. Others have come into existence as society found the need for them.

The states also found the need for regulatory agencies, and they followed the pattern established by the federal government.

Today the average state has many quasi-judicial regulatory agencies: the Registry of Motor Vehicles, rate setting boards for hospitals and insurance matters, a Commission against Discrimination, a Civil Service Commission, a Public Utilities Commission, an Alcoholic Beverages Control Commission, a Parole Board, an Industrial Accident Board, various agencies that regulate professions or crafts such as boards on physicians, plumbers, electricians, barbers, and so on.

Over the years the powers of federal and state regulatory bodies have kept increasing. They investigate complaints, negotiate settlements, issue various rules and regulations, and decide disputes. Usually these regulatory boards were created by statute; and often the statute that created the boards merely outlined general objectives and left the methods of accomplishing those objectives up to the board. The result was that the board often became the real lawmaker. Cases were decided and these became precedents with the force of law. Statutes creating these boards almost always provided that there could be a judicial review of the decisions of the board, agency or commission. However, experience has shown that the courts usually sustain administrative rulings unless there is very good reason to overrule them. Even though there is an appeal from the semi-judicial agency to the courts themselves, as a practical matter the decision of the administrative agency is almost always final. If the record shows "substantial evidence" to sustain the board's finding, the courts will not overturn it.

Most states have an "administrative procedure act" which spells out rules and regulations that must be followed by the agency. These statutes invariably require that a person be given reasonable notice of the time and place of a hearing upon some matter in dispute, that the parties be allowed to call witnesses and to cross-examine the opposition, and that there be evidence to support a finding of the board. The agency decision usually must be given in writing, spelling out the reasons for it, and notifying an aggrieved party that he has the right to a judicial review in the courts. While the hearing itself is more informal than a trial in court, the rights of the parties are protected and the agencies do follow some rules of evidence.

At one time the agency official who sat as a judge was called a Hearing Officer. That title has been changed to the more appropriate one of Administrative Law Judge. It is expected that further changes will be made in the future in connection with administrative procedures but it is safe to say that any changes made will be in favor of a person seeking his rights by appealing to such semi-judicial bodies.

THE COMMISSION AGAINST DISCRIMINATION

One of the semi-judicial agencies that the layman should be familiar with is the Commission against Discrimination. Most states have such a body. Its main function is to prevent discrimination based on race, color, creed, sex, age, political affiliation, national origin, or anything else. The state will usually have statutes referring specifically to living accommodations, employment, and public accommodations or recreation. There often are reasonable exceptions made for religious concerns, for example, which might have to do with only people of a certain religion.

Many states have laws that prevent discrimination by stores in extending credit to consumers; by finance companies in lending money; by employers who refuse to hire *solely* because of age or physical handicap or union activities; by educational institutions in accepting applications by students; and so on.

Some states have statutes that prevent landlords from trying to exclude children in living accommodations and that penalize employers who are not restoring employment to women after maternity leaves.

A book could be written on the many types of discrimination that might be practiced and the statutes and rules and regulations that seek to prevent it. You should know what general types exist and the methods of preventing them. The statutes or agencies of each state should be checked to ascertain the situation in a particular case.

TO HECK WITH 'EM ALL!

SURE I JUST GOT HERE... BUT I'M HUNGRY.

WORKMEN'S COMPENSATION

The Industrial Accident Board, the Workmen's Compensation Commission, or whatever it may be called in a particular state, is the semi-judicial agency that hears cases of employees who sustained injuries arising out of, and in the course of, employment. These cases are tried practically the same way a legal trial is heard, the only difference being that they are slightly less formal. But most testimony is medical because the most important question is the extent of the claimant's disability.

If a person is injured at work, he probably will be covered by this compensatory system. It does not cover, and was not intended to cover, pain and suffering or all loss of income or other damages (which are usually recoverable in non-employment injuries). In Workmen's Compensation claims, the question of fault or negligence is immaterial. The only question is: Did the employee's injuries arise out of and in the course of employment? The usual Workmen's Compensation system calls for payment of medical bills and a schedule of payments to the injured worker made on a percentage of the weekly wages. They are classified as compensation for total disability or partial disability. There are also specific payments made on the loss of such specific parts of the body as an arm, a leg or an eye—even including one for the loss of the tip of a finger. In addition, dependents are covered for death payments and other benefits.

Workmen's Compensation is compulsory in most states, although ordinarily there are exceptions for firms that employ less than three or four persons, or for workers in farm, domestic, or "casual" fields of employment. The employer may insure himself or obtain the insurance from a private concern.

Boards or agencies that handle Workmen's Compensation claims always favor the injured employee. In addition, the trend of legislative statutes and judicial decisions in such matters is to favor the employee. For example, the question often arises of when employment begins and ends. The tendency has been to constantly extend the interpretation to cover the employee. And even if the employee is away from the place of employment, if he is on the employer's business by some reasonable interpretation, he will be covered. Almost the only time the employee is not protected is if the injury is intentionally inflicted or if it is sustained during activities the law calls "skylarking": fooling around and not tending to business.

We hear a great deal about "no-fault" recovery: the injured person is compensated, regardless of whether he was to blame for the injury or not. The theory is that a member of society should be made whole again as quickly as possible and that, basically, it really does not matter how he sustained his injuries. Recent years have seen that philosophy applied to automobile accident cases. Workmen's Compensation cases are based on the same fundamental concept.

SOCIAL SECURITY BENEFITS

The Social Security Administration of the Health, Education and Welfare Department has Administrative Law Judges who hear cases involving claims concerning retirement, survivors, disability, and hospital insurance benefits. Often the individual is not aware of his rights in these matters. The claimant needs to present testimony about his employment record, his medical condition, or other evidence bearing on the particular issue. There are many benefits available and the Social Security Administration has personnel who are ready and willing to assist in processing such claims. The layman should know about the availability of such assistance.

PUBLIC UTILITIES

Every state has a Department of Public Utilities, a Public Utilities Commission or some equivalent agency that conducts semi-judicial hearings on a variety of matters affecting the consumer. The consumer can look to this agency for relief from any improper or unfair rates imposed by gas, electric, telephone, water or other public utility companies. The hearings conducted by Public Utility Commissions are usually fairly formal and closely resemble court proceedings.

WELFARE

Every state has a Welfare Department, and communities may have their own. For some time there has been considerable discussion over whether welfare is a right or a privilege. Currently the law *seems* to be that the welfare recipient does not have a *right* to assistance but the government does not have the total right to cut off a recipient's aid or to reduce it at will.

The case of *Goldberg v. Kelly*, 397 U.S. 254 (a five to three decision of the U.S. Supreme Court) held that a person receiving welfare assistance cannot be deprived of it without notice and the right to a hearing. The Rosado and Dandridge cases established the "balancing of interests" test, holding that the basic question is whether the recipient's loss outweighs the government's interests. These cases held that the government's interests were more important.

In addition to general welfare, states had at least four different categories of assistance: Assistance to Families with Dependent Children (AFDC), Old Age Assistance (OAA), Disability Assistance (DA), and Medical Assistance. The federal government has taken over most of these programs. The Federal Social Security Act prescribes that all claimants under any category have a right to a fair hearing on any claim. The states provide that claims will be considered under the state's Administrative Procedures Act.

The federal statutes provide that the requirements for a state plan must include a fair hearing for anyone whose claim is denied; the hearing must be conducted by an impartial official of the state agency at a convenient time and place; the claimant has the right to examine all records and to have counsel and witnesses; and the agency hearing officer's recommendation must be based exclusively on evidence adduced at the hearing.

The federal statutes also provide that a request for a hearing is any expression (oral or written) by the claimant or anyone speaking for him.

There are also provisions for federal financial participation in providing transportation for the claimant, his lawyer and witnesses, and other costs related to the hearing.

The various states have different welfare procedures, the claimant having the right to appeal from the agency to the court. In states that have an administrative procedures act, judicial review is in accordance with its provisions. In Massachusetts, General Laws Chapter 18, Section 16 says that any person aggrieved by the failure of the Department of Public Welfare to render adequate aid has a right to a hearing that is subject to judicial review under General Laws Chapter 30A (the Administrative Procedures Act).

There are countless boards, commissions, and agencies in every state that are available to a claimant in a variety of situations. They are intended to provide quick, inexpensive, and adequate relief to an aggrieved person. The layman should know of their existence and what they can do for him.

ENVIRONMENTAL PROTECTION

When administrative agencies fail to protect the public, statutes may be written to correct the situation. In recent years we have begun to hear a great deal about "environmental protection," "pollution," and other terms indicating a belated awakening to the realization that for generations we have been despoiling nature to the great detriment of society. We have lately thought to do something about this by passing laws to protect ourselves and future generations from short-sighted policies of despoilment. The overall federal protective legislation is the National Environmental Protection Act (1970)—enacted because federal agencies were not doing enough to prevent the exploitation and destruction of our natural environment. This Act requires federal agencies to state what effect their contemplated actions may have on the environment; and individuals or groups are given legal standing to force agencies to act.

At the present time there are many federal and state laws that prevent air pollution, dumping refuse in waters, and similar acts. Practically all states (including Massachusetts, New York, and Connecticut) have such laws and penalties and we are bound to see more cases arising out of their enforcement. The layman who knows about the existence of such laws may be able to help insist on their enforcement. Basically and fundamentally, the protection of our environment must come from interested and informed citizens rather than lawyers.

The federal and state governments can do a great deal to protect and preserve the environment—and informed citizens can influence or force governments to act. Governments, whether state or federal, are sovereign; and sovereignty means power. Let's examine the doctrine of sovereignty.

15
The Doctrine of Sovereignty

THE LAW OF EVERY JURISDICTION has a doctrine called "sovereignty." The "sovereign" means the ultimate ruler, whether it be king, nation, state or locality—and the doctrine of sovereignty holds that no one can sue the sovereign without the consent of the sovereign. Over the centuries, this resulted in various kinds of injustices when the sovereign injured some citizen through its negligence or fault. The history of the law in the United States has been to keep whittling away at complete sovereignty by making exceptions to the original complete immunity. Either by legislative statute or court decision, all the states have ruled that the sovereign may be sued for various infringements of the rights of its citizens. That is why the land owner may recover payment for his land taken by the state through eminent domain (the power to take property of one individual for the benefit of all). It is also why a traveler may sue the state for injury sustained because of a defect in the highway. On the local level, we are familiar with lawsuits by pedestrians who have fallen on snow and ice the city negligently allowed to collect in sidewalk defects.

Originally the state or city would not have had to pay for such causes of action by damaged citizens—the doctrine of sovereignty held that no one could compel such recovery—but the sovereign itself (through its legislative and judicial organs) has now ruled otherwise and has given its consent to be sued. To determine in what type of case and to what extent it may be sued, the statutes or ordinances of the local jurisdiction must be consulted.

111

"CHARITABLE IMMUNITY"

A similar doctrine called "charitable immunity" protected "charitable institutions" such as hospitals that, theoretically, at least, were supposedly not commercial or profit-making in character. Neither the hospital nor its agents (doctors and nurses, for example) could be held responsible for injuries sustained by a patient through the negligence or carelessness of the hospital or its personnel. But so many patients suffered injury that the law (through the legislatures and the courts) was gradually changed throughout the nation. Today in practically every state the doctrine of charitable immunity has disappeared as part of the protective armor of hospitals and other similar institutions: if you are injured through the negligence of a "charitable institution" your chances of recovering compensation are excellent.

The trend in every jurisdiction is to eliminate or reduce the freedom from responsibility for injury that has been enjoyed over the years by "sovereigns" and "charitable institutions"; and the pace and scope of that trend has accelerated and broadened.

DON'T STUB YOUR TOE ON PROCEDURAL STEPS

A note of caution: While the immunity has been reduced, the injured person may legally stub his toe on procedural steps he must follow before he is qualified to bring suit. These can be extremely strict and technical—and the courts will be equally strict and technical in insisting that they be followed to the exact letter of the law. Let me illustrate by a personal example that still sears my memory. As a young lawyer, I had occasion to notify the city of injuries sustained by a client in a fall on a defective sidewalk. The statute spelled out the kind of notification that had to be given to the mayor of the city: the date, the cause of injury, and the specific location of the defect. Such notice had to be given to the city within a certain number of days.

I gave notice within the required time and shortly thereafter, by letter which is automatically sent out in all such cases, as I later learned, the City Solicitor (the title of the lawyer for the city) acknowledged the notice but requested more specific information as to the defect's exact location by feet and inches. Since I had stated its location in more general terms—"the north side of Jones Street between Smith and Green Street, a hole in the sidewalk in front of the entrance to 250 Jones Street"—I went out to the defect and measured its exact location in feet and inches from various landmarks in the area. I then proceeded to answer the City Solicitor's letter which had requested such information.

The case proceeded through various stages until, some two years later, I had to drop it in great embarrassment when it developed that I should have sent my second letter to the *Mayor*, not the City Solicitor. Even though the City Solicitor had written to me, the statute said "notify the Mayor." Although the City Solicitor was the Mayor's official lawyer, had written on the Mayor's stationery as the duly authorized representative of the Mayor, and, although as a matter of legal ethics, a lawyer is supposed to communicate only with the other party's lawyer, not the party himself, the statute said "notify the Mayor." I had not followed the exact words of the statute, and the courts insist that they be followed with complete technicality, strictness, and exactness. The moral is that while sovereignty may be diminished, beware of the terms of the procedural qualifications that may accompany the diminution.

That particular statute has since been changed to prevent the repetition of such a fluke by any other person. But the fact that one particular statute was modified to give more protection to the victim does not mean that there are not still hundreds or thousands of deceptive ordinances, by-laws, statutes, and court decisions still on the books in many states. The unwary layman had better consult a lawyer on *any* matter involving any sovereignty or charitable institution. And he also should consult a lawyer in any dispute involving contracts—the subject of the next chapter.

16
Contracts

IF THERE IS AN argument about a "contract," probably only a lawyer can determine the legal consequences of whatever agreement is in dispute. The layman needs to know generalities about contracts, but when technicalities arise, it is dangerous for anyone but a lawyer to try to resolve them.

Who can be a party to a contract? In the ordinary case, anyone who is of legal age and sound mind can enter into an agreement. The states differ as to what constitutes "legal age."

What form must a contract take? With a few exceptions—mostly matters concerning real estate, long term contracts, or promises for the benefit of a third party—the contract can be either oral or written. There is a doctrine or principle called "Statute of Frauds" which requires certain agreements to be in writing: claims concerning land, promises to pay the debt of someone else, agreements that cannot be performed within a year, etc. Anything involving the Statute of Frauds is not for the layman; if the term is involved in any dispute, the services of a lawyer are essential. You should be aware that some contracts *must* be in writing and that something called the Statute of Frauds may come into play—and then realize if there is a real dispute about the meaning of the effect of the contract, a lawyer is needed.

What must the terms of a contract include? In general, they must be specific and be understandable. And they must include a legal term called "consideration," which means that each side must give something. The consideration may be goods or services or a promise or action or refraining from action—but it must be *something*. The consideration cannot be just on one side.

114

The courts often talk of a "meeting of the minds" of the contracting parties. This recognizes the principle that the parties must be talking about, or considering, the same subject matter, and with the same understanding of the terms. Each should understand what the other has in mind; otherwise, there is no "meeting of the minds," and such a meeting is essential to a valid contract.

Must the terms of a contract be carried out? Ordinarily, yes. A person is not excused from liability simply because unforeseen circumstances prevent him from carrying out his part of the bargain, or performance would cause him unexpected hardship. There is usually no legal excuse for failing to carry out the contract unless the failure is caused by an act of God or a war. Such things as a flood or lightning are acts of God—pregnancy is not. An act of God is usually defined as some act caused by violence of nature—something that proceeds from physical causes alone without the intervention of a human.

IMPLIED CONTRACTS

In addition to formal contracts, there is something the law calls an "implied contract." This merely means that there never was an actual formal agreement of any kind but both parties acted in such a way that it would be fair and reasonable to assume that both expected each was acting on the basis of an unspoken agreement. That explanation is oversimplified, but it is perhaps the easiest way of having some general understanding of "implied contracts." This is a subject about which volumes could be written and lawyers are not in unanimous agreement. However, you should know that your actions could bring into being something that has the legal force and effect of a contract—so don't assume there is no binding contract simply because there was no oral or written agreement.

For example, I say to a passing tramp: "How would you like to mow the lawn?" He says nothing but takes off his coat while I go to the garage and bring the lawn mower out. I read on the porch while the tramp mows the lawn. There has been nothing said about what he will get for compensation, if anything. Under circumstances such as these, there has been no oral or written contract—but there has been an "implied contract." The law would say that, by implied contract, I had agreed to pay the tramp fair and reasonable compensation for his work. From my actions, it would be fair to assume that he would have expected some compensation for his services

115

and that I was aware of it and would have expected to pay him something.

Many cases in the law seem to distinguish a contract that bears a seal from one that does not. The states and the decisions are not consistent on the point. The earlier cases used to say that a seal imports consideration, meaning that the presence of the seal indicated legally that the case would be considered as though something had been given as consideration. The more recent cases do not take the same point of view. In the absence of a statute or a decision to the contrary, the layman should probably assume that the presence or absence of a seal on a written agreement does not have any particular meaning.

As to witnesses to a contract: of course it is always good to have witnesses for anything. However, the question of whether or not a contract was entered into is a question for the court if there is a dispute. The presence or absence of witnesses usually means only that it is easier or more difficult to prove the existence of the contract.

"ADULTS BEWARE" OF THE INFANT'S CONTRACT

The subject of contracts made by an "infant" is a thorny one and should be entitled "Adults Beware."

The law is peculiarly easy on someone who is legally an infant— even if the infant is a sophisticated scoundrel who knows his way around every corner in the world of business or law. The law says that an infant may "avoid" his contract, which means that (if he chooses to do so) the infant can simply decide that he does not want to be bound by his promise. If he has received anything from the other party, he then must return it *if he still has it*. If he does not have anything, then the other party is out of luck.

For example, if the "infant" has paid $2,000 for an automobile, drives it a block and smashes it beyond repair, he can return the totally wrecked car and demand the entire $2,000 back from the seller. He has this right even if he had misrepresented his age to the seller by showing a false identification card. If he is an infant, he has the right to avoid his contract for anything except necessaries, such as food, clothing, and other essential items. Incidentally, there are some highly legal technical questions as to what qualifies as a "necessary" and whether the situation is changed if the infant has a parent who is ready, able, and willing to provide such necessaries. Such technicalities become a matter for the lawyer.

116

An "infant" is someone below whatever the legal age is in his particular state. In most states that age would be either eighteen or twenty-one but, in addition, there may be statutory exceptions below the "legal age." In Massachusetts, for example, under Chapter 168, Section 37A of the General Laws, a student who borrows from the Higher Education Loan Plan (HELP) is subject to all the obligations of a person of full age. Your state may also have an exception about a minor who purchases an automobile, or similar statutory exception. The law of the individual state must be checked.

Sometimes the status of a person may impose contractual obligations upon him. For example, a husband or a parent may find that he is liable on some sort of implied contract for something about which he knows nothing. The parent is responsible for the support of the youngster and, under certain circumstances, he may find that he is obligated to pay some bill that has been incurred by the child. This may be changed by "emancipation"—the child is working and supporting himself. But the subject of "emancipation" is quite technical. A husband is similarly responsible for certain debts of the wife, but this, too, is changing with the advance of Women's Liberation.

Any layman who is dealing with an "infant" should exercise caution: the infant has incredible rights even if he has been guilty of fraud, misrepresentation or anything else. To the maxim, Buyer Beware, you had better add another one: Adult Beware.

TAKE THE CAR...WHERE'S MY MONEY?

17
Bailments and Liens

SOMETHING AKIN TO A contract is a "bailment": an act by which the owner or possessor of personal property transfers its possession temporarily to another. Title is not transferred, merely possession. The usual case is taking clothing to the cleaner or leaving an automobile in a parking lot, etc. The owner is called the bailor; the one given temporary possession is the bailee. The bailee must take reasonable care of the property and, in the absence of an agreement to the contrary, is liable for negligence—but he is not liable for damage if he has not been negligent. For example. if you lend me your automobile and a third person negligently runs into me and damages your car without any fault on my part, I am not responsible for the damage done.

IS THE PARKING LOT OWNER RESPONSIBLE FOR DAMAGE DONE TO YOUR CAR?

The main knowledge the layman needs is that the bailee—the parking lot owner, the dry cleaner, etc.—does owe an obligation to him to take proper care of the article entrusted to him. That means the particular article for the particular purpose; for example, the garage owner is responsible for such items in the trunk as the jack, the wrench or the spare tire, but cannot be held liable for damage to a fur coat or wallet left there. Those were not articles that would normally be in such a place.

The bailee can attempt to limit his liability by putting up "not responsible" signs, having similar small print on the claim stub, and other such protective measures, but such tactics aren't necessarily binding. The courts differ as the facts differ and no general rule applies to every situation. Some cases held that there was no

118

reason for the automobile owner to realize there were any liability-limiting words on the claim ticket: he might reasonably have assumed it was merely a claim check. The state may even have a statute; e.g., in Massachusetts, General Laws Chapter 231, Section 85M says that such disclaimers of liability in parking lots are void.

The moral to the layman is: the bailee *may* be liable in damage for any damage to your property whether there are or are not disclaimers of liability on any signs or claim ticket. So, the bailee should beware—and the bailor should be aware.

Any matter concerning bailments often involves the subject of liens. A lien is usually defined as a charge or security or an encumbrance upon property. It is something like a mortgage and perhaps easiest to understand if we say that nothing can be done to transfer title in the property upon which there is a lien unless something is first done to satisfy or discharge the lien.

The usual claim of a lien arises when you have entrusted personal property to the bailee for a certain purpose, and the purpose having been accomplished, the bailee will not release the property until he has been paid. Illustrations might be the garage repair man not releasing the automobile until he has been paid or the dry cleaner not giving up the clothing until the bill is paid.

The various states differ on whether a lien does or does not exist in a specific situation—the law in the particular state must be checked. Ordinarily every jurisdiction will recognize there will be liens to protect the artisan, craftsman, repairman, mechanic, etc. How such liens came into existence may differ, too. A lien may exist by statute if the legislature passed a law granting such a lien. Or the court may have created liens by decisions based on factual situations. In general, whether generated by the legislature or the courts, if an article of personal property is stored or repaired or worked on by a jeweler, mechanic, repairman, garageman, furrier, or other such bailee, there is probably a lien on the article to protect such person for any payment due him.

If you rent a room, the innkeeper almost certainly has a lien on your luggage or other personal property brought there by you.

Of course there are legal procedural steps a bailee must take before he can sell the article to satisfy his claim, the balance of the proceeds going to the bailor. These steps must be taken carefully and exactly.

Many people think the hospital has a lien on a new baby: it does not. If the proud father is told he cannot have the baby until he pays the bill, he should tell the hospital that either he gets the baby at once or he will see his lawyer. The hospital will give up the baby. Incidentally, the employee demanding payment will probably be acting as an *agent* of the hospital—we will examine this relationship in the next chapter.

18

Agency: How You May Be Held Responsible for Another's Acts

AN IMPORTANT DOCTRINE OF law is agency: the performance of an act through someone else. If there is a true principal-agent relationship, the act of the agent is the act of the principal. But before such responsibility is established, it must be shown that whatever the agent did was something within the scope of his authority and had the expressed or implied consent of the principal.

An employee is an agent only for those matters that come within the scope of his employment; other matters may be beyond his authority. For example, a pedestrian is injured by the negligent driving of a bus operator employed by the defendant corporation. In a suit by the pedestrian against the defendant corporation, the principal-agent relationship will cause the driver's negligent act to be the defendant corporation's negligent act: driving was within the scope of his authority. If the bus driver orally admitted to the police that the accident was his fault because of his negligence, such admission would not bind the defendant corporation: the driver was not employed to make admissions on liability or to speak for the corporation. As the statement was beyond the scope of his authority, the principal is not bound by the agent's statement. (If the driver is also being sued, the statement is admissible against *him*.)

The law of agency can become very complicated as it revolves around various types or degrees of authority. If an agent is specifically authorized to act for the principal in some way, he has *actual* authority. If the agent had no specific authorization but his actions were those normally within the employment, then he may have *implied* authority. If the principal holds him out in such a way that any reasonable person would believe the agent was empowered

121

to act for the principal in such matters, then the agent may have *apparent* authority. There are many legal technicalities involved and the relationship of principal and agent may or may not exist depending upon the particular circumstances of a case.

There is a question that usually arises in any dispute about principal and agent: is the status that of independent contractor rather than agent? An independent contractor is merely told the end result desired and exercises his own independent judgment and authority in achieving that goal. It is often difficult to distinguish the two relationships. An oversimplified illustration might be two taxicab trips taken to New York by principals A and B. Each tells his respective driver: "I want you to drive me to New York City." Then principal A sits back and lets his driver determine for himself the route he will take, the speeds at which he will travel, and other decisions that must be made in order to get to the destination. Principal B, on the other hand, is a "back seat driver" who directs the taxicab driver on what streets to turn, what speeds to travel, and exactly what to do as various situations arise during the trip to New York City. The law would probably determine that principal A's driver was an independent contractor whereas principal B's driver was an agent.

The important distinction between the two classifications is one of responsibility or liability in case of damage done by the wrongful act of the driver. If A's driver injures a pedestrian, A is not responsible: his driver is not his agent but is an independent contractor. But if B's driver injures a pedestrian, B is responsible because B's driver is his agent and the principal is liable for the act of his agent, the so-called doctrine of *respondeat superior* (let the master answer).

In determining whether someone is an agent or an independent contractor, the usual test is whether he had independent judgment and control to achieve the desired result. If he does, the person is probably an independent contractor; if he does not, the person is an agent.

The layman should be aware of the fact that, in having someone perform some act for him, he may be creating a relationship that will make him responsible as principal for the acts of his agent.

Likewise, in dealing with someone who is not the principal, the layman should be alert to the possibility that such person may be acting beyond the scope of his authority and may not be able to legally bind the principal. There is no hard and fast rule of thumb that can guide the layman in either situation; all he can do is be aware of this possibility and conduct himself accordingly.

CHILD DRIVES PARENT'S CAR: WHO IS RESPONSIBLE?

A common case of questionable agency arises when a parent lets his youngster take the automobile for some purpose. The basic question is: For what purpose? Other questions may help: For whose benefit? Just what is comprehended by the "consent"?

If the car is used on an errand for the parent, then the relationship of principal-agent has been established and the parent (as well as the child) is responsible for any injury caused by the child. On the other hand, if the child is solely on his own "business"—a joy-ride with a friend or going to the movies or a dance, etc.—then there is no principal-agent status, no *respondeat superior,* and no liability on the parent. Mere consent does not establish agency.

In criminal law, the person who directs or hires another to commit a crime is himself liable criminally. In most jurisdictions, he is equally liable with his agent; and, in all jurisdictions, he has at least some degree of criminal liability. Over the years the law has designated such a person an accessory, principal, conspirator or accomplice; but, whatever he is called, the law punishes as a criminal the person who hires, procures, counsels, directs, assists or in any way participates in the commission of a crime by another. This is true even if the "agent" is a non-human—for example, if someone commands a vicious dog to kill or puts a poisonous snake where it will bite. The moral is: if you can't do it legally yourself, you can't do it legally via someone else.

WHAT ABOUT BUSINESS ACTIVITIES?

There are, of course, other ways in which one person can be held responsible for the acts of another. Many of them have to do with business or commercial activities—so let's take a look at the business world.

19

Business Law and Negotiable Instruments

(For practical literature on how to start a business write to The Small Business Administration, Washington, D.C.)

SO YOU'RE GOING into business? Well, of course it's advisable to have a lawyer or an accountant give you some advice. In fact, in today's sophisticated and complex society the average layman cannot be in business very long without needing professional services of one or both.

Anyone going into business should have at least a "speaking acquaintanceship" with sales agreements, negotiable instruments, warranties, and many other concepts that govern business dealings in addition to the general laws of contracts and torts.

Probably your first consideration is whether you go into business as an individual, a partner, or a corporation. Some laws affect all forms of business organizations in the same way while others do not. Let's try to touch on the differences but, a big caveat, we will not cover every difference and will be oversimplifying a little for the sake of clarity. Let's illustrate by assuming that you're going to invest $5,000 to open a variety store. We will assume that you have determined that the area is zoned for business and that the local authorities don't require any kind of license for that type of commercial enterprise.

INDIVIDUAL BUSINESSES

If you plan to "go it alone" in your own name, you simply put up a sign and start business. If you plan to use some name other than your own for example, The Corner Variety Store, you may be in a state or locality that requires you to file a certificate stating that you are doing business as the Corner Variety Store at a given address. The "doing business as" laws or regulations are to protect anyone who needs to know who is operating The Corner Variety Store: it lets the public know the name and address of the real owner. So, if you are "doing business as," check with the city or town clerk or the proper authority to find out what kind of form you must fill out and where to file it.

That's about all there is to it if you're going into business for yourself. But what if you're going into business with one or more persons?

PARTNERSHIPS

If you go into business as a partnership with one or more others you can use your own names or you can select a company or firm name. In the latter case you are "doing business as" the chosen name. The essence of a partnership is that two or more persons join as co-owners to carry on a business for profit. Almost every state has laws modeled after the Uniform Partnership Act to govern such a business. (This is one of various "model" Acts drawn by the American Law Institute in the hope that states will copy them in order to have uniformity throughout the country on the same subjects.)

The partnership is treated as a firm although it is not a legal entity in the sense that a corporation is. Unlike a corporation, a partnership does not have to obtain the state's permission to exist and it doesn't have to file reports. The key terms in partnership law are "co-owner," "carrying on a business," and "sharing profits and losses." The law says that a partnership does not come into being unless the parties so intended but intent is determined by acts as well as words. Consequently, circumstances may prove the existence of a partnership even if the parties have expressly said that none exists. The usual tests of this are the sharing of profits and losses and a voice in control.

CO-OWNERSHIP

If you're going into business by partnership of course you should have some kind of agreement with your partners, whether it be oral or written. Each partner owes a fiduciary duty to the other partners: all must be scrupulously honest and candid with each other. You're inviting trouble and possible litigation if you

125

don't insist on something in writing. There is an old Chinese proverb that the palest ink is more reliable than the most retentive memory.

The law holds that in the absence of agreement otherwise, partners share profits and losses equally, regardless of the contribution each makes. And (again, unless the agreement indicates the contrary) a partner is not entitled to wages—his compensation is his share of the profits.

As a partner, you are personally liable for all the obligations of the partnership—and "personally liable" means whatever you have, whether it's partnership property or not. If you are a general partner your liability is substantially the same as if you were carrying on the business in your own name and is not limited to just your investment as it is in a corporation, for example.

CARRYING ON BUSINESS FOR PROFIT

To "carry on" a business there usually must be more than simply a single transaction. Carrying on business involves continuity.

The word *business* means an enterprise from which participants expect and hope to realize profits. A charitable venture does not ordinarily constitute "carrying on a business for profit."

Who manages or controls the partnership? Unless the partnership agreement indicates otherwise, the partners have an equal voice in management; each has one vote regardless of the amount of his investment. If a dispute arises on any point that the partners cannot settle between themselves, the disagreement cannot be resolved by the court. The only action that a partner can take is to seek dissolution of the business upon terms to be decided by the partners themselves, or if they cannot agree, by the court at that time.

THIRD PERSONS

The law is somewhat unsettled on the rights of third persons who deal with the partnership. There is no question that in the ordinary partnership every partner is the agent of the firm and is therefore authorized to carry on its business. But suppose the partnership agreement has limited the right of one partner who nevertheless enters into some unauthorized transaction with a third party? The Uniform Partnership Act (which is followed in almost all states) says that "persons who are not partners as to each other are not partners as to third persons." However, many cases have held that, if a transaction is within the usual course of partnership business, and the third person does not know about the internal limitations on a partner, the partnership is bound, even though the transaction was not an authorized one.

What it all comes down to is this: if you're a third party dealing with a partnership, and the transaction is within the usual course of partnership business, you're probably safe in assuming the partnership is bound by the partner's act, provided you had no reason to question any limitation of his authority. But you had better be sure that the one on whose authority you're relying is actually a partner.

What's the partner's liability as concerns torts (wrongs, injuries) or crimes committed by another partner? In torts, the partner's liability is determined by the law of agency (see chapter 18). Under criminal law, one partner is not responsible for a crime committed by another partner unless he participated in it.

Upon the death of a partner, that partner's share in the business goes to his heirs unless there is an agreement to the contrary. Because that often causes a disruption of business (especially since partners who get along with each other may not find widows or sons as compatible) many partnerships take out insurance covering the share of each partner, together with a provision of the partnership agreement that the deceased partner's share shall be bought by a surviving partner. In that way, the partner's heirs get the value of his share and the surviving partner gets the business.

LIMITED PARTNERSHIPS

A restricted formal partnership called *limited partnership* is permitted by statute in most states. The business is controlled by one or more "general" partners and the partnership has any number of "limited" partners—the liability of a limited partner being limited to his share invested. A person who takes a part in the active management of the partnership cannot be a limited partner. If a limited partner exercises any control over the business, he becomes liable as a general partner. As of this writing, 42 states allow "limited partnerships." This type of partnership must file with the state a certificate disclosing information about the business to be conducted, including the names and addresses of all the partners.

Still another business entity is the joint venture—often called a syndicate, pool or a joint enterprise. It is very much like a partnership, the main distinction being that it is limited to a particular venture or transaction and is not really the "carrying on" of a business.

CORPORATIONS

If you decide that you, whether alone or together with other business associates, want to be a corporation, it's more complicated. A corporation is a "legal person" chartered by the state. Forms must be filed detailing the name of the corporation and its purpose, the names of those organizing it, the kind of stock that investors will receive, and all kinds of other information. Later by-laws must be adopted, directors elected, annual reports filed, and other requirements met. A corporation must also pay certain filing fees and special taxes.

Money for the corporation is raised by issuing stocks, bonds, or other securities to investors.

Corporations are strictly supervised. The Securities Exchange Commission regulates inter-state sales of stock and supervises the activities of such corporations; and all states have "Blue Sky" laws to protect investors in intra-state corporations. The regulatory authorities are very strict so if you're organizing a corporation, you had better be very careful to comply with all the extremely technical rules and regulations or you'll get into serious trouble.

You also owe some very important duties to the other stockholders—and the courts will strictly enforce them. The "promoter"—the term given the one who organizes and starts a corporation—owes a fiduciary duty to the corporation. That means you hold a position of trust requiring scrupulous good faith and you cannot take advantage of any knowledge or opportunity to profit that you may have except whatever is of benefit to the corporation. For example, if you had in mind buying a piece of land for $500 and selling to the corporation for $5000, forget it. That's letting you, as an individual, profit at the expense of the corporation. You cannot do that because you and the corporation technically are two separate entities. Moreover, the average corporation has minority stockholders whose rights are zealously protected by the courts. Incidentally, if you're a minority stockholder you'll be pleased to know that minority stockholders can sue to prevent directors from siphoning off profits by various devices, such as paying excessively high salaries to officers or favorite employees.

The law concerning corporations changes from time to time (as most law does). As of this writing, the concept of "ultra-vires" acts is in a transitional stage. "Ultra-vires" means "beyond the powers" or "beyond the authority"—and in this connection it refers to some act committed by the corporation that is beyond its power, as the corporation's authority is spelled out in its charter and statutes of the state or federal government.

At one time, the defense of ultra-vires was practically a customary pleading by every corporation that was sued. However, that is no longer the situation. The Model Business Corporation Act and the decisions of many state courts have largely eliminated the defense of ultra-vires.

THE MASSACHUSETTS TRUST

In addition to partnerships and corporations, there is also a hybrid entity known as a Massachusetts Trust, named for the state where it originated. This is a business trust where each member receives a trust certificate in the amount of his investment. The Massachusetts Trust is managed by a Board of Trustees. The investors incur no liability for the torts or contracts of the Trustees who are managers. Most states do not allow business entities with the characteristics of the Massachusetts Trust.

THE LEGAL ASPECTS OF DOING BUSINESS

To summarize the *legal* situation (not the "commercial" or "business") that confronts you when you are trying to decide whether to begin business as an individual, a partnership, or a corporation: as an individual, you do not have to get the consent of the state or anyone; you do not have to file any application or forms (except possibly a doing-business-as form if the business is to be conducted other than in a name of your own); you pay no special fees or taxes; you make all the decisions and control the business; and you are personally liable and responsible for any and all debts and obligations incurred in operating the business.

As a partnership, you enter into specific agreements with the other partners as to how expenses and profits will be shared; the partnership does not have to file any application or form (except possibly a doing-business-as form); it pays no special fees or taxes; as a general partner you make decisions and control the business equally with other partners unless the partnership agreement indicates otherwise; as a general partner you are personally liable and responsible for any and all debts incurred by the partnership in operating the business; and you may be responsible for the conduct of a partner that an outsider dealing with the partnership would reasonably think was authorized.

As a corporation, you invest and receive stock (or bonds or other securities) on the same terms as the other stockholders; an application and various forms have to be filed with the state; the corporation pays special filing fees and taxes; you and your stockholders elect directors who make decisions and control the business; if you are a director, your knowledge and ability must be exercised solely in the best interest of the corporation.

You can probably "get by" without the services of a lawyer or an accountant to help you begin business as an individual or a partnership but, if it's to be a corporation, you almost certainly cannot. And just the fees and rock-bottom expenses for even a simple "shoe-string" corporation and a friendly lawyer will probably run to at least $300 (at the date of this writing), depending upon the locality and the complexity of the corporation. A corporation also is more expensive to operate after its formation but its big advantage from a business standpoint is that a stockholder's liability is limited to his investment in the corporation.

If you are going into business you should also know at least a little about the Uniform Sales Act. Many court decisions, statutes, and commercial customs have been codified in the Uniform Sales Act, which buyers and sellers are presumed to follow. Agreements between buyers and sellers do not always have all the provisions they should have in order to clearly establish what the parties had in mind—but over the years the courts have resolved at least some of the uncertainties. Let's just mention a few of the ones that seem to keep popping up.

When the parties agree on terms, and they may agree on anything and everything, there's not much need of trying to interpret or guess at what they intended. But what if they don't?

130

For example, if there is no time stated for "performance" (when each does what the contract calls on him to do) is the time a day, a week, a month, a year, or what? The courts have had the question in innumerable cases and the answer is: if no time of performance is expressly provided for in the agreement, then a party has a "reasonable" time to perform. And what is reasonable of course varies with the facts of each case: it may be anything from seconds to years.

When does "title" pass? This is of vital importance because the subject of the sale may be destroyed or damaged—and which party has to suffer the loss? For example: Smith sells his horse to Jones for $100—and the horse dies after the agreement is signed but before Jones has taken the animal. Who suffers the loss?

Or Brown sells Green all the grain in Brown's warehouse—and a fire destroys it all before Green has removed it. Is it Brown's or Green's loss?

The answer to such a question usually depends upon the determination of when title passes. If the horse is Jones' as soon as the agreement was signed, it's Jones' loss even though the animal never left Smith's stable. If the grain remains the seller's property until the buyer removes it, it's the seller's loss even though the buyer had paid for it and had the right to remove it.

When title passes depends upon the agreement between the parties (the buyer and seller). If it is not covered by the agreement, then title passes when the seller has completed his part as to delivery. For example, if the seller is to ship goods, title passes when they are delivered to the railroad or other carrier. On the other hand, if the contract requires delivery to the buyer's premises, then title would not pass to the buyer until they arrive there. If the sale is "on approval" the risk of loss remains with the seller even though the goods have arrived on the buyer's premises. The buyer has not yet accepted them by approval.

The question of when title passes is so highly technical and may be so affected by conduct, words, custom, statute, legal cases, and so many other factors that anyone who may be involved in a question of this kind is simply foolish not to engage an attorney to obtain proper advice in advance as to how to deal with the question.

Is there any legal excuse for non-performance at the time a party is supposed to do something? The law accepts an excuse of unforeseeable conditions that make performance commercially impracticable—for example, transportation facilities unexpectedly not available.

Another interesting circumstance is that if a party reasonably deems himself "insecure"—it looks as if the other party is not going to be able to carry out his part of the contract—the one feeling insecure may demand "assurance" before proceeding with his performance. If the other party fails to provide assurance within 30 days, the demanding party is justified in repudiating the contract.

NEGOTIABLE INSTRUMENTS

Anyone going into business should also have a general knowledge of negotiable instruments, which are certain written instruments that have been given special legal effect in order to conduct business. Negotiable instruments include checks, promissory notes, bills of exchange, drafts, and other such items. If the layman becomes involved in a legal dispute over any of these, he should consult a lawyer.

You should have some general knowledge of what the various negotiable instruments are. Basically, negotiable instruments are documents that can be negotiated—transferred from one person to another by signatures called endorsements, or sometimes by delivery without any signature—in commercial transactions. A check is a familiar example: an order to your bank to pay someone a certain amount of money out of your account. When someone endorses it—signs his name on the back—he is representing that the check is "good." In other words, the endorser is saying that the maker of the check has that amount of money in the bank to meet the order and that he, the endorser, is willing to be liable to anyone who relies on such a representation.

A promissory note is a piece of paper on which the maker has promised to pay the promisee—or his order, which merely means whoever else is so designated by the one to whom the maker has promised payment—a certain sum of money by a certain date.

HOW TO PROTECT YOURSELF FROM "BAD CHECKS"

A layman should know that, in signing his name on any kind of a negotiable instrument, he is usually making himself responsible

132

for the validity of the instrument or incurring personal liability in some other way.

Once a check has been endorsed, it is like cash in the sense that usually it can be endorsed again and passed by anyone into whose hands it falls. For this reason, many people protect themselves by writing "For deposit only" above their signature, thus notifying one and all that the check cannot be endorsed and passed again. It has a qualified endorsement—for deposit only—which means that it must be deposited only to the account of the qualified endorser.

In theory, a negotiable instrument may be written in pencil or crayon and on any sort of material: paper, wood, slate, anything. But even though such an article may be perfectly legal, by practice and usage neither a bank nor anyone else will honor anything except a writing in ink, and on paper normally used in business.

A few questions that usually arise: Do the words "in full settlement" have any legal consequence? Most people think they mean exactly that, and they *may* mean exactly that. But there are circumstances when those words have no such effect. The law in most states takes the position that, if the amount due is *not* in dispute, a check for a lesser amount does not settle the claim even if it says "in full settlement." On the other hand, if the amount is in dispute, such words do settle the claim and the person who accepts the check cannot sue to collect the balance. It might not be easy to do but, if someone who owes John Jones $100 wants to give him a check for $50 "in full settlement," Jones probably can safely accept the check and still sue for the balance if he can get his debtor to write something like: "While I owe John Jones $100, I am paying him $50 in full settlement of such debt." On the other hand, if the person paying the money wants to protect himself, he perhaps can best do it by writing something like: "The amount owed being in dispute, this $50 is accepted in full settlement of such debt." What the layman should remember is that the words "in full settlement" may or may not mean what they say: it depends on whether or not there is a dispute about the amount due.

Most people deposit or cash a check soon after they receive it. It should be done promptly or, at most, within a reasonable time after its receipt. The maker may be discharged from responsibility for any loss caused by neglect to deposit it within a reasonable time: for example, if the bank fails. When does a check become "stale"? *Probably* not sooner than a month after its receipt; and, equally probably, it's almost certainly "stale" if it's held as long as six months before cashing it. In between is an uncertain area where courts might differ or, in layman's language, "It's anyone's guess." Don't take the chance of losing money because of delay in cashing or depositing a check.

Everyone who has a checking account should examine his cancelled checks reasonably soon after they are sent to him by his bank. He has a duty to notify the bank of any impropriety he notices such as a forged check or a "raised" check (where the amount has been altered) or other irregularity. If he has negligently failed to do so, he may be responsible for any loss to the bank and cannot hold the bank liable for any losses sustained by forgeries or alterations of the checks.

The usual "bad check" is one where the maker of it does not have sufficient funds in the bank to meet it. If the maker issued it with knowledge of such fact, he may be criminally liable for larceny. A different situation usually arises if the check is "post-dated"—bears a date sometime in the future. The very act of post-dating is usually interpreted as serving notice that the maker is not representing that he has sufficient funds in the bank at the time of making out the check but he expects or hopes to have enough in to meet it by the time of the future date the check bears. If he actually is not able to meet a post-dated check, although it is of course a "bad check," most states do not regard the making of such a check as a criminal act (unless the maker never had the intention of meeting it, which is almost impossible to prove).

Just as in real estate transactions (see Chapter 30) sometimes the question of what is legal tender becomes involved: is a check legal tender? The layman must be very careful if he is involved in a transaction that calls for payment at a specified time and place. Depending upon the contract (and sometimes the particular law or custom in a state) nothing but money, hard cash, may sometimes constitute "legal tender." (A common example is in contracts with furniture movers.) In such a situation, the tender of a check does not qualify as meeting the requirement of the payment of "legal tender." That is true of an ordinary check and it is usually also true of a certified check or a bank check. The question depends upon the specific contract and the law in the particular state; the layman had better carefully check if he is a party to a contract that calls for payment at a specific time.

Incidentally, the difference between "bank checks," "certified checks," and "treasurer's checks" is very slight. While there are legal differences, as a practical matter they are usually all checks issued by a bank with the bank's promise or representation or guarantee that the check will be honored by the bank. There is, of course, no such representation by the bank for a depositor's check.

Sometimes there will be inconsistencies apparent on the face of a document. For example, in a check the amount is handwritten in the figures "125" and the words "one hundred twenty" are written. Or two words (one printed, one typed) that should be the same are not. What controls? The courts have decided: handwritten prevails over typewritten or printed; as between typewritten and printed, the typewritten prevails. As between words and figures, words prevail.

In cases involving negotiable instruments, unlike other instruments the phrase "holder in due course" often appears. A holder in due course of a negotiable instrument is often designated as someone who is "an innocent purchaser for value." It is the legal terminology to describe someone who has in good faith paid money for the document without any reason to know of any defects in it. Such a holder takes a negotiable instrument free from any defenses that might be available to the original parties without being prejudiced in his rights by defects or flaws in the title of the original parties or by personal defenses available to the original parties among themselves.

A person is not a "holder in due course" if he had reason to recognize defects in the instruments: for example, some material term is not included or the instrument is overdue. Either circumstance should have put him on notice that something might be amiss.

What's the situation if death or incompetency occurs? For example, you have a check from John Smith who died (or became insane) the day after he signed the check but three days before you present the check to the bank on which it was drawn. Under the law of Agency, death or other incompetence terminates the agency at the time it occurs—which would have meant the check has become invalid. However, the Uniform Commercial Code has superseded the old law of Agency in such matters—and the bank (if it wants to) is protected if it cashes the check within 10 days of

135

the death or disability, unless a stop payment order is given the bank by the potential heirs of the person who drew the check.

Incidentally, a "stop payment" order is only binding for 14 days if it's oral, whereas a written one holds for 6 months (and may be extended).

In business (or for personal reasons) you'll perhaps have occasion to use a power of attorney. It is a document by which the principal (you) empowers the agent (a trusted friend, usually) to act for you with as much authority and effect as you yourself would have. The power of attorney may be as broad and all-inclusive or as narrow and limited as you specify. It can be as long or as short as you desire—subject only to its termination by the principal's death or other incapacities such as insanity. You can obtain a power of attorney form at a legal stationary store or simply write it out yourself. Something like the following will do: "I, John Smith, name Robert Green as my attorney in fact to act for me and in my name to (whatever it is you want him to do)." Date it and sign it, preferably before a notary public because some states require this formality.

Knowledge of legal concepts known as bailments, liens, agency, mortgage, warranty, and product liability is important to anyone doing business as a buyer or seller of any product. Bailments and liens are discussed in Chapter 17, agency in Chapter 18, and Chapter 22 touches on mortgages, warranties, and product liability. The businessman should also understand the legal ramifications of bankruptcy. Let's take a look at it.

(The author acknowledges his appreciation of the helpful suggestions for this chapter made by attorney-professor Michael J. Princi of Hyannis, Massachusetts and attorney Sidney Friedman of New York, New York.)

20

Bankruptcy: A Legal Antidote to a Financial Disease

WHEN WE HEAR THE word "bankruptcy," the average person thinks of financial doomsday and social ostracism. We believe it carries some sort of stigma, either financial, moral, or social. We're afraid it must indicate a fatal defect in character, a flaw in business acumen or some kind of sharpness or dishonesty that has led to the brink of fraud or chicanery. And as for a credit rating, if anyone ever had a chance to get credit, it's gone with the bankruptcy decree.

That's what we think—and we couldn't be more wrong. Bankruptcy should be none of those things, and it actually is not. It may have been at one time in the distant past, but not today. Just as a medical doctor might recommend amputation, corrective surgery or the injection of a drug, so might the financial "doctor" urge bankruptcy, or an assignment for the benefit of creditors, or some type of agreement by creditors that allows the debtor to discharge his obligations by the payment of only a fraction of what is owed. Bankruptcy is merely a legal antidote to a financial disease that might have fatally poisoned the entire body. So let's begin our discussion of bankruptcy with the realization that it is not a scare word, but merely a legal word that offers a haven to people caught in a financial storm.

Just what is bankruptcy? What does it mean? What does it do, how, and why?

There are two types of bankruptcy: voluntary and involuntary. The voluntary type is where the person in debt himself decides he wants to go into bankruptcy. The involuntary type is where a debtor owes over a thousand dollars and at least three creditors decide they want him put into bankruptcy. Since the person has no choice

137

about involuntary bankruptcy, let's discuss the voluntary types.

Whatever is it that causes a person to begin wondering if the answer to his problems is bankruptcy? The thought never occurs to anyone unless his debts have mounted to such a degree that he is finding it virtually impossible to meet them. Once that happens, it is only a matter of time until he begins to experience the harassment and embarrassment of "dunning" by his creditors. Then he begins to wonder about bankruptcy, a legal eraser that cleans the financial blackboard of virtually all debts.

The mechanics of bankruptcy, greatly oversimplified, are that the court appoints someone called a Trustee in Bankruptcy to whom the debtor turns over all his property, together with a list of his debts. Out of the bankrupt's "estate," the trustee pays every creditor proportionately so that all are treated equally: if the debtor's total assets amount to $1,000 (after expenses of bankruptcy are deducted) and the debts total $10,000 every creditor will receive ten percent of his debt. And that extinguishes the debt; *the slate is wiped clean*. That is the important fact about bankruptcy: the debtor is freed of his burden and gets a fresh start. Imagine a dog-tired man loaded down with a hundred-pound burden trying to climb up an endless hill—when suddenly the burden is lifted from his shoulders and the hill is leveled. Bankruptcy gives a debtor the same kind of fresh financial start.

But suppose the debtor really wants to pay off one or all of his creditors once he gets on his feet? Fine! He can do so if he wishes but the choice is up to him.

Can bankruptcy eliminate every debt the person has? It all depends on the kind of debts. There are a few (such as unpaid taxes) that cannot be wiped out; but in most cases, bankruptcy discharges all the debts.

Is bankruptcy expensive or very time-consuming? No. The main expense is the lawyer—who, sensibly, is customarily paid in advance. An uncomplicated bankruptcy proceeding takes very little of either the lawyer's or the client's time.

Will bankruptcy affect your social standing? Probably not. The only people who care very much one way or the other are your creditors—and they probably are not too happy with you in any event. And of course if there is any one of them whom you particularly want to please—say your doctor—you can always pay him even after his bill has been discharged in bankruptcy. It will improve your standing with him if you pay a debt that the court has officially ruled is no longer owed.

BANKRUPTCY CAN IMPROVE YOUR CREDIT RATING

But what does bankruptcy do to your credit rating? Strangely enough, bankruptcy probably will improve your credit rating. How can that be? Doesn't bankruptcy prove that the bankrupt is the kind of person who will run out on his debts, who cannot be trusted, who should not be extended credit under any circumstances? Well, perhaps the logical answer to all those questions should be in the affirmative, but experience shows that this is not the correct answer. The fact is that today's merchants will extend credit more quickly to the person who has just gone through bankruptcy than to another person who is struggling to pay a back-breaking load of bills. Why? Because the bankrupt is starting afresh with a clean slate and with no creditors.

Make the decision yourself: two of your customers want to buy five hundred dollars' worth of goods on credit. Both are steady workers at the same manufacturing plant, each making $200 a week. Jones has just gone through bankruptcy, wiping out $10,000 worth of claims against him by other merchants. Smith still owes $10,000 to other merchants and he is being hounded by them to increase the weekly payments he is making on each bill. Out of the $200 weekly pay check, Jones has no debts to pay—they have all been discharged in bankruptcy. But Smith is paying $75 a week in debts out of his paycheck—his creditors have legal claims against him. Which one looks like the better "risk" to you?

The final clincher is that Jones cannot go into another bankruptcy for at least six years—that's the law—whereas Smith can go into bankruptcy anytime he wishes. If you have to sue either, you have the choice of Jones who legally owes nothing to anyone else or Smith, who owes everybody in sight. And Smith might go into bankruptcy, listing his debt to you, tomorrow. Which one looks like the better "risk" to you?

So, strange and illogical as it seems, bankruptcy probably will improve your credit rating if you are in desperate financial straits, no matter how the local credit bureau might have you listed in its official records.

We are not recommending bankruptcy—quite the opposite. If you can pay your bills, keep your good credit rating, and avoid a mental or physical breakdown without bankruptcy, by all means it's best to avoid bankruptcy. But if the only way to avoid a worse fate is by bankruptcy, then it's not a bad road to take. If financial conditions are so bad you're having trouble keeping your head above water, don't refrain from at least considering bankruptcy. If the obstacle is your conscience, you can salve it by remembering that you can always pay any debt you want to after you have been discharged in bankruptcy.

There's another avenue of relief from creditor harassment that may be something to consider: assignment for the benefit of creditors. If you want to avoid bankruptcy, and if your creditors are agreeable, it is possible to assign all your assets to a trustee who will then make agreed-upon weekly or monthly payments to gradually clean up your bills. It's a lengthy process, it doesn't give you an immediate clean slate, and it does not avoid payment of your bills—but it may give you relief. Again, like bankruptcy, it's an avenue to be explored by a debtor who is being harassed or embarrassed by creditors.

Both bankruptcy or an assignment for the benefit of creditors call for the services of an attorney. Don't try to become an expert in such matters or think you can perform adequately with a "do-it-yourself" legal kit. The layman needs to know that there are such reliefs available, and then see a lawyer to recommend the proper one.

The topic of bankruptcy always brings to mind something that has inevitably preceded it: the collection (or attempted collection) of debts. Being on either end of that problem is an uncomfortable position.

WHAT THE BILL COLLECTOR CANNOT DO

The creditor cannot attempt to collect his debt by any method that appeals to him. He could at one time, but the abuse of this privilege led most states to pass legislation preventing extraordinary methods. Where the legislature did not act, usually the courts have protected the debtor from collection methods that border on harassment.

In general, debts cannot be collected in an unfair or a deceptive manner. It is considered unfair if the creditor uses threats of one kind or another. Ordinary threats have included such things as threatening to communicate the facts of such debt to the public in general or to interested persons; or words on an envelope that would indicate that the communication is about a debt.

140

Most courts hold that it is undue harassment or embarrassment of the debtor if he is telephoned at unreasonable hours or with unreasonable frequency, if offensive language is used by the caller, or if the creditor is threatening to use unusual steps to collect the debt. The courts are also very strict about the use of forms that simulate the appearance of judicial process. At one time, it was fairly common for a creditor to send the debtor a notice that had words or a form that made it appear that it came from some court. Today such methods are illegal in most states and, in addition, many courts regard use of such simulated process as being in contempt of court. In Massachusetts, for example, Chapter 272, Section 97A of the General Laws forbids the use of demands and notices resembling court process and provides for contempt of court proceedings for violation of the statute. Chapter 93, Section 49, forbids the collection of debts in an unfair or deceptive manner.

Some states are particularly careful to protect the homeowner from being harassed about any debt that he may have incurred primarily for a family or household purpose.

So far as debts are concerned, the law is a two-edged sword: if someone owes you, it can be used to help you collect. On the other hand, if you're debt-ridden, the law can help you avoid embarrassment and harassment by your creditors or, if the burden is too heavy, bankruptcy can eliminate either all or most of your debts. The layman does not have to become expert in using this sword; but he should know that it is available to him for either purpose.

One last word about debt. If there's a judgment against a debtor that says he owes a creditor some money, the courts have a procedure that is usually called "supplementary process," "poor debtor proceedings," or something similar. Under it, the creditor has the debtor brought into court, examines him under oath, and the judge can then make an order determining what the debtor must do to satisfy the judgment.

The usual questions asked by the creditor (or his attorney) have to do with the debtor's financial situation: How much does he make a week? How much is in his bank account? Does he own a house or automobile? How much is the mortgage on it? And so forth.

The debtor counters by showing how much money he needs for himself and his family, what other obligations he has, and so on.

The judge steers a course between the two positions and makes an appropriate order. He might order the debtor to pay the whole debt immediately, decide that the debtor is unable to pay anything at that time, order the debtor to pay $2 a week, or whatever else fits the situation.

The judge's decision is a practical one, based on the debtor's financial position in light of his domestic situation. If the debtor does not obey the judicial command, he is in contempt of court and may be punished by a fine or confinement. This is not considered peonage or enforced servitude or jail for debt. The debtor does not get a jail sentence because he owes money—he is confined because he is in contempt of court in disobeying the court order. Sometimes the only way a creditor can avoid this trap is to go into bankruptcy. That may be his only hope that he—and not the judge—will have the last word.

No one really wins in bankruptcy—but torts is a different matter. Let's turn to that.

THE CONSTITUTION GUARANTEES PRIVACY.

21
Torts: Accidents, Injuries and Damages

ONE IMPORTANT FIELD OF law is the law of torts. Most tort actions are based on negligence by the defendant that injured the plaintiff. In addition, the plaintiff may have to show that he himself was not contributorily negligent.

A tort is usually defined as a private or civil wrong for which the law provides a remedy in money damages. If someone is injured through the carelessness of another person—his fault or his negligence—the law inquires into the question of who was "wrong," to what extent, and whether the injured person himself contributed to the accident. This gets involved with standards of care and the law has established certain criteria. While there are exceptions to everything—as is always true of any legal doctrine—the law talks about the degree of care that should be exercised by a reasonable person in the circumstances.

It is all theoretical because no such person as the Reasonable Man ever existed; and, even if he did, it would be impossible to determine scientifically what is meant by "careful" and "careless." Nevertheless, the law says that if you are injured by another person's negligence, you may recover damages if you were "in the exercise of due care"—doing whatever the Reasonable Man would do in the circumstances—and were not yourself contributorily negligent.

There are many ramifications in the law of torts, and the various states have different decisions on liability: the question of who is responsible for the injury. Some states say contributory negligence bars recovery; but others take the position that comparative negligence may decrease the amount of recovery but does not bar it. So if the plaintiff—the injured person—was ten percent at fault as against the defendant's ninety percent, whether he recovers or not depends upon whether he is in a "contributory negligence" or "comparative negligence" state. If the injury was sustained in the former, the plaintiff's contributory negligence bars his recovery of anything. If the case were in the latter, the jury determines what damages would be awarded if the plaintiff were not at fault in any way and then decreases the amount by the degree of negligence of the plaintiff—in this hypothetical case, by ten percent.

WHO WAS AT FAULT?

When we talk of negligence and torts, we must think in terms of fault—that is the basis of both the plaintiff's claim and the defendant's defense. As a general rule, the injured person's right to recover damages depends upon his proving that the defendant was at fault and he himself was free of blame. Or, to put it legally, that he himself was exercising the due care of a reasonable man in the circumstances, but was injured because of the negligence of the defendant.

In an action of tort, the general rule is that the plaintiff may recover for all the "natural and probable consequences" of the defendant's negligent act. The amount recovered is usually the actual damages suffered, but there are rare occasions when punitive awards are allowed by statute.

We must also remember that, regardless of what the law itself says, it is not unusual for juries to completely disregard legal doctrines that might deny recovery to someone who has sustained serious injuries. The generous or compassionate juror may say: "The man was hurt, wasn't he? Then let them pay!" The likelihood of such sentiments is increased if the defendant is a corporation or if the defendant apparently carries insurance. The layman should know that, while the law books have all the legal definitions and doctrines, it is a jury composed of laymen who have the last word.

The injured person who loses his case may find some consolation in the customary practice of the tort lawyer to work on a contingent fee basis: the fee is a percentage of the amount of recovery. If the injured person loses his case, at least he doesn't have to lose any money paying the lawyer. That's the silver lining in the dark cloud of injury and defeat.

22
Consumer Protection - Knowledge That Saves You Money

THE CONSUMER IS YOU and I: any person who buys a product for consumption, not for resale or profit or commercial use. Over the centuries the consumer has always been the low man on the legal totem pole. This is no longer true. Today the consumer is king. Gone are the days when the consumer bought at his peril, or when he did not know whom to sue for a defective product or shoddy merchandise: today the merchandiser sells at his peril and the buyer has the choice of defendants to hold responsible. *Caveat emptor*—let the buyer beware—has been replaced by a new rhyme: let the seller be fair. The changes were fought for by consumer advocates such as Ralph Nader, and aided and abetted by the whole new philosophy of law that followed the growth and development of today's society with its modernized methods of production and marketing.

The transition has been little short of miraculous. In the beginning, the seller showed his wares, told lies about them, and did whatever was most calculated to result in a sale—and the buyer could take it or leave it. If he took it, he did so at his own peril. The law Latinized the mantle of protection it threw around the seller: *Caveat emptor.* And if the buyer did not beware, he was hurt; it was as simple as that.

Gradually changes came into being. The gut-fighting rules of the marketplace were softened somewhat. The seller could not tell outright lies about the product—the most he could do was "puff," which is Madison Avenue terminology for telling lies that should be recognized as such by anyone with common sense. So, legally, the seller could "puff" his product but he could not defraud or make the kind of substantial misstatements that could not be detected by

145

a careful buyer. However, *caveat emptor* was still pretty much in the saddle.

The marketing evils were of many kinds but, basically, they added up to the fact that even the careful buyer was taken advantage of by modern advertising, salesmanship, marketing methods, and fine print: even the smartest housewife doesn't have the time or knowledge to keep up with commercial techniques that would baffle a Philadelphia lawyer. It was easy to be taken in by words that seemed to be representations but were not such technically and legally. And there were scores of deceptive practices that were perfectly legal even if they were sharp, immoral or unethical.

RETAILER, WHOLESALER, MANUFACTURER—WHOM CAN YOU SUE FOR DEFECTIVE PRODUCTS?

Legal rights themselves were vague and unsatisfactory. While it was easy to be misled by advertisements, it was not easy to hold anyone responsible for the product that turned out to be shoddy or defective. Let me illustrate: the corner store sold Mrs. Housewife a bar of soap that turned out to have lye in it that burned her skin. Mr. Retailer, the owner of the corner store, could say, "I didn't make any representations about the soap. The customer picked it out herself." If there was no liability there for that reason, perhaps she should see the wholesaler. "Oh, no," Mr. Wholesaler could argue, "I have nothing to do with it. I don't even know Mrs. Housewife. I had dealings with no one but Mr. Retailer." Legally, Mrs. Housewife is a stranger to Mr. Wholesaler—there is no "privity of contract" between the customers of the corner store and the wholesaler in some distant community.

Another problem was (and is) that many retailers are "judgment proof"—that is, they do not have any money or other assets to pay anyone who sues and wins the case. The plaintiff (the person suing) may get a piece of paper from the court saying he has been awarded so many dollars in damages—but that is only a judgment. It is not much help to you if the defendant (the person sued) is "judgment proof." While this is not a legal impediment, unless bankruptcy enters the picture, it is a very practical one—and it is cold comfort to the victim to say that the law, which has provided a remedy, is not at fault simply because the defendant has no money to satisfy the remedy provided.

What about the manufacturer itself? If any suit based on contract law is not possible because there was no contract between Mrs. Housewife and Mr. Producer, what about negligence? Isn't a manufacturer responsible for negligently letting a poisonous substance get into the product? Perhaps. But the law said it was up to the consumer suing to prove the point: Mrs. Housewife had the "burden of proof" to show in just what way the manufacturer had been negligent. Can you even imagine where she would begin? Of course you cannot, and neither could anyone else in most cases—so injustices were built into the judicial system regarding consumer law.

One thing the law cannot tolerate forever is injustice. So the law began to change—slowly, as is its custom; but decidedly. The very law that had been the shield of the seller gradually was forged into a sword for the buyer, sharpened by legal words called "warranties." Articles that were merchandise became legally tagged with expressed or implied warranties.

WARRANTIES PROTECT THE CONSUMER

At present, the consumer is usually protected by statutes or judicial decisions that refer to warranty, express warranty, implied warranty, warranty of fitness, breach of warranty, and other similar principles of law. Technically, a warranty is a promise that a proposition of fact is true. It has varied meanings in laws referring to real property or the sale of personal property or in contracts, and so on. Perhaps the easiest way to understand "warranty" is to think of it as a representation relied on by the person to whom it is made. It is like a guarantee of something, too. An express warranty is a direct representation or statement made in so many words; an implied warranty is one that is not stated but is understood to exist because of the nature of the transaction or of the relative situation of the parties to it. Whether the warranty is express or implied, the buyer is protected by it: the law says that the buyer is entitled to rely on the representation, whether the seller made it in so many words or is simply assumed to have made it.

When we refer to an "express warranty," we mean a direct or explicit statement made by the seller or the person to be bound. The words are said, the promise is specific, the transaction is exact.

An "implied warranty" is one where the specific words are not said, and we cannot point to an exact promise; but we can show a

147

transaction or situation such that a representation or guarantee is understood by the parties concerned.

Here are a few illustrations of the distinction. If I say to you, "This carving knife is sharp," that is an express warranty that the knife is sharp and will cut. If I say to you, "This is a good carving knife," that is an implied warranty that the knife is sharp and will cut. If the hardware store salesman says, "This lawnmower has sharp blades," that is an express warranty that the lawnmower has sharp blades. If the hardware salesman said, "This is a good lawnmower," or "This lawnmower will do the job," that is an implied warranty that the lawnmower has blades sharp enough to cut the grass.

While there may be implied warranties of various kinds, the most common as well as the most important to the layman is the implied warranty of "merchantability"—that is, that the product is fit for use for the purpose for which it is sold. The buyer of a bicycle does not have to look for an express warranty that the pedals will turn the wheels satisfactorily so it may be ridden: there is an implied warranty to that effect. If the striking head of a hammer turns out to be putty, the seller has violated an implied warranty of merchantability: the purpose of the hammer was to pound nails into wood. If the article will not satisfactorily perform the function for which it was manufactured or produced or sold, it is not "merchantable." The court gave consumers a powerful weapon when the doctrine of implied warranty was declared to be the law governing sales.

A warranty of fitness is where the seller of merchandise is told by the buyer of the particular purpose for which the article is needed, and it is apparent that the buyer is relying on the seller's experience and knowledge that it is reasonably fit for such purpose. In such circumstances, if the article is not fit for the purpose, there has been a breach of warranty and the seller may be liable for any damages caused to the buyer. Such implied warranty could be involved when a customer orders a meal in a restaurant, purchases a suit in a clothing store, or buys cold cream in a drug store.

The law has many technicalities when the purchaser himself selects the article, either using his own judgment or in reliance on a trade name. In such a case, the immediate seller may not be liable for any damage caused by defects in it. The theory of law here is often that the buyer did not rely on the seller's knowledge or judgment but on his own. Similar reasoning comes into play when the buyer orders an article by some well-known brand name: "Give me a pack of Camel cigarettes." Such a buyer is relying on the name and reputation of the particular brand, and not on the judgment or expertise of the man behind the tobacco counter.

There are also cases where the buyer may be relying on both the immediate seller and the brand name. These are situations where both the man behind the counter and the manufacturer or producer in some distant state may be liable for any damages caused by a defective product.

When we talk about the various kinds of warranty, we are getting into deep legal waters; and anything involving a dispute about breach of warranty calls for the services of a lawyer.

"PRODUCT LIABILITY" PUTS THE RESPONSIBILITY ON THE MANUFACTURER

Closely related to the subject of warranty is the concept of "product liability." While the whole subject of product liability has been on the books for years, it is constantly changing and growing along with society. The trend of law today is to hold the distant manufacturer liable—responsible for damage—for any injury or loss caused by any defect in the product. At one time, the law took the position that the buyer of an automobile or loaf of bread or toothbrush or other product could look only to the immediate seller of the article if there were any defects in it. The best legal thinking of just a few years ago was that the buyer had had no business with the distant manufacturer, had not relied on anything said by that manufacturer, and had no claim against the manufacturer. They were legal "strangers" and an important legal ingredient called "privity of contract" was missing. The buyer's business had been with the local retailer who was selling that automobile, loaf of bread or toothbrush; he had relied either on himself or that retailer, and he had no claim against anyone but that retailer.

Today most of that thinking has changed and legal authorities take the position that the distant manufacturer may well be liable to a purchaser he has never seen or even heard of. Practically an entire new field of law practice—something called product liability —came into existence in the 1950's and 1960's and has been steadily expanding the risk of responsibility of manufacturers and producers until it is now in many ways the greatest protection the consumer has. No longer does the average buyer have to look solely to some judgment-proof local retailer to compensate him for

149

damage caused by a defective product: he now usually can go after the financial resources of the giant company that manufactured or produced it. The law of product liability gives the consumer a defendant such as a huge manufacturing corporation instead of the virtually bankrupt owner of the Mom and Pop store that sold him the product.

Let me illustrate "product liability." You are walking down the sidewalk when the axle of a passing automobile breaks, the wheel comes off, bounds up on the sidewalk, and injures you severely. Who compensates you for your medical bills, lost wages, pain and suffering, and other damages? Well, you do not have a contract action against anyone because you have never had any agreement of any kind with anyone concerning that automobile. No one told you, directly or indirectly, that it wouldn't have a defective axle and no one assured you it would be in good working condition.

When you turn to another field of law—the possibility of a tort action for injuries sustained because of someone's negligence or carelessness—you quickly find out that the driver of the automobile had not been negligent or at fault in any way. He was driving carefully and he had no reason to know (or even suspect) that there might be anything wrong with the axle. In fact, he himself has been badly injured and has the same question as you: whom does he sue?

Today, in both cases, the lawyer would undoubtedly advise that there is every likelihood that the remote manufacturer of the automobile—a concern that doesn't know either you or the driver and never had any contract or business of any kind with either of you—is responsible. You can look to that manufacturer for damages. You do not have to prove you had a contract with him or that he was negligent or careless in manufacturing the car: you must show that he manufactured the car, it had a defective axle, and you were injured as a result. The newly recognized doctrine of product liability gives you that virtually complete protection—not from some "judgment proof" small retailer, but from the manufacturer or producer who undoubtedly has assets you can reach. If you win your product liability case, you're going to get your money.

It sounds simple, but don't be deceived. Product liability cases are strictly for lawyers. They are complicated, technical, and require expert handling. But you certainly should know that there is something called product liability and, if you are injured in some way by anything that is "wrong" in a product—machinery that

150

breaks, food that's bad, toys that burn fingers, steel that doesn't hold walls, anything that doesn't do its job—you should see a lawyer. You probably have a good product liability claim and you may win it—but, almost certainly, only if you see a lawyer who understands not only the possibilities of such cases but also their complexities.

The protection given a consumer by laws relating to warranty and product liability may be codified in the statutes or judicial decisions of any state. The consumer must of course consult the authorities in his particular jurisdiction. You should know that it is virtually certain that every state affords such protection to the consumer—as does the federal law in federal situations. You should also understand that, if there is any controversy about any important aspect of cases involving warranty or product liability, the services of a good lawyer are essential. It is not law for a layman.

"BAIT AND SWITCH" PRACTICES THAT LURE THE CUSTOMER

The legislatures of virtually all states have passed many other kinds of statutes intended to give greater protection to the buyer. For example, one common practice of retailers was the notorious "bait and switch" gambit. A newspaper or window advertisement would feature some article at a price so low that it could not be resisted. This was the "bait" that lured the customer into the store. Once inside, the clerk would explain that the last of the low-priced class had unfortunately been sold but, "Here is a much better model at just a little higher price." Or a meat store might advertise steak at $3 a pound when it was selling for twice that, and then have an inedible sample available at that price next to good looking steaks at $5—knowing that no customer would take the $3 "bargain." The "bait and switch" merchants had a field day in higher-priced areas like used cars where the salesman would "confidentially" tell the customer everything that was wrong with the $890 advertised car but, "This other one, now, for just $1,280—there's the real bargain."

Most state legislatures have put a stop to "bait and switch" practices. If you run into it, your local Chamber of Commerce, Better Business Bureau or similar agency can usually tell you whether it's illegal in the particular example. Give them a telephone call. Or, if you're really upset, call the Consumers Division in the State House (most states either already have one or

151

are in the process of getting one, usually in the Attorney General's Office). Most of the time you don't have to go that far: the mere threat of such action may bring the retailer to terms in short order.

The automobiles discussed above bring to mind the question of repossession because autos are frequently repossessed due to the failure of a buyer to keep up installment payments. Repossession, the taking back of the thing sold, may be tied in with something called "deficiency judgment." Let's digress for a moment to discuss deficiency judgment.

"DEFICIENCY JUDGMENTS" CAN REALLY HURT YOU

Suppose you have bought a car by making a down payment of $1,000 to be followed by monthly payments of $100 until the full purchase price of $5,000 has been paid. You make a couple of payments, then lose your job or have family sickness that prevents you from keeping up your monthly payments of $100. By the time the auto dealer (or the finance company, in the usual case) repossesses your car—takes it back because of failure to keep up the monthly installments—you have paid $500 in monthly installments which, added to your $1,000 down payment, means you have paid $1,500 on the car and still owe $3,500. The auto dealer or its finance company auctions off the car for $2,500. This means that they have received $4,000 for the car (your $1,500 plus the $2,500 from the buyer at auction)—and that total is $1,000 less than the agreed $5,000 purchase price. There is a "deficiency" of $1,000. If the auto dealer (or finance company) sues you on your contract to purchase the car for $5,000, they will get a judgment against you for $1,000—the deficiency or difference between what you promised to pay and what they actually received. This is called a "deficiency judgment."

Deficiency judgments often occur in other situations, perhaps the most serious being in real estate mortgages. Most borrowers have a mortgage on their property—a piece of paper held by the bank (usually) which says that the home owner owes the bank a certain amount of money which will be paid in stated monthly or yearly installments. If you buy a home for $25,000, let us assume you have $10,000 available. The seller must get $25,000. So you borrow $15,000 from a bank (paying interest to it, of course). As security, to be certain you will repay the loan, the bank has you sign a promissory note (called a mortgage note) in which you promise to pay the $15,000 in certain stated installments over a certain period of years. You also sign a document called a mortgage which, in substance, gives the bank ownership of your home if you do not keep up your payments. (While this definition is not technically exact, it is practically correct.) The bank is willing to lend you the $15,000 on this security (or collateral) because it believes your home is worth more than $15,000—if you don't pay, they have the house, which is as good or better than the money itself. But suppose you cannot keep up your payments. The bank "forecloses." That means they bring a legal action that says, "You didn't keep up your payments so we're going to take your house. Remember that mortgage note you signed?" The bank may feel sorry for you, but that's business. Misfortune has struck.

Occasionally misfortune may seem to strike the bank next. Perhaps your house was foreclosed at a time when the real estate market had gone down. When the bank auctioned off your house (to get the $15,000 you owe it) the highest bid was $12,000. The bank takes that $12,000, but now it's $3,000 short. It's true that misfortune has struck again—but it's probably you who is hurt, not the bank. Why? Because of the legal words "deficiency judgment" —which means that the bank can sue you for the deficiency, the difference between what you owe and what it has received. If so, you not only have lost the house but also have to pay the difference between the amount you owed and the amount the house brought at the auction.

Here is another area in which the consumer is gaining. Deficiency judgments still exist in some states, but they're on the way out. For example, they have been legislated out of existence in Massachusetts, Connecticut, and many other consumer-minded states—but in others (New York, for example) the courts still enforce them. The trend definitely is to outlaw deficiency judgments, the theory being that the seller or lender has a choice: he can repossess (foreclose) or sue, but not both. If the choice is to repossess (or foreclose) the seller or finance company can take the article or the real estate and that is all. If its sale brings less than the original contract called for, there is no remedy—the money lender should have anticipated that possibility. Those who follow this line of thought believe that the average money lender is usually in a better position than the average purchaser or consumer to understand and appreciate the possible risks involved.

INSTALLMENT CONTRACTS AND REPOSSESSION

The states are giving the consumer more and more relief from the once widely used mechanism of repossession. It is increasingly difficult for merchants to recover furniture and household articles sold on installment contracts.

The deceptive installment contract is another "come-on" that is well on its way to complete extinction. There is a necessary place for a genuine installment contract and it serves a useful purpose in helping people "buy now, pay later" for essential items that are beyond their instant purchasing capacity. Consumer protection statutes do not interfere with this type of installment buying. All that legislatures in most states have done (or are doing) is to require that the installment contract be fair to the consumer. No longer does he sign a contract only to find out that the financial terms were concealed in the fine print or buried under technical legal phrases that were just so much gibberish to the average buyer. Consumer protection statutes compel the seller to put all this information in large print and in readable language. If the interest rate is two percent a month, then the contract must state in large letters in a prominent place that it is TWENTY-FOUR PERCENT A YEAR. If there are any penalties for late or missed payments, the penalty clause must be so prominent that the customer is sure to see it.

In most state legislatures there has been particular emphasis on the statutes that insist on truth in lending because many consumers have been taken advantage of by installment contracts with exorbitant interest rates. For instance, the Massachusetts Truth in Lending Act, General Laws Chapter 140C, provides that interest, taxes, insurance, annual percentage rate, carrying charges and other financial details have to be printed conspicuously in sales contracts. The so-called Federal Regulation Z has the same effect.

Another law that many states have is similar to the Massachusetts Consumer Protection statute. Under it (General Laws Chapter 93A) Section 2 makes unlawful any unfair methods of competition or deceptive acts in the conduct of any trade. Section 4 provides for injunctions by the Attorney General to stop such practices, and Section 9 enables consumers to sue for possible damages. Chapter 93, Section 48 allows the buyer to cancel a contract for goods or services that was made at other than the seller's place of business, and Section 49 bars debt collection by unfair or deceptive methods.

The trend in every state is to compel merchants to be fair in advertising and in the extension of credit or installment contracts. Most states have a Consumer's Advocate Division either as an independent agency or in the office of the Attorney General of the state. It has the responsibility of protecting the consumer and in most instances it is very active in prosecuting those who are cheating the consumer.

A cautionary note should be inserted here. There is one way to circumvent the protection that is supposed to be given the consumer, which all states have not yet remedied. This problem arises when a retail store immediately assigns an installment contract to a bank, gets its money now, and leaves it to the bank to collect the installments from the buyer. If the consumer has a good defense of some kind against the seller—for example, some fraud or deception or illegality in the installment contract itself—will that defense carry over and be good against the bank? The states have differed on the point. Some states take the position the bank was not a party to the installment contract, had nothing to do with any illegality or defect in it, and has already paid over the bank's money in good faith to the retail store in return for the installment contract being assigned to the bank—in brief, that the bank is entitled to its money from the consumer, and any defense of illegality the consumer might have had against the retailer is not good against the bank. And so the consumer must pay the bank the installments due and then sue the retailer for the illegality in the installment contract. This, theoretically at least, gives the consumer a complete remedy.

Other states take a different position and hold that the bank takes the assignment of the installment contract at its own risk; and if there are any illegalities or deceptions in it that would give the purchaser a good defense against the retail seller, then that defense is also good against the assignee bank. These states are of the opinion that making the consumer pay the bank and then sue the retailer may be theoretically a remedy but, practically speaking, it is not. (To this writer, it seems that this is the sounder view and is more in keeping with the trend to protect the consumer against those who should understand the risks.)

The federal government as well as the states affords protection to the consumer, both by statute and by regulations of the Federal Trade Commission and other regulatory agencies.

155

The federal Fair Credit Reporting Act allows anyone to see a credit agency's file and to demand proper corrections in it. Civil suits for substantial damages are also available to anyone injured by a false credit report. (In fact, even if the report is not false, it still may be legally damaging.)

In virtually every state, the individual is protected from various legal attachments of his property by creditors. Exempt articles almost always include necessary wearing apparel for the person and his family, household furniture, tools or equipment necessary in carrying on a trade or business, and so on. In addition, a substantial part of the wage-earner's wages are exempt; and many states do not allow a motor vehicle to be attached without the permission of a court. Some states also exempt at least some part of savings accounts.

Federal laws have similar exemptions from attachment.

MAIL ORDER FRAUDS

One area that often concerns the consumer is his liability or responsibility in mail order situations. Unrequested books, records or other articles may suddenly arrive on your doorstep accompanied by a form note saying, "If not satisfied with them after 10 days, return to sender without any obligation on your part." The law in most states now relieves you of any obligation to pay for such articles or to return them at your own expense. Usually the only obligation the person has is to notify the sender that he does not want the articles and will return them if the sender forwards sufficient postage to do so. And some states even allow the recipient of unsolicited goods or services to use them without any obligation to pay for them.

Of course the situation is completely different if the recipient of the merchandise either accepts and uses it, or had requested that it be sent, or had accepted an offer to examine and return, or was a party to other similar conditions. In that case the recipient has accepted the obligation of either paying for the articles or returning them.

Mail order business has become something of a nuisance to many people. But under most conditions, you no longer have an obligation to accept or pay for or return unrequested merchandise. Your only duty is usually simply not to damage it by your negligence or unreasonable conduct.

Similarly, protective measures have been aimed directly at those door-to-door salesmen who fast-talk the unwary housewife into signing up for aluminum siding, wall-to-wall carpeting, a swimming pool, or other "bargains" that are irresistible. Legislatures have put a crimp in such tactics by passing "buyer's remorse" laws that allow the buyer to rescind (change his mind and withdraw agreement) such contracts the next day or within a couple of days.

And there are countless other recent changes in statutes and court decisions along the same lines. Neither the layman nor any lawyer will know them all—but you should at least know that there is every probability that your state now gives such protection. When a particular situation arises, check it out with one of the business agencies or consumer protection departments in your area. Most of the time you will find that—regardless of what you have signed—the "bargain" must be an honest one and without unfair strings or deceptive practices or you are fully protected. The protection varies all the way from a quick "your money back" to more complicated and time-consuming remedies that allow you damages from the retailer and also criminal penalties of fines or jail on the head of the offender.

CLASS ACTIONS: THE CONSUMER'S BLOCKBUSTER WEAPON

Don't forget the real blockbuster weapon that the consumer has: most states now permit the injured consumer to institute a class action. That means he brings suit not only for himself and his $10 damage but also for everyone in the same class, greatly increasing the potential liability of the merchant. The consumer's $10 action may suddenly have become a $10 million class suit.

To further assist the consumer, all states have various boards and agencies that regulate virtually every trade, occupation, profession, and calling. If the vendor's job or profession has to have any kind of a license, and most do, there is some official board or agency that holds absolute power over it. If he is a lawyer or a doctor or dentist, there's a grievance or ethics committee that can suspend or revoke the practitioner's license, which means taking away his livelihood. Barbers, beauticians, real estate brokers, collection agencies, liquor dealers, funeral directors, all are regulated by some state agency. All are subject to rules and ethics and if they cheat you, the consumer, they can be penalized by the regulating agency.

157

The consumer has other help available, too, from federal and state boards and departments such as the Department of Public Utilities, the Federal Trade Commission, the Food and Drug Administration, and countless others, discussed in Chapter 14.

THERE IS NO PROTECTION FOR A FOOLISH CONSUMER

Now for a word of common sense. All the laws, regulations, and protective devices in the world, together with all the courts, boards, and agencies that can be dreamed up to enforce them, don't amount to a thing if the consumer is a fool. No one can protect a person from his own foolishness. Let me illustrate with an actual case from the Consumer's Division in the Department of the Attorney General of Massachusetts. A nice little old lady came in to tell the following story: a young man in a truck knocked on her door and explained that he was representing a company with a special that week on aluminum siding for $1,000 instead of the normal $3,000 charge. He would be back the next day for the $1,000 if she wanted to take advantage of this wonderful opportunity. She did, he returned, and she gave him the $1,000 in cash. It then developed that his company could not start work for another week. That was all right with her. However, three weeks passed and she had not seen him or anyone from his company. Someone suggested that the Consumer's Division could help her out in such a situation.

"Positively, madam," said an Assistant Attorney General, "that's what we're here for."

"Fine," responded the old lady. "Then I want to make a complaint based on the facts I've outlined to you."

"Against whom?"

"That nice young man or, rather, that nice young man's company. He himself was quite young and quite nice, too. I wouldn't want to hurt him at all."

"Okay. What's the name of the company?"

"Dear me, he didn't say."

"Well, maybe it's on the receipt he gave you for the $1,000 cash."

"But he didn't give me a receipt."

"Well, then, what's the name of the nice young man?"

"It was John."

"John what?"

"Actually, that's his first name. He said everyone called him by his first name. He was so young, you know."

"Was there a name of the firm on the truck?"

"Oh, no, it wasn't a truck. It was just an automobile."

"Well, then, did you get the license number of it?"

"No, but it was a black car and it had either two doors or four doors, one or the other. And now that I think of it, I'm not sure whether the car was black or dark green or maybe blue."

"Madam, I'm afraid we can't help you."

"But isn't there anything I can do?"

"Yes, there is. Repeat after me: 'Our Father who art in heaven . . .' "

Some schemers will go to great lengths in order to put a potential easy mark into a situation or frame of mind where the victim actually feels grateful for the opportunity of spending his money. Here's one example: Mr. Green was reading his paper at home on a freezing cold Saturday morning when, following an authoritative knock on the door, he opened it to see a man dressed in the uniform of a lieutenant in the Fire Department. It seems it was boiler inspection time, a good precaution to prevent fires from defective furnaces that might overheat. After five minutes in the basement, he delivered the bad news: "Sorry, but I've got to order you to shut off your heat—defective boiler. You're lucky it hasn't exploded. That's why it has to be disconnected immediately." And it was.

By good fortune, less than an hour later a boiler salesman appeared. He just happened to have a good used boiler for an immediate installation before Mr. Green and family would be frozen out of their home, and for only $400. Mr. Green not only gave up the $400 but he accompanied it with thanks to Providence for sending a salesman in such a time of need.

Later, in comparing notes with neighbors, Mr. Green learned that several had had visits from a fire lieutenant and, coincidentally, a boiler salesman. While no one could be certain, all suspected that nothing more had taken place than an exchange of boilers in something comparable to a game of musical chairs— accompanied, of course, by the movement of money from the pockets of the purchasers to the pockets of the seller.

Both stories point to this moral: the state can provide laws, policing agencies can provide help, and the courts can provide justice—but none of them can give the consumer protection without the exercise of some degree of care and common sense by the citizen himself. While the law now implies "seller be fair," the smart person will still remember "buyer beware." Being right in a dispute

159

with someone you cannot find is no better than being wrong in a case against someone around the corner.

Sometimes legal problems can arise closer to home—or even in the home itself. In such cases we may have to enter the arena of divorce and domestic relations, described in the next chapter.

YOU WANT TO READ IT?

23
Divorce and Domestic Relations

THE DIVORCE COURT HAS many official names: Probate Court and Surrogate Court are among its titles. Whatever it is called, most of the people who frequent it are women. Divorce cases may be either contested or uncontested; if uncontested, usually the husband allows the wife to obtain the divorce. And if a witness is needed—either to attest to cruelty or to prove the legal papers were properly served on the husband—the witness is usually a woman friend of the wife. It all adds up to the average divorce court being a woman's court. Even so, there are occasional judges who have the reputation of being partial to husbands in the matter of alimony or other support orders.

In most states, to get a divorce there must be a cause. The legislature will have passed a statute or statutes spelling out the causes for a justified dissolution of the marriage. They will vary from those of a conservative state, which might only recognize adultery, to those of a liberal state that allows a divorce simply upon the representation that the two adults are incompatible. Most states are between the two extremes. In Massachusetts, for example, the cause may be adultery, impotence, gross intoxication, cruelty, desertion, or a prison sentence. In addition, non-support by the husband is a cause—but the reverse is not true as of this writing.

Most states have some qualifications about jurisdiction: usually the parties must have lived in the state as husband and wife or the person seeking the divorce must have lived in the state for a certain period of time. The particular state statute must be checked.

CUSTODY AND ALIMONY

In most instances the only questions to be settled between husband and wife are support and custody of the children. The

161

usual agreement on such matters sees custody of the children (especially if they are under the age of 16) given to the wife with the husband having reasonable rights of visitation.

Theoretically the husband is also eligible for alimony from the wife but, as a practical matter, alimony is usually solely for the wife. In a community property state the division of property is fifty-fifty; in other states it may not be so simple.

When both parties want a divorce and are agreed upon it, the obtaining of it is simple and easy to accomplish. In some states the parties must be careful to avoid collusion—obtaining something by improper agreement—which may prevent the divorce.

Another shoal to be avoided is a foreign divorce that will not be recognized. In general, if someone leaves his home state to go to Mexico, Nevada, Florida or some other jurisdiction which is reputed to have easier divorce laws, there may be a question about the validity of the divorce. If such a question arises, the services of a lawyer are essential. The divorce is probably illegal and usually will not be recognized if the party challenging its validity has done nothing to assist in its granting.

A divorce action is often called a libel. In such states, the person bringing it is called a libellant and the person against whom it is sought is the libellee.

Laws about divorce are becoming more and more "liberal." The general tendency is to allow divorces where both parties have agreed there is no point in trying to continue the marriage.

You may have heard of "no-fault" divorce. Several states, following California's lead, now permit divorces on the grounds of "irreconcilable differences." This means that neither party has to accuse the other of anything to obtain a divorce. "No-fault" can prevent bitter recriminations between parties to a divorce, as well as making unnecessary the lying or faked evidence that sometimes had to be employed to end a marriage in which both husband and wife simply wanted out.

Merely living apart does not end the responsibilities of marriage, but a legal separation can be obtained. A separation agreement may be agreed to voluntarily by both husband and wife. The agreement spells out the responsibilities of each in such matters as support or custody of children. If approved by the court, the partners then have none of the normal responsibilities of marriage toward each other, except the ones agreed to in the document.

If only one party wants a legal separation, the court may be asked to define the terms of an agreement. This procedure is sometimes called "separate maintenance" or "limited divorce," since the partners could not remarry under its terms.

ANNULMENT OR DIVORCE?

Annulment is similar to divorce in that it dissolves a marriage. However, there are basic differences in both the cause needed and the legal effect of each. Most states have statutes that spell out the conditions under which an annulment may be granted. The usual cause is fraud, but it must be the type of fraud that "goes to the essence" of the marriage contract. Mere concealment of such matters as pregnancy, disease or financial condition are generally not considered to go to the essence of the marriage contract; marrying with the intention of not carrying out any part of the marriage contract may be.

In general, it is easier to annul an unconsummated marriage than one where the parties have lived together.

A divorce recognizes that there has been a valid legal marriage between the two parties (in the usual case). If an annulment is granted, it means the marriage is void *ab initio* (from the beginning)—that is, no valid marriage ever existed.

The layman should remember that, although a marriage of record may be void or voidable for some reason, it is nevertheless still "of record" and there may be the need of some other action of record—such as annulment or divorce—to erase it. In such a situation, a lawyer must be consulted.

Divorce can be a tragic matter for the parties involved; the only thing more tragic might be compelling two adults to remain married when they are miserable together.

Annulment is usually not such a sad matter because, in the ordinary annulment case, there are no children and the parties have not really "lived together." Most people (and courts) don't even consider the possibility of annulment if there are children because, the marriage being void from the beginning, any child would be rendered illegitimate by the annulment.

Domestic relations concerns the law as it relates to families. The relationships are many and varied and they raise very practical questions: Between husband and wife, who supports whom? What about the children? What about a destitute parent?

163

There are many questions but a basic one is what will happen if support is not forthcoming. In most instances, the answer is welfare. And, since welfare comes from the taxpayers, the legislatures are motivated to pass strong statutes enforcing support. The judiciary also comes into play, not simply to dispense justice but also to try to prevent anyone from becoming a charge on welfare. When a judge hears the ordinary criminal case, the question in his mind is: Did the defendant do this? But in an illegitimacy case, the judge also has another problem in mind: If this defendant is not found guilty, who is going to support the child?

Laws concerning domestic relations come in many forms. Let's examine the more common ones.

SUPPORT

Most states require a man to support his wife but, if his failure is not unreasonable, the law will not punish him. The father also has the duty of supporting a minor child and that responsibility is absolute. Underlying these laws is the fear that the wife or minor child who is abandoned may become a burden on the public.

Some states also provide punishment for a mother who willfully neglects or refuses to provide for her minor child. In addition, there may be a penalty for any custodian of a child who willfully fails to provide proper physical, educational or moral care and guidance for the child.

In illegitimacy cases, if the defendant is found guilty, he is usually put under an order to make weekly payments to support the child. He either pays or goes to jail for contempt of court. In addition, the court may order him to pay confinement expenses of the mother.

Often these cases are disposed of by a lump sum settlement in lieu of weekly payments. Judges are reluctant to approve inadequate settlements because they usually mean that the child becomes a charge on welfare sooner than would be the case if the weekly payments were ordered. Legally, the mother of the illegitimate child has the duty of supporting it. She is relieved only to the extent that assistance can be obtained from the father.

An illegitimate child's domicile follows the mother, whereas a legitimate child's follows the father. The illegitimate child may be "legitimized" by his father, the usual ways being by marrying the child's mother or by "publicly acknowledging" the child.

164

The children also have a duty to support a destitute parent. If a child is of legal age and of sufficient means, and if the parent is destitute without fault, a child of sufficient means cannot unreasonably neglect to help support such parent. If there is more than one child, each has only a proportionate responsibility.

Many support cases involve more than one state because the person who has the duty to support, usually a husband, has left the state where the responsibility arose. As a result of this situation all states have adopted the so-called Uniform Reciprocal Support Act. Under its terms, the person to whom support is owed can commence proceedings in the state where such person, usually the wife, lives. That court sends the proper papers to the state where the person who owes the support lives.

In theory, at least, it greatly simplifies support proceedings and eliminates (again, in theory) many of the difficulties encountered when the wife was in one state and the husband in another. The Uniform Reciprocal Support Act does not always work satisfactorily but it is certainly a great improvement over earlier legislation. The layman should be familiar with the possibilities it offers. Since it operates through the probation departments of the courts, there is no charge to those who avail themselves of its provisions.

If there is a court order for alimony or child-support, a 1975 federal law allows attachment (or garnishment, as it is called in many states) of government checks due federal employees or retirees. Persons who may benefit from this law should investigate the possibility of help under it (and probably the assistance of an attorney will be needed here).

ADOPTION

The probate court also has a major interest in overseeing the welfare of children who come before it for adoption. In general, in adoption matters, the prime concern of the court is that of the child's welfare. Some states pay attention to the wishes of the child's natural parents so far as religion is concerned—the child may be adopted only by parents of the same religion as its natural parents—but the tendency today is simply to take into account whether the general welfare of the child will be promoted by the adoption.

Adoption drastically changes the rights, duties, and the entire relationship of the adopted child with his natural parents and his adoptive parents. The two sets of parents legally change places: the

165

child no longer inherits from the natural parents (in most states, including Massachusetts, Connecticut, and New York) but instead inherits from the adoptive parents; and the child's duty is no longer to the natural parents but to the adoptive parents.

As far as the adoption procedure itself is concerned, it is simplified and facilitated by the consent of the natural parents. While all the states agree on this, they differ on the effects of a change of mind by the natural parents. From the point of view of adopting parents, the best state is Florida: once consent to an adoption has been given by the natural parents, it is irrevocable. Other states are less inflexible.

In virtually all states, a mature child's consent to adoption is necessary. While the age differs in various states, it usually is set at twelve or fourteen years—for example, it is twelve in Massachusetts and fourteen in Connecticut and New York.

It is against the law for anyone to pay the natural parents money for a consent to adoption. However, it is common knowledge that this law is violated in many instances.

Considering domestic relations and the rights of wives, children, and others, naturally leads to problems that arise when people live together—as well as when they die. So let's look at some that arise in life and some after death.

ONE THING, YOU'LL NEVER GET ME PREGNANT.

24
"Live-in Partnerships" in the Eyes of the Law

HOW DOES THE LAW view live-in arrangements—a way of life selected by a substantial number of Americans? Do parties who live together have legal rights against each other? What happens in case the parties later agree to end the relationship, or if one party walks out, or if one dies? These questions deserve careful consideration because living together is a relatively recent social phenomenon that is creating all kinds of legal problems and repercussions.

The number of couples who live together without being bound by the traditional tie of marriage is not known. Based on a sample survey in March 1978, the Bureau of the Census estimated the number at 1,137,000 couples. Some marketing estimates presently place the figure as high as up to six million couples. More recent estimates are higher but, whatever the correct figure, the number of unmarried couples living together is a significant part of the population. In the terminology of the Census, live-in arrangements are "unmarried persons of opposite sex sharing living quarters."

There are many reasons couples "share quarters without being married." Many are young people who are not ready for marriage economically or psychologically. Some couples do not believe in technical formalities or rebel against conventional relationships. Others wish to try a "live-in" arrangement to test whether marriage should follow. Some are unable to marry because they are not legally divorced even though they live apart from their spouses. Still others are divorced persons who are unwilling to marry because re-marriage might terminate alimony or other support they receive from their former spouses. Still others deliberately wish to avoid the obligations the law imposes in a marital relationship.

167

Some of the live-in couples are elderly and include widows and widowers who might lose pension or other benefits if they married, etc.

Marriage and its rights and legal obligations, are subject to laws which vary from state to state. However, every state confers some important rights and benefits on persons merely by virtue of the marriage. But, a simple "living together" arrangement deprives one or more of the partners of most legal benefits applicable to married persons, and traditionally it is the woman who loses out.

Should live-in partners lose the benefits and privileges the law confers upon married partners? Can the partners by agreement confer upon each other the rights of married persons without marriage? Let's discuss these consequences, not from a standpoint of morality or convention, but simply from the standpoint of common sense.

LIVE-IN PARTNERSHIPS vs. COMMON LAW MARRIAGES

From a legal standpoint, the usual live-in arrangement should be differentiated from a common-law marriage. A few states, such as Alabama, Georgia, Iowa and Texas still recognize common-law marriage in which a man and woman live together, freely acknowledge the union, and hold themselves, out as "married" rather than just living together, even though a formal marriage ceremony has not taken place. In such states, (and in any other jurisdiction that gives full faith and credit to the laws of another state), if a common-law marriage is proved, the parties have the protection of the laws applicable to formally married couples. But the situation is vastly different if a state does not recognize common-law marriages, and very few states do. Moreover, an increasing number of states, such as New York and New Jersey (as well as many others,) which at one time recognized common-law marriages have outlawed them.

THE DECK IS STACKED AGAINST LIVING-IN

Let's examine the law as it exists at this time, and how it is likely to exist tomorrow in the vast majority of states.

In the case of married partners, the husband is usually responsible to pay for necessaries such as clothing, furniture, food, medical and legal services furnished by third parties to the wife at her request. This is *not* true of a live-in arrangement. In that case

168

neither party has an obligation to support the other although they are living together.

Many couples who live together regard their relationship seriously. Others, however, enter the arrangement believing they are free to walk away at any time without obligations. Generally they are—but, one partner is likely to suffer. Often the woman is the victim of the arrangement as she may be without a job or involved with duties toward a child.

A spouse who is legally married has a right to support, usually called alimony or maintenance, if the parties later separate and the facts indicate that the other spouse should provide it. Usually the wife gets financial aid from the husband but occasionally it is the other way around. In either case, the support is based on a legal marriage. All the prevailing party has to show is the fact of marriage, the need for support and the ability of the other spouse to pay. It's a simple remedy based on the recognized legal status of marriage.

In the case of the unmarried couple living together, the facts are virtually identical: the couple has been living together, loving together, sleeping together. But they are not married, even though the neighbors may think they are, and that creates an entirely different legal situation. The party seeking support or maintenance, still usually the woman, can produce all the proof necessary to make out a case except a marriage certificate. But without that certificate, the best she fares is a long, difficult, and expensive lawsuit with the legal cards and precedents stacked against her.

LIVING-IN MAY NOT PAY

Remember the case of movie star Lee Marvin? Marvin's live-in partner, Michelle Triola Marvin, would have won a huge amount in a breeze if she had a marriage certificate. Michelle had a live-in arrangement with Lee Marvin for about six years. In an action she brought in California against Marvin she unsuccessfully claimed both alimony and fifty percent of six million dollars which she estimated as Marvin's earnings in the period they lived together. The court ruled that California law does not equate unmarried cohabitation with marital rights as far as alimony and property rights were concerned. Michelle was denied the large amounts she would have received if the parties had been legally married. The bottom line was that living with Marvin without marriage did not pay off for Michelle.

The judge did allow Michelle $104,000 as a one-time rehabilitative allowance under the special circumstances of the case, as she had surrendered her career as a singer earning $1,000 per week in order to live with Marvin. But even that award, relatively small in the light of Marvin's great wealth, would not have been allowed in most states.

INHERITANCE

What about inheritance? If a married person dies without leaving a will, the surviving spouse has certain rights of inheritance, generally one-third or one-half of the decedent's estate. But to be a "surviving spouse" in law, the parties must have gone through a formal marriage ceremony (except in the few states that still recognize common-law marriages).

In general, people can dispose of their property by will any way they wish. Thus a partner can leave a valid will disinheriting the survivor. But in most states a surviving spouse of a legal marriage inherits a substantial part of the estate, usually one-third or one-half, even if the decedent leaves a will cutting off the survivor without a dime. But to be a surviving spouse the survivor again must be a lawful surviving spouse and not a mere live-in partner.

Additionally, most states have some other benefits or privileges for widows. For example in some states a widow has the use of the marital home rent free for several months, or she may be protected against having furniture or other marital property re-possessed by creditors, or she may receive some concessions regarding real estate taxes or other legal benefits. But again, it must be understood that a surviving widow is one who was legally married.

LIVE-IN PARTNERS LOSE BENEFITS

A similar situation exists relating to Social Security, pensions, or other retirement benefits. The Social Security Law has many provisions which benefit a "surviving spouse," but again that means a legally married person, and a surviving live-in partner does not partake of these benefits. Additionally, many private pension plans provide that the beneficiary must be either a legally married spouse of the wage-earner or a lawful child. Where does that leave the live-in partner or a child of the relationship? Generally speaking they are without remedy.

savings. Alternatively, married persons are allowed to file separate returns if they find it results in tax savings in their particular case. The law does not give live-in partners a similar choice. They must file separate returns regardless of the tax consequences. In some cases tax-bracket schedules can be one-third higher for single people living together than for married couples with identical incomes who file joint returns.

There was a quirk in the income tax laws under which, in some circumstances, an unmarried couple had a tax advantage over the married couple. However that so-called "marriage penalty" was reduced in the 1981 tax law (see Chapter 26). As a practical matter, tax laws have always favored marriage and will undoubtedly continue to do so—that's part of our mores.

Husband and wives are able to take advantage of other important tax savings which are not available to live-in partners. For example, a married person who dies can leave as much as one-half of his or her estate to the surviving spouse free of inheritance taxes. This substantial saving does not apply to live-in partners. Similarly married persons can make gifts in their lifetime and pay lesser gift taxes than live-in partners who make the same gifts.

OTHER DISADVANTAGES FOR
UNMARRIED COUPLES

Many additional illustrations can be given where advantages are given to legally married persons but not to others who just live like married couples without a marriage ceremony. For example, let us look at charge accounts. If *Mrs.* Jones wishes to open a charge account the store may give her credit on the strength of her husband's job and credit rating. But if *Miss* Jones wishes to open a charge account in the same store she is strictly on her own. She cannot obtain a charge account based on the job or credit rating of her live-in partner. The store knows that a husband usually is responsible to pay for a wife's purchases but a live-in partner has no legal responsibility for bills of the roommate.

Suppose the couple wishes to buy a home and applies for a bank mortgage. As far as the bank is concerned, the application will be treated as made by two separate and unrelated persons. The banks will say they are not concerned with the private morals of the applicants, and indeed the bank may approve some mortgage loans to unmarried couples. But there can be no doubt that in fact it is more difficult for unmarried couples to obtain a mortgage loan than for a married couple. In practice, banks are conservative and often seek to cultivate an image of morality. Moreover, they proceed from the assumption that an unmarried relationship is not as stable as a marital relationship.

Suppose an unmarried couple wishes to vacation at a hotel. Will the hotel permit them to occupy the same room although their names are different or must they go through the charade of registering as Mr. and Mrs.? Also, they can run the risk of violating some local law by occupying the same room.

CHILDREN OF A LIVE-IN ARRANGEMENT

Suppose there is a baby. What is the situation as to child support? Legally, parents are responsible for child support whether they are married or not. If the child is not supported authorities of a state can sue the alleged father to compel him to support the child. But notice the words "alleged father." Paternity has to be proven against the unmarried father. On the other hand, if the parties are married, the husband is presumed to be the father. This presumption of legitimacy is so strong that in many situations courts will not even permit proof that the husband is not the real father. Thus lawful marriage has a great significance in the realm of child support.

If a married person dies without leaving a will, a child of the marriage inherits from the deceased father or mother. But a child of a live-in partnership, in being illegitimate in the eyes of the law, generally does not inherit from the father but only from the mother.

A child, whether legitimate or illegitimate, is entitled to social security benefits accruing through the mother. A legitimate child automatically can receive social security benefits derived from the father but a child of a live-in arrangement cannot receive similar benefits unless the father takes certain steps which the law regards as proof that he has acknowledged paternity. The fact that the man and woman were living together is not enough by itself to qualify the child for social security benefits derived from the father.

On the subject of children let me mention a problem encountered by unmarried couples who wish to adopt a child.

Almost without exception adoption agencies and the law frown upon an application from unmarried couples even if their other qualifications such as character, health, home environment and other conditions are excellent. An unmarried couple planning adoption should not be optimistic about succeeding. The stumbling blocks in their way are very difficult to overcome.

BREAKING UP

Of course, whether couples are legally married or not, they often break up. One of the supposed advantages of not being legally tied together is the widely held belief that it's easier for a couple to "walk away" from each other if they have never been legally married. As we have seen, that is true in many respects, but breaking up still can bring many problems to the unmarried former live-in partners. Let me cite just a few examples of what I mean.

John and Mary, the live-in partners, have an automobile that they thought they both owned. Although it was registered in John's name, each had assumed liability for the finance payments because both signed the purchase papers. Now John has disappeared with the car after he and Mary agreed to part company. Since John cannot be found but Mary is available, the finance company may seek to collect solely from Mary.

Or, John and Mary are sharing expenses of an apartment in Mary's name, including telephone, gas, electricity, and other services. John decides to leave for greener pastures. When Mary tries to tell the utility companies that she is responsible for only half the bills, she will rapidly find out that she is stuck for the entire amount. If she wants John to keep his part of the bargain, it's up to her (not the utility company) to try to force him to keep his part of the bargain.

Or, John and Mary may have contributed to the purchase of furniture for their apartment. Who owns the furniture when they break up?

Countless illustrations can be given of problems that arise when the unmarried couple breaks up.

As we have seen, the law does not favor live-in relationships. As the man is usually still the breadwinner, or at least the major one, in general the live-in partnership is more likely to be unfavorable to the woman rather than the man.

LEGAL REMEDIES FOR LIVE-IN PARTNERS?

Can anything be done, short of marriage, to change the situation and assure full legal rights to partners in a long term live-in relationship? One step might be to try to get legislation in the various states that would give unmarried persons living together the same rights and obligations toward each other that married couples have. That's easier said than done. In the first place, many, if not most, legislators would bitterly oppose such a proposal whether for political reasons or on grounds of morality, religion, convention, public policy or otherwise. If by chance it did meet with legislative approval, there would be the possibility of a gubernatorial veto. Assuming the Governor approved the legislation, what might the courts do to it? The legislation still might be challenged in court in its entirety or given a limited application. So, legislation perhaps may not be the answer.

A CONTRACT FOR LIVE-IN PARTNERS

What about some sort of contract between the live-in partners? It is not too difficult to draw up a document that states the understanding of the parties, the legal consideration flowing from each to the other, and the duties and responsibilities of each. The contract could include provisions that cannot be changed without mutual consent, and with safeguards relating to insurance policies, deeds, stocks and bonds, bank accounts, and other property rights.

The following is an example of the kind of agreement the parties may wish to consider. A sample contract might include provisions such as these: (1) The two parties living together John Smith and Mary Brown, agree that they owe each other the same duties and responsibilities that legally married husbands and wives owe to each other; (2) Mary Brown is to be named beneficiary of a $10,000 policy of insurance on John Smith's life, the premiums to be paid by John Smith, and the beneficiary shall not be changed without Mary Brown's written consent (or the couple might take out cross policies in which each is a beneficiary of the other); (3) All bank accounts, stocks, and bonds (and other personal property if so desired) of either party are to be held in joint ownership by both, and neither is to change such title without the written consent of the other; (4) The title to any real estate now in the name of either party, or acquired hereafter by either, shall be held

174

jointly by the two parties; (5) The parties will each make a will leaving the other not less than half of the estate of the first to die, and such will may not be changed without the written consent of the other; (6) If any provision of the contract be invalid for any reason, the others are still to be of full force and effect.

Let me stress that this sample is not intended to be complete and its validity cannot be assured. It merely illustrates some of the things that might be considered by the parties. After they have discussed the agreements they want they should retain an attorney to draw up a document that will be as legal and binding as possible. This sort of thing is not law for a layman: *a lawyer is an absolute must.*

Even with a lawyer, there is no assurance that such a contract will be upheld by the courts. The contract, or some of its provisions, might be ruled invalid for a number of reasons. The courts may trot out an old standby and decide that the contract, or a particular provision, is invalid as based on a meretricious relationship. When parties make a contract based on a live-in arrangement, the courts may say that public policy does not permit such a contract or at least all of its terms. However, at least some of the provisions may be ruled valid.

But, even if such a contract eventually is determined not to be legally binding, what do live-in partners have to lose by trying to arrive at an over-all understanding of their rights and obligations before they start the relationship? Indeed, if a proposed partner will not agree in advance to reasonable provisions that is a clear danger signal that the relationship is doomed to failure.

A SOCIAL DILEMMA

Sometimes couples are confronted by a dilemma which is really social rather than economic or legal: How should they introduce each other? It is simple for married people to introduce each other to friends, relatives or others. The introduction "This is my husband John," or "This is my wife Mary," or some equivalent, is of course standard and conveys the status of a spouse. Mention might be made that married persons sometimes encounter awkwardness in an entirely different direction—addressing their in-laws. "Mother" or "Dad," may not come naturally; "Mr." or "Mrs.," usually is too formal; first names may be too intimate; and some other satisfactory appelation may not have been found. For example, what would you think about the term "Chief" for a father-in-law? It has dignity, respect and affection. Isn't the in-law entitled to it?

Unlike married persons, live-in partners often find it difficult or awkward to introduce *each other* to friends, relatives or others. You may have heard the introduction "Meet my boyfriend," or "Say hello to my girl," or "This is my old man," or some euphamism or just stammering. Perhaps the most usual form of introduction is just "This is John," or "This is Mary." But who is he or she, and what status does he or she have?

What should we call live-in partners? They are less than married but more than friends or lovers or just dates. There are millions of people—youngsters, oldsters, in-betweensters—who have a special status in the never-never land of human relationships, because they are living together although they are not married.

Both are entitled to an introduction that says to everyone: "Treat this person as my wife (or husband) because she (or he) is a spouse in everything but the eyes of the law." Both are owed a special title that would save them from embarrassing explanations like: "We're sleeping together" or "We're practically married," and so on. An easy first step to recognition is a meaningful title for the partner. What about a title, "Faithful Comrade" (which might be objectionable because of the Communist connotation) or "Faithful Companion"? I think either title carries warmth and dignity while describing the actual relationship. What do you think?

A word of warning is appropriate. Legal consequences may flow from the title used for a live-in partner. If a title is used which connotes a lawful marriage, it may not only be deceptive but the parties will be deemed married if this title is used in the states which still recognize common-law marriages.

In conclusion, while live-in partnerships may fit the requirements of various persons it is important to recognize the adverse legal consequences—especially to a woman—which may result unless they are corrected by a valid contract between the partners or by changes in the law.

25
Writing a Will

WILLS ARE HIGHLY TECHNICAL and the various states have different laws pertaining to them. But basically, all these laws are intended to guarantee that a person's property will go to whomever he wants to have it, and every effort is made to accomplish that purpose. However, a heavy burden is put upon the testator—the one making the will—to compel him to follow to the exact letter every detail of every procedure that is essential to a valid will. For example, one of the requirements in Massachusetts (at this writing) is that there be three witnesses who attest to the will by signing in the presence of the testator and in the presence of each other. If one of the witnesses happens to step into the next room for a second during the ceremony, even if the others acknowledge their signatures, the will becomes invalid upon a contest establishing that fact. The point is: making a will is highly technical and even the most absurd technicality must be followed.

If you are drawing a will, go to a lawyer. The fee will be nominal in most instances. If you are determined not to go to a lawyer, as risky as such a decision is, then the next best thing is to go to a stationery store, obtain a form for a will, and follow its every provision as exactly as you can. Don't just write something and assume it will be all right; the chances are a thousand to one it will be invalid.

The court that has jurisdiction of wills and estates may be called the Probate Court (as in Massachusetts), the Surrogate Court (as in New York), the Orphans Court, or something else in another state.

The will of the deceased must be presented to such a court to have its validity established and to have an executor or administrator appointed to distribute the estate. If the deceased

177

died intestate (did not leave a will), then some interested person (usually an heir who expects to inherit) will file a petition in this court stating that the deceased left an estate but no will, and asking the court to appoint someone to administer the estate. The executor (if there is a will) and the administrator (if there is no will) perform the same function: each collects the assets, pays whatever may be the debts of the estate, and then distributes to those entitled to inherit. Each must file an account with the court, and everything is under the supervision of the court, including the appointment of a guardian to protect the rights of minor heirs or other persons. It is a very strict procedure and every precaution is taken to insure that the estate is properly distributed and that there are no unwarranted expenses incurred in the administration of the estate.

If a person dies without a will, each state has statutes that determine who the heirs will be. The spouse and children are in a special category in every state, with the estate usually being divided between them to the exclusion of other relatives of the deceased. If there are no children, in most states the spouse will inherit the bulk of the estate and then relatives of the deceased may get a share. It usually depends on the size of the estate, and, if the estate is small, it is likely that the surviving widow will inherit it all.

Usually the spouse—and as a practical matter this means the wife—has special rights of which she cannot be deprived, regardless of the husband's wishes. The states have provisions about the wife's "right to waive" the provisions of the will if they are not as generous to her as the rights given to her by statute. In most states, children have no similar right unless they can establish that the parent has absolutely forgotten their existence when making out the will. If the child can prove such an unintentional oversight, the child may inherit his statutory share. It is for this reason that a testator who wants to cut off a child will name him in the will.

Anyone who made a will before September 12, 1981, should have it carefully reviewed to see if it should be changed to obtain liberalized estate-tax changes made in the Economic Recovery Tax Act of 1981. That Act removed the limitations on the marital deduction for both estate and gift tax purposes. Unlimited amounts of property can now be transferred between spouses without imposition of an estate or gift tax.

People close to the testator should remember that a beneficiary cannot be a witness to the will. To qualify as an "independent witness" (which is the usual requirement of wills) the person must be someone who does not benefit under the terms of the will.

While all states have very technical requirements before a will is recognized as valid, many states make an exception for a holographic will—one without witnesses but completely written in the hand of the testator, and thus apparently trustworthy This exception originated with wills that were handwritten by soldiers and sailors during wartime, and under circumstances such that it would have been impractical to have witnesses. Holographic wills are still recognized in many states, but not in others, including Massachusetts, Connecticut, and New York.

CONTESTING A WILL

The usual grounds for attacking the ordinary will are first, that the testator did not have legal testamentary capacity—he did not understand the nature of his act, the extent of his property, or remember his loved ones; and second, there was undue influence—the will was drawn without a free and independent mind.

The courts try in every possible way to see that the wishes of the testator are carried out. It is very difficult to "break" a will, particularly if those who inherit under it are the natural objects of the testator's bounty and affection. However, when making a will, the testator should be very careful to see that all technicalities are met and that the witnesses are reliable and trustworthy people. If a great deal of property is involved, and especially if the person making the will is along in years, it is thought to be a sensible precaution to have a doctor or expert talk with the testator to be able to later testify as to the frame of mind and strength of will and purpose of the testator.

HOW TO LEAVE YOUR PROPERTY TO WHOMEVER YOU WISH BUT AVOID PAYING TAXES

A will is a very important document intended to insure that property will go to whomever and in whatever proportions the owner of the property wishes. However, when property passes at death, the expenses of the estate through inheritance and other taxes may be very heavy. For that reason, many people try to avoid leaving property either by will or by intestacy (death without a will). There are many ways of doing this. Sometimes the property owner will have his bank account in two or more names, constituting a joint account from which either party may withdraw funds. Real estate may be held by some sort of deed that, at death, passes entire ownership of the property to someone named in the deed as a joint owner. Trusts of various kinds can be created under which the person owning the property holds it "in trust" for the named beneficiary, to whom it goes after the death of the person holding it in trust. There are various methods of controlling property during the owner's lifetime and yet having it go as he wishes after his death, without using a will—but they are all methods that absolutely require the services of a lawyer who is skilled in such matters. You should know about these possibilities, but should not try to put them into practice without the services of an expert.*

You may not want to have a will because—not that you're superstitious—you just don't want to tempt fate. Well, just remember that, if you don't dictate the terms of your will, someone is going to do it for you. And do you know who the someone is? It's the state legislature yes, that same state legislature that you've always judged to be composed of idiots, jackasses, buffoons, thieves, and whatever other terms you've used to describe them. And *your* will not mine or his or hers but *your's* is going to be written by those legislators. *They* will decide where *your* property goes. Why? Because you haven't written your own will and left your property the way you wanted—and so your property goes by the laws of intestacy [the legal term for the disposition of the estate of a person who died without a will].

Who writes the laws of intestacy? Not you, of course. They're written by the legislators of your states—so it is not you who decides what happens to your property. Who lets them decide? You and anyone else who hasn't selected the terms of his or her own will. So just remember a fact that's usually overlooked: all of us have a will written by someone, whether we know it or not. Who's deciding who gets your property?

Each state has its own laws on wills and inheritance—again, the layman should consult a lawyer to determine what his rights may be. If he is determined not to do so, then his best policy would be to stop in the office of the Clerk of Court that handles such matters and ask some questions. One question he does not have to ask is whether the occasion will eventually arise when the laws of inheritance will be of concern to him and his loved ones. Whether he "puts his affairs in order" or not, death is inevitable.

*For a more detailed examination of some of these legal tax-reducing possibilities, see *Build Family Finances & Reduce Risks & Taxes,* by Fred Nauheim (Acropolis Books, Washington, D.C., 1975).

26
The Inevitability of Taxes

AS INEVITABLE AS DEATH are taxes. Every state and the federal government have many laws concerning taxation, the principal ones relating to income and real estate. As you have undoubtedly discovered, there are also taxes on virtually everything else: sales taxes on items you buy as well as personal property taxes on items you already own; entertainment, tobacco and liquor taxes as well as taxes on necessities such as utilities.

PREPARING INCOME TAX RETURNS

Problems often arise in preparing income tax returns. Many good paperback books are available at very reasonable prices, some published by the Internal Revenue Service. Most are in simple language and have charts and diagrams that make the text relatively easy to follow. It's not a bad idea to get one.

If your questions are not answered in the book, telephone the Internal Revenue Service in your area. Their experts will answer your questions or help you by suggestions. They are as willing to save you money as they are to extract it from you for the government.

If the taxpayer needs additional help, or if his income is substantial, an accountant or lawyer should be consulted. The entire subject of taxation can be technical and complex, and the chances of possible savings or big penalties are far too great to be entrusted to any amateur.

The taxpayer is responsible for filing a correct return even if he pays a commercial tax service to prepare it. If the preparer makes a mistake, the taxpayer—not the preparer—is liable for any extra taxes owed the government, as well as any penalties the government may assess.

If there is disagreement between the taxpayer and the Internal Revenue Service over the amount owed, the IRS may call the taxpayer in to audit his return; this involves examining all his records and deductions very carefully. Usually such disputes are settled out of court between the individual and the IRS, generally in the government's favor or on some sort of compromise basis. (Here is where a good lawyer or accountant can be especially useful.) If some new interpretation of the tax laws may be required, the case could be decided in U.S. Tax Court. A surprising number of these cases are decided in the taxpayers' favor.

PROPERTY TAXES

Taxes on your home or other property are usually assessed by officials in the local community. If they have placed too high a value on the realty, the owner can take steps to remedy the situation. One is to seek an abatement—a reduction. This usually involves getting a form and filling it out, stating the reasons why you believe the tax bill should be reduced. Most states have laws that grant some relief to widows, veterans, the blind or disabled, low-income elderly persons, and other classifications. The law of the particular state should be checked but usually a telephone call to the local tax assessors' office will disclose the possibility of savings in the particular case. Some states have an appellate tax board to which a property owner may appeal decisions of the local tax assessors, but here the services of a lawyer are essential.

Excises—usually a tax on ownership of automobiles—are subject to abatement, too. Again, the form should be obtained from the local tax assessors. The usual reason for an abatement here is that the vehicle had been sold or disposed of during the year.

THE ECONOMIC RECOVERY TAX ACT OF 1981

This federal enactment of August 13, 1981, made some sweeping changes in the tax law. Anyone who has a business or substantial income should consult an accountant or a tax lawyer to take every possible advantage under it. The law also tries to correct the so-called "marriage penalty" that two-income couples often suffered; and it changes the amounts a person can contribute under qualified retirement plans or for an Individual Retirement Account (IRA) or an HR-10 Keogh Plan. It's far too complex a law for this book but, if you're affected by its provisions, you should be familiar with it.

You probably are affected because about 48% of the population (more than 28 million families) have annual incomes of $15,000 to $35,000. Earning too much to qualify for government programs of assistance but too little to take advantage of most tax shelters and investments, they have found it increasingly difficult to get ahead or even to stay abreast of the cost of living.

Typical price increases in family costs since 1971 (sources: Federal Home Loan Bank Board; U.S. Departments of Commerce, Agriculture, Energy, and Labor; the Social Security Administration; the National Center for Education Statistics):

> Monthly home mortgage payment: up 372%
> Annual fuel oil bill for homes: up 393%
> Social Security taxes (minimum): up 387%
> Monthly electric bill: up 195%
> Annual medical payment: up 161%
> Monthly car payment: up 128%
> Weekly food bill: up 128%
> Private college education: up 113%

And during the same 10 year period (1971 to 1981) median family income rose only 130%.

The Economic Recovery Tax Act of 1981 brought about many changes in the tax laws. Some of the important ones concern the tax rate, the "marriage penalty," Individual Retirement Accounts, the Keogh Plan, interest and dividend exclusion, estate and gift tax exemptions, Americans working abroad, child care, adoption, withholding taxes, and countless others. We'll just touch on a few in the appendix (pp. 247, 248, 249).

27
Minors and Juvenile Delinquency

THE FEDERAL GOVERNMENT AND all state governments have laws that determine whether a person is a "minor"—an infant, a child, someone below the age of legal competence or, practically speaking, someone who is so young that he is not his own boss.

There are various statutes that touch on specific ages when a person is not old enough to vote, to marry, to consent to intercourse, to disobey parents, and so on. These ages are not always the same; in fact, they differ greatly both by subject matter and also by state. Yet every state has treated the same subjects by a similar approach. The net result is that "minors" are treated differently than adults—and the difference may be a benefit or detriment, depending on the point of view.

The first question: Under what conditions is a person considered a minor? We cannot answer that categorically because a person may be considered as an adult for some purposes and as a minor for others. We'll have to take the situations one by one.

The voting age differs with different jurisdictions. A person who is eighteen years old may vote in federal elections. Most states follow suit although some have kept their voting age at twenty-one.

The age where a person might be drafted for military service has varied over the years, usually having been set at eighteen.

The states have different ideas in their laws pertaining to the right to own or operate automobiles. The trend has been to lower the age to sixteen or eighteen in most states.

The use of liquor by minors is governed by various state laws, city ordinances, and rules and regulations by alcoholic beverage control commissions that usually set the drinking age at either eighteen or twenty-one.

At the present time there is considerable agitation about legalizing marijuana. A great deal of the discussion centers around establishing an age, such as sixteen or eighteen, at which marijuana might be legally bought.

When we examine the reasons behind all these protective statutes that forbid minors to purchase various drugs or operate automobiles, we see that the basic intent of the law is to protect the minor against himself. The statutes are protective or parental in their general philosophy.

Marriage laws vary in the different states. All have some age below which consent to marriage is void or voidable. The states also have different ages when minors may marry with the consent of the parents. Interestingly enough, in many states the age differs with the sex of the minor. In Massachusetts, for example, minors under the age of eighteen need the consent of the parents to marry. If the male is under fourteen or the female is under twelve, the marriage is void without court action if the parties have separated during nonage.

In sexual matters, a female below a specified age cannot give a valid consent to intercourse. If she is below the statutory age, intercourse with her is rape even if the female was the aggressor. The "age of consent" varies in the different states but is usually not below the age of sixteen. If the girl is below the "age of consent," the male is guilty of statutory rape or carnal abuse of a female child, or a crime that carries some such terminology, without regard to the fact that she willingly consented to the intercourse. The law says she cannot consent and, since that means there was intercourse without consent, in the eyes of the law it is rape.

WHO IS LIABLE—PARENT OR CHILD?

In contractual matters, all states protect minors against liability from contracts they have made. Although the basic idea is that the child should be protected from unscrupulous adults, the fact is that the shoe is often on the other foot. The child may avoid his contract (except for necessaries and then only if he has no parent to provide) even if it has been a very good bargain for him and a great loss to the adult. (See chapter 16 for illustrations.)

The situation differs in tort matters: an infant is liable for his wrongful acts that injure others. The practical problem, however, is

185

that the average infant is judgment-proof. You may bring your suit against him but what property or wages does he have out of which you can satisfy your judgment?

In some states, the parent may be responsible for the acts of the child under certain circumstances. For example, if the parent allows the child habitually to do something dangerous to others, the parent may be liable. Some states have statutes on various points. Massachusetts offers some examples of the kind of liability the state may impose on a parent. In that state, general laws Chapter 231, Section 85G, imposes liability up to $300 on the parent for the willful act of a child between the ages of seven and seventeen which injures the person or property of another. That same statute increases the figure to $1,000 if the damage is to some cemetery property. Massachusetts General Laws Chapter 40, Section 155 holds the parent liable for damage done by the dog of the minor.

General Laws Chapter 112, Section 12E, says that a minor who is twelve years old or over, if he is found by two physicians to be drug dependent, may consent to medical treatment without notification to the parents; and the parent is not liable for such treatment.

Chapter 168, Section 37A provides that a student who borrows from the Higher Education Loan Plan is as liable as a person of legal age would be.

Chapter 90, Section 2C (passed when "legal" age was twenty-one), says that where a minor of eighteen years or over, with the parent's consent, has a motor vehicle purchased, repaired, or financed, the minor is responsible.

These statutes are cited merely to give the layman some idea of the kinds of laws a state *may* have on a variety of subjects pertaining to minors: the law of your particular state would have to be checked.

And of course most states have the doctrine of Emancipation: with the consent of the parents, a child may be "on his own." The usual criteria of Emancipation are that, with the parent's consent, the child is working and supporting himself and is regarded as being out in the world. Emancipation has a bearing on various legal points concerning responsibility of both the child and the parent.

"STUBBORN CHILD" LAWS

The criminal law of every state treats minors differently from adults. Many states have so-called "stubborn child" laws. These are based on the philosophy that, since the parents have the

186

obligation of supporting and educating the child, they have the right to control him and exercise whatever authority is really necessary. If the child does not obey reasonable commands of the parent, the child may be punished criminally.

The Massachusetts Stubborn Child statute (in effect until it was changed in 1973) may be found in General Laws Chapter 272, Section 53, which, interestingly, names several kinds of law violators who may be punished by confinement up to six months. The list includes disturbers of the peace, prostitutes, and stubborn children! The constitutionality of the Massachusetts statute on Stubborn Children was tested in the case of *Commonwealth v. Brasher* 270 N.E. (2) 389 and was found to be constitutional.

Stubborn Child laws may seem to be tough on youngsters but, in general, the criminal laws in most states are very gentle on young offenders. The law in most states conclusively presumes that a youngster under the age of seven is incapable of committing a crime. From age seven to seventeen, in most states, the law treats the criminal offender as a juvenile delinquent even for such crimes as burglary, rape, or murder. The judge is usually allowed to determine whether the accused of such age will be tried as a juvenile delinquent or as a young adult accused of a specific crime.

THE JUVENILE DELINQUENT

To be considered a "juvenile delinquent" means the offender is treated as a person who is more than a child and less than an adult. The aim in treating a juvenile is to accord him the compassionate treatment of a child and still give him the benefit of all the rights of a criminal adult. The courts try to handle his case informally—for his benefit—and yet to keep for him all the formal rights of an adult—again, for his benefit.

All this may be done by provisions in a statute passed by the legislature or simply by decisions by the judiciary. Whichever way it is done, the juvenile benefits.

Some states' statutes go so far as to say that proceedings against the juvenile are not criminal proceedings. Others provide special favored treatment for him: the record may not be used against him, his parent or a probation officer must be notified before he can be questioned, his name may not be publicized, proceedings against him must be in some room other than that used for criminal adults, and so on.

187

The judge may hear juvenile cases informally, including the presentation of evidence and the questioning of witnesses. This procedure can be a two-edged sword because technical objections are not tolerated but, as actually used, it is favorable to the juvenile.

Either by law or by custom in various states, every effort is made to protect the child from association with criminal adults. In fact, in progressive states, he may not be confined in the same institution with them.

The problem of juvenile runaways has plagued most states. As a result, an Interstate Compact on Juveniles has been entered into by a great many of them. It provides for cooperation between the states in the form of notifying parents, returning runaways, and other similar measures.

The difficulties that may be encountered in a juvenile matter were pointed out by the case of *Gault v. Arizona* (387 U.S. 1). The practical situation was that, treating the fifteen-year-old defendant as a juvenile meant that he could face possible confinement until he was twenty-one years old, while if he were treated as an adult the most severe sentence he could be given was six months. Would he face six years (if he was to be treated as a juvenile) or six months (if he was treated as an adult)? In the actual case, Gault's conviction as a juvenile was reversed because his constitutional rights had been violated in many ways: his parents had not been given adequate notice or time to prepare for trial, he was not afforded counsel, he had no opportunity to confront witnesses against him, and his confession was used although he had not been given the Miranda warnings.

The Gault case was a good indication that the United States Supreme Court was making it clear that a juvenile had to be given all the rights available to a criminal defendant. The Gault case also pointed out the possibility that a juvenile defendant might actually face a greater penalty than an adult for the identical offense.

In most states, a juvenile's record is not admissible against him as it would be if he had been treated as an adult. In addition, in those states that have measures providing for the sealing or expunging of records, the juvenile is given preferred treatment.

Whenever we discuss juveniles, the Latin words *in loco parentis*, in place of the parent, are heard. For instance, it is often said that while the youngster is in school the teacher or principal stands in the shoes of the parent during school hours. In recent years this concept of the teacher-student relationship has been virtually abandoned as far as older students are concerned. As students are treated more like adults, the idea that the school stands *in loco parentis* is no longer the absolute rule it once was. There has been a trend to recognize that our institutions are not parents, and that older students are citizens, not children. The theory of *in loco parentis* has disappeared from colleges and very little of it is left in high schools.

The schools have many problems peculiar to them. Let us examine a few.

28
The Rights of the Student

SCHOOLS AND STUDENTS CREATE many problems in law. What do we do to protect teachers, guidance counselors, principals, nurses, and others who are often thrown into situations where law, practicality, ethics, and humanitarianism may be in conflict?

What should the teacher do if she sees a youngster in obvious physical distress? If there is a nurse or doctor in attendance, the teacher's decision may be simple: call the person who is medically qualified. But what should the teacher do if there is no such person available? In many states the teacher acts at her peril. The teacher may possibly avoid legal liability by doing nothing; but what about the moral responsibility? A teacher who refuses to avoid the issue may find that she is acting at her peril. The law in many states is that the "good Samaritan" is legally responsible for any harm caused by negligence, regardless of the good faith in interfering in an effort to be helpful. Other states have "Good Samaritan" statutes that protect certain persons—often limited to doctors and nurses—from any suits as long as there was an emergency and the person who tried to help acted in good faith. The law differs in the different states. Enlightened legislation (for example, Massachusetts General Laws, Chapter 71, Section 55A) protects school personnel: the principal, teacher, and nurse are all given immunity against any suit based on injury suffered by the student as a result of first-aid or transportation furnished to a student who needed assistance.

DRUGS IN THE SCHOOLS

The widespread use of drugs has raised many questions. What

should a teacher do who sees a student smoking marijuana or passing drugs? If she tells anyone about it, she may be threatened with a slander suit: saying someone violated the criminal law is a touchy thing. What should a teacher do if she sees an illegal drug in the classroom? If she picks it up, is she not then in violation of a criminal law that forbids possession of such a drug?

What are the drug laws in this country? The penal statutes of most states are patterned after legislation in Congress dating back to the 1914 Harrison Act and the 1937 Marijuana Tax Act. The more recent federal Controlled Substances Act is being followed by similar legislation in the states in the seventies. The aim, of course, is to have some degree of uniformity throughout the nation.

The punishments decreed by most states are very similar in that usually they distinguish between users and sellers; and they usually also have more severe punishments where the "harder" drugs are involved.

For almost fifty years the law passed by Congress classified marijuana as a narcotic—which it is not. Chemically, medically, scientifically, and historically it has always been classified and recognized as a hallucinogen. A narcotic deadens your senses, quiets you, and causes you to nod. A hallucinogenic drug—which marijuana is—tends to excite you, alter your mind, and have you see visions. Hallucinogens and narcotics are two different classes of drugs—which today's kids know even if Congress didn't.

The drug laws in many states—Massachusetts, for example—were based on the federal statutes so, of course, marijuana was for decades legally classified as a narcotic in most states, which permitted the kids to poke fun at the state law as well as the federal.

At least one state's law had another apparent absurdity in its distinction between the maximum sentence for possession and that for being in the company of someone who illegally possesses drugs. The possession penalty was three and a half years whereas the penalty for being present was five years. Did you ever try to justify that to an audience of young people?

Most state legislatures have mistakenly classified marijuana as a narcotic because Congress did; and most states have various absurdities in their statutes, too. One state even had a life penalty for possession of marijuana and many states have committed defendants to prison for several years merely for using marijuana. Actually, by the time you read this, the federal law has properly reclassified marijuana, and state courts are following suit.

Returning to other student problems, what about searching a student or his locker? There is no hard-and-fast answer to such questions that bear upon constitutional rights. Chapter 3 discusses some of the problems.

These and dozens of other questions are difficult even for experienced lawyers. The law itself will differ in various jurisdictions and will even change at different times in the same jurisdiction. But the layman should know that the legal ice is thin, and he should be alert to the questions even though it is not possible to give easy and ready answers to them. Sometimes it is important to be aware of the question even if we do not have a satisfactory answer.

IS THE LAW OF CONFIDENTIALITY VALID?

Another area that should intrigue the layman is the law of confidentiality or privileged communications. Can a teacher, or a guidance counselor in the probable situation, truthfully assure the student that whatever is said is disclosed in confidence and will not be revealed? Is there any legal privilege that protects the confidentiality of disclosures by students? Most teachers and guidance counselors think there is; but the fact is that there probably is not. It depends upon the law in the particular state. Some states have statutes or decisions that protect the student—and the teacher or guidance counselor—by ruling that no one can compel the disclosure of such communications between a student and his teacher or guidance counselor. Many do not. The state of Massachusetts, for example, by 1974 had thrown the mantle of confidentiality around disclosures by client to lawyer, penitent to priest or patient to psychiatrist (under certain conditions) but not to the secrets of a young student to the school nurse, teacher or guidance counselor. Some states are more protective of the youngster, some are not. The lesson is: as in many situations, there is no overall solution except to be alert to the problem. Forewarned is forearmed—and half the battle in law is to be forearmed, in the schools as well as in the home.

RESIDENCY REQUIREMENTS

We may feel on safer ground discussing the home, but the legal question of "residence" is sometimes a thorny one, especially for college students. States may have different laws that apply to the length of time a person must live in a place in order to qualify for voting rights, welfare assistance, occupational preference as a fireman or policeman or other benefits or privileges. There are different criteria that determine what makes a person a "resident": length of time in the state, occupation or property there, where "home" is, and so on. A ticklish question arises for students who spend several months at an educational institution but whose "real home" is elsewhere.

There is no one answer that can be given to a residency requirement question, even within one jurisdiction. The length of residency necessary to obtain welfare benefits may differ from that required in order to be eligible to vote, for example. You should know that there may be residency requirements to qualify for different programs or objectives: and you should also know that the courts may regard some requirements as being so arbitrary, capricious, unreasonable or unrealistic that they will declare them unconstitutional or invalid.

There is also no question but that the trend in virtually all states is to liberalize the interpretation of residency requirements. The prevailing view is to follow an interpretation that will favor the person claiming residency, and to eliminate or nullify technical requirements that would prevent it. This trend exists in both statutory law and judicial decisions when that particular issue arises. This is a field where the lawyer may not be able to predict the outcome with more accuracy than the layman. That is because it is a situation that is peculiarly susceptible to the mercurial thoughts and opinions of a society in ferment; and whenever change is in the air, the lawyer's predictions suffer in reliability.

29

The Landlord-Tenant Relationship

THE LANDLORD-TENANT RELATIONSHIP is based on an agreement, oral or written, between the lessor and the lessee (the owner and tenant). There are various kinds of tenancy: for years, at will, and at sufferance. Before we can answer most questions, we must first know the kind of tenancy that exists.

LEASES

In a tenancy for years, the lease must be in writing and be certain and definite both in its commencement and in its termination.

A tenancy at will is a lease for an uncertain and indefinite term. An oral lease is a tenancy at will. The most common tenancy at will is one that runs from month to month.

A tenancy at sufferance is where there is a holding over by the tenant, without any agreement, express or implied. It can be converted into a tenancy at will by certain conduct, such as a tenant paying and the landlord accepting the rent.

A lease of land conveys an interest in land and, under a concept known in law as the doctrine of Statute of Frauds, the lease must be in writing. A lease transfers possession to the lessee.

A license, on the other hand, does not convey any interest and it may be oral. When someone rents a room in a hotel or rooming house, it is legally regarded as a license and not a lease. The hotel or rooming house's occupant is regarded as a licensee, but not a tenant (there may be an exception to this if the person is a long-term continuous resident).

When a question arises, before we can answer it, we must first know if the occupier of the premises is a tenant or a licensee; if he is a tenant, what classification of tenant. As a practical matter, he

194

will be a tenant for years (having a definite, written lease), or at will (an oral lease), or at sufferance (no lease of any kind), or a licensee (someone who temporarily occupies a room in a hotel or rooming house).

REPAIRS

In the absence of any agreement or statute to the contrary, the landlord is not liable for repairs. Most landlords do make repairs but usually it is because it's good business, not because of any legal responsibility. The tenant has the obligation to return the premises in the condition in which he found them, reasonable wear and tear being excepted. That is the general law but most states now have statutes calling for the landlord to make repairs if the premises are in an unsafe condition or are unfit for human habitation. Massachusetts statutes, General Laws Chapter 111, Section 127L and Chapter 239, Section 8A impose an obligation on the landlord to meet this requirement of the law.

EVICTION

If the landlord wants to evict the tenant, he must give him reasonable notice. The particular state statute spells out the details of what this notice must be. The Massachusetts statute, General Laws Chapter 186, Sections 12 and 13, requires the landlord to give a notice equal to the time between rent payment days or thirty days, whichever is longer. If the eviction is for non-payment of the rent, Section 11 allows fourteen days' written notice.

State statutes now make it clear that a landlord may be criminally punished for failing to provide water or heat. The Massachusetts statute is Chapter 186, Section 14. There may be civil liability, too, as in Massachusetts by a 1973 amendment.

Any provisions in the lease that provide non-liability for the landlord or waive eviction notices are rendered void in Massachusetts by Chapter 186, Sections 15 and 15A. Section 16 renders void any agreement that allows the landlord to terminate the lease if the tenant has a child. The tenant is further protected by Section 18, which provides damages if the landlord threatens the tenant for reporting him to the Board of Health or for activity in the tenants' union. Many other states have comparable protection for tenants; the law of the particular jurisdiction must be checked in specific cases.

Unless there is some law to the contrary, or provision in the lease, the general rule is that the tenant may keep a domestic pet, such as a dog or cat, and may sublet.

If the landlord has required a money deposit, many states have statutes that protect the tenant. In Massachusetts, Chapter 186, Section 15B makes the landlord pay interest after a year, and he is liable in double damages if he fails to return the deposit.

RENT CONTROL

If the premises are in an area covered by rent control, the tenant is afforded whatever protection the rent control statute provides. The landlord must comply with rent control regulations in addition to the general statutes of the state. Most states have some statute under which, by vote of the residents, a community can decide for itself whether or not it wants to have rent control. The layman may want to take action to inaugurate or eliminate rent control in his area.

WHO OWNS THE FIXTURES?

In any landlord-tenant relationship, the question of "fixtures" is apt to arise. Fixtures are chattels that have been placed on the rented premises. (A "chattel" is an article of personal property.) On the question of who owns the fixtures, assuming there is no agreement covering the point, the test is whether the chattels have been so annexed to the realty as to lose their identity, whether they can be removed without material injury to the realty or the chattel, and whether they were especially designed for use on the premises. The tenant has the right to remove fixtures he has installed if they have not become a part of the realty and can be removed without damaging them or the realty.

In commercial property, the general rule is the trade fixtures installed by the tenant may be removed by him during the term of the lease.

If a problem arises in any of the matters touched on here, the layman should check the statutes and other rules and regulations that apply in his area. It is probable that they will provide most of the remedies that have been illustrated here by the Massachusetts statutes.

The layman should also realize that many landlord-tenant difficulties have no real solution either legally or practically: they are often problems in human relations. The law of landlord-tenant must be considered and understood within that framework.

Maybe the simplest course is just to be your own landlord. Ever think of buying a home?

REPUBLICAN OR DEMOCRAT, IT DON'T MATTER. THEY'RE ALL WITH THE TENANT.

30

Buying a Home

BUYING A HOUSE, YOUR future home, is probably the second most important step you will take in life (marriage being the first). It is also the single biggest expenditure you will make in a lifetime (buying an automobile is second.) Isn't it important enough to retain an attorney for advice about it? In the ordinary case, the fee may be anything from $100 to $750 (in 1980), depending upon the locality and the attorney. For a purchase that could run from $35,000 to $200,000 isn't it sensible to spend another few hundred dollars on full protection? So, if you're buying a house, get an attorney. It's the least expensive thing you can do. But whether you choose to retain an attorney or not, read on and find out what kinds of things you, as well as your legal eagle, need to know before buying a home.

COMMON SENSE AND HOUSE BUYING

A person buying a house needs to have at least two things: legal knowledge and common sense. The knowledge of law can be minimal but the common sense should be great. All the legal expertise in the world doesn't amount to much if you don't have enough horse sense to require representations by the seller that the roof doesn't leak, there are no termites, the heating bill for the year was under "x" dollars, and so on. And of course you or some competent friend should have personally examined the foundation, walls, ceilings, gutters, and other places for signs of leaks and need of maintenance. Using common sense to consider such matters may save you from getting into a situation where knowledge of law is required.

THE REAL ESTATE AGENT

Usually a real estate agent will be showing the property and telling you about it. While most of them are probably honest and ethical, you must remember that whether technically they are representing the buyer or the seller, they only get paid if the sale is consummated. All of them are aware of which side their bread is buttered on—and the real estate agent (who usually is the seller's representative) rarely volunteers anything that would kill a sale. So ask questions. Don't expect him (or her, because most agents are women) to volunteer information that may be adverse to the seller's position. But the average real estate agent will answer questions honestly, even if the information hurts the seller's presentation. And of course you should check on what the answers are, anyway.

If it's a newly built house and you'll be the first occupant, be sure to carefully investigate the builder's reputation and qualifications. If he has built other houses in the area, make it a point to inquire of those owners about their satisfaction. The knowledge may be extremely valuable.

EXAMINING THE NEIGHBORHOOD

Whether it's a new or old house, inquire about the neighborhood itself. Is it changing in character in any way? Is a new type of family moving into the area? Maybe you don't care and maybe you do; however, if you care you should at least know the situation before you buy. If there's a vacant lot on the corner, inquiry may reveal whether a gas station or high-rise apartment is going on it and this knowledge may affect your decision. What about traffic conditions, schools, churches, cafes, bus service, garbage collection, or television reception? Are there zoning regulations that might be of concern? For example, if you planned to have a medical office, hair dressing parlor or photography studio in one part of your home, you might be surprised to learn that you cannot because the section is zoned for strictly residential purposes.

A friend of mine was buying a "three family house" largely because he planned to rent the two top floors. Quite by accident he learned that zoning regulations of that neighborhood forbade renting the third floor to anyone except members of the family.

199

It's wise to check for these restrictions because zoning laws may turn out to be of great importance to you, too.

A LEGAL REPRESENTATIVE HELPS
PROTECT THE BUYER

There are dozens of questions you should ask even if you had 50 lawyers representing you; so ask. And then check on the answers given to you. Speaking of lawyers, do I need a lawyer? Yes, you do. Checking the title to be sure there are no mortgages, liens, incumbrances or other clouds on it requires a lawyer. Also, there are other technicalities involving the transfer where it's comfortable to have a lawyer even if it isn't absolutely necessary. However, if you're troubled by the expense of engaging a lawyer, keep in mind the fact that you almost certainly are financing the purchase by a mortgage from a bank—and the bank will insist on having its own lawyer examine the title before lending you any money on the strength of a "clear" title. So there is a lawyer in the picture somewhere, even if he technically is not representing you.

Who pays the fee of the bank's lawyer? You do. Yes, you do even if you have also engaged your own attorney to examine the title. Why do you have to pay the bank's lawyer? Well, you either agree to pay or the bank will not lend you the money for the mortgage—it's as simple as that. So, as a practical matter, you already have a lawyer for the most important legal phase, searching the title, because your interest is identical with the bank's in wanting to be sure the title is "clear." Practically speaking, you are as well protected as the bank on that point, and believe me, the bank's trying to be as well protected as possible.

THE BINDER OR PURCHASE AND
SALES AGREEMENT

Let's assume you've checked out the property, the neighborhood, taxes, services, schools, and everything else, and decided to buy. What next? First, keep in mind that agreements concerning real estate or houses must be in writing or else they cannot be enforced except in extremely rare cases. So the next step is a document that is called a "binder" or a "purchase and sales" agreement or some similar designation, depending on the local custom. (Hereafter it will be referred to as a binder.) This document (which incidentally, is almost always a binding contract and should be entered into with full realization of its legal consequences) briefly spells out the terms of the sale.

The binder is a deposit of money by the buyer (usually held by the real estate agent) as a manifestation that the buyer is in good faith or is really in earnest about binding the bargain. This agreement gives a buyer a brief amount of time (usually 30 days) to arrange for financing, title search, and other such details. Since most houses already have a mortgage, the buyer usually goes to that same bank or to one recommended by the real estate agent. If the deal goes through, the good faith deposit (perhaps $500 or $1,000 for houses selling for less than $100,000) is applied to the purchase price.

It is unfortunate that most laymen seem to regard the binder as merely sort of a memorandum. It is a binding legal contract and, before entering into it, the party should have the advice of a lawyer. Too many people do not call in their own lawyer until the "closing" (the actual passing of papers). Would you sign a binding contract to purchase an automobile and then call in a mechanic to look it over? Or, would you have the mechanic "check it out" before you signed the contract? Of course you'd have the mechanical expert look the car over before you signed an agreement to buy it, and of course you should have the legal expert look over the binder agreement before you sign it. It contains the terms that you are legally bound to carry out or face a lawsuit. Don't be misled because some people characterize the binder or purchase and sales agreement as sort of a legal "handshake." It is, but don't forget it's a handshake with teeth.

If the sale is not completed there may be a legal hassle about what happens to the deposit. If the buyer backed out without good reason, the seller may claim the deposit on the grounds that another purchaser was lost or that he had the right to its retention. Both the buyer and seller should know that in some states the seller must give specific reasons for not returning the deposit; if they are not valid, the buyer can sue for triple the damages he claims to have incurred.

The buyer should be certain to see that the binder agreement protects him; for example, there should be a provision excusing him from carrying out the agreement if the bank won't advance the required mortgage. Since disposal of the deposit is often the most troublesome item if the sale does not go through, both parties should be especially careful to see that the terms of the binder agreement are crystal clear.

The binder should spell out exactly when and where the final sale will be made, and specifically whether the payment may be made by personal check or bank check or what. Remember that (unless the particular state has a statute or law to the contrary) "legal tender" means hard, cold coins or greenbacks—unless the binder gives the buyer the right to pay by certified check or bank check (no sane seller will agree to anything less).

Why is it so necessary to protect the buyer in this regard? The reason is a seller might want to back out of a contract because a better offer may have been made for the property or its value may have increased due to some unexpected development. The seller is legally entitled to refuse any payment except "legal tender" (hard cash)—no matter how unreasonable such an attitude may be—and who walks around with $20,000 or $30,000 in cash? A bank or certified check (or one signed by Rockefeller) may be "as good as gold" to the average layman, but in most places it is not the "legal tender" required by law unless the binder agreement specifies it as such.

The seller doesn't need any protection on this point. He has the option of taking the bank check, a library card, insisting on cash, or whatever. The buyer has no such option. Unless the binder agreement says otherwise, the buyer cannot insist on performance by the seller unless he puts "legal tender" on the table; and this probably means hard cash.

Other important items are such matters as insurance, taxes, shrubbery, furniture, fixtures, and various house expenses that usually are billed annually or semi-annually (e.g. water bill). Does the purchase price include washing machines and other utilities? What about the wall to wall carpet? The TV antenna? It's not a bad idea to even refer to the shrubbery, especially if it's easily removable.

The binder agreement should specify the "fixtures" that do not go to the purchaser: for example, the dining room chandelier, the living room drapes, the air-conditioners, and the dishwasher. Many buyers claim (and believe) that the purchase price includes whatever they "see" when they toured the house.

LEGAL ASSISTANCE FOR OLDER PEOPLE

Older persons should also look into the possible availability of legal services based on the federal Older Americans Act. The Act was amended in 1975 to mandate that every state Title III plan should provide for the establishment of at least one of four listed priority services for the aged. One of the four is legal services (the other three being transportation, home care, and housing renovation). Your state may have a plan that provides legal services, and the assistance might be quite comprehensive. For example, the Boston (Massachusetts) office of Legal Research and Services for the Elderly (LRSE) has 42 lawyers and 91 paralegals (as of August, 1978, an increase from 12 lawyers and 22 paralegals in 1975). These local area agencies usually provide their services at no cost to the elderly and the legal personnel are paid out of grants from the federal government. Legal service agencies usually take only problems in such matters as social security, medicaid and other non-fee generating cases. If there is a fee-generating problem, the case is usually referred to the private bar. If the legal agency does handle a matter that requires a fee, it is usually on a sliding scale where the elderly person pays only a part of it.

In recent years (largely because of the trend in consumer protection) many state or local governments have had statutes or regulations requiring the house-owner to make repairs or renovations before being permitted to sell. For example, a Detroit friend of mine had to spend $5,000 on repairs before he could get a permit from the city authorities allowing him to sell. If you're a seller, you had better check your locality on the point. On the other hand, since all states don't have that protection for the purchaser, a buyer had better be aware of the fact that there have been situations where the Board of Health or other local authority has stepped in *after* the purchase to tell the new owner that he could not live on the premises until certain conditions have been corrected. For example, a Boston purchaser was not allowed to move into his newly acquired home until he had eliminated a lead poisoning hazard that existed because of the type of paint on the house. It cost him quite a bit to remove and resulted in a very unexpected expenditure. The binder agreement should have had a provision anticipating such a contingency.

The buyer should be particularly careful to ascertain the status of the insurance, if any, and whether it sufficiently protects him during the negotiations. There have been cases where, because fire insurance coverage terminated immediately after the transfer of title, the property was unprotected from that hazard. It's not a bad idea for the buyer to confer with the insurance agent to verify the exact situation.

CHECKLISTS AND ADJUSTMENTS

Since sales are made at all times of the year, the usual transaction calls for "adjustments" between the parties concerning assessments for taxes, premiums for insurance, and other bills that will be coming due or the seller has already paid for the year. If there is oil heat, how full is the tank? And is the oil included in the price or does the seller expect the buyer to pay for it? The sales document should spell it ut. A buyer would be well advised to prepare a very extensive "check list" before going out to look at any property. List all the questions—at least every one detailed in this chapter and as many more that you can think of—and get answers to them. When you decide it's the house you want, check out the answers *before* you conclude the transaction.

If you have an attorney, be sure you have gone over your check list with him. It will increase both his knowledge of the transaction and his respect for your acumen—and he may be more cautious about what he charges such a careful person.

CONVEYING TITLE: THE DEED

The official document by which title is conveyed from the seller to the buyer is a contract called the "deed." Unless there are some special agreements or provisions between the parties, the usual deed is purchased at the legal stationery store and the blank spaces are filled in by whoever makes out the deed. Blank spaces always include the names of buyer and seller, the purchase price and a description of the property, usually also identifying it by reference to the book and page on which it is recorded in the office of the County Recorder, County Clerk, the Registry of Deeds, Land Court or proper agency of the particular state. If any question ever arises concerning title to the property, the courts will almost certainly only recognize a recorded deed to establish ownership. The official recording the deed will place documentary tax stamps on it, which conform to the consideration paid for the property.

The aim of both the buyer and the seller is the transfer of something that is called a "marketable title," which means that the buyer has no reasonable objections, the title has only minor defects, or that the property is free of debts except those specified. As a practical matter, the only kind of title that is good is one that is marketable. If it is not marketable, no one will buy the property or lend any money on its security. So of course the seller must assure the buyer that the seller's title is marketable. That is done by the deed, which states the particular conditions under which the transfer is made: by "warranty," "quit claim" or "subject to" such and such a lien, mortgage, easement, covenant or other restrictions or encumbrances. The deed tells both parties (and everyone else, when recorded) exactly what is being transferred and under what conditions. The type of deed a purchaser will receive depends upon the terms of the binder contract, which is another good reason for having a lawyer represent you right from the beginning.

A lien or mortgage is most easily understood if we regard it as a claim against the property itself that somebody has, usually because the property was pledged as security for money loaned to the owner by the one holding the mortgage or lien. An easement is usually access to the property by a path or the right of some person or the public to use the property in some way. For example, perhaps some owner gave the electric light company the right to have an underground cable on the property.

Covenants are legal agreements (made by some earlier owner) that limit the future use of the property and may restrict the rights of even the owners. For example, there may be a "real" covenant (one that runs with the land, in the words of the law) that forbids the owner to subdivide the property or add another story on the house or use it for commercial purposes, and so forth. Or there may be a restrictive covenant to prevent sale to certain ethnic groups (such a covenant has been held to be unconstitutional, but who wants a law suit on some recorded documents?) Various covenants may have been entered into by former owners of a neighborhood who felt it was necessary to protect the value of their property. Before purchasing, a buyer should know about such agreements: it might affect his decision.

WARRANTY DEEDS vs. QUIT CLAIMS

Most states distinguish warranty deeds from quit claim ones in that in the former the seller "warrants" (guarantees, represents, promises) that he has a marketable title; one to which the buyer has no reasonable objection or one that has no mortgages, liens, incumbrances or serious legal defects except those stated. Whereas in the quit claim deed the seller merely transfers whatever title or interest he has in the property, without any guarantee or representation that his title is good. The usual "bargain and sale" deed is somewhere between the two: the seller makes no warranties or guarantees but, by implication, he represents that his title is marketable. Of course the bargain and sale may include whatever representations the parties agree upon; and that is called a bargain and sale deed "with covenant" as distinguished from one without covenants.

What happens if the property is not as represented? In a transfer by quit claim deed, the buyer has no basis for a law suit against the seller if it turns out that the seller's title really wasn't "good" because it was clouded by the various mortgages and liens on the property. The seller represented merely that he was transferring only whatever title he had, good, bad, or indifferent. On the other hand, if it were a warranty deed, the transfer would give the buyer a good law suit against the seller if the seller's title was not marketable. If the buyer wins in a lawsuit based on the seller's failure to deliver a marketable title, he is entitled to money damages to compensate him for whatever losses he has sustained, all of which are a matter of proof. Or, if he chooses to force an unwilling seller to do so, the court will order the seller to specifically perform his promise and transfer the property to the buyer. In the eyes of a court of equity, the buyer is entitled to this particular piece of property because it is distinctive in that nothing of value (including money) is identical to it.

If the seller wins, he cannot compel the buyer to accept a transfer of the property but the court will order the buyer to pay whatever damages the seller has sustained, usually the profit that would have been made if the sale had been consumated.

In some areas, property is transferred by various kinds of deeds; in others, the custom is for merely one type to be used. Custom is by area and not necessarily by state. For example, in western

Massachusetts most transactions are by warranty deed whereas the quit claim deed is customarily used in the eastern part of the state. Many realtors resolve the problem by recommending the use of title insurance companies which, as the name suggests, guarantee the title against any defects and provide for the payment of money if events prove the title is not as "good" as it is supposed to be.

THE CLOSING

The final step is the "closing" or "passing of papers" which describes the exchange of deed for money. It customarily takes place in the appropriate governmental office where the deed is to be recorded after a last minute search of records to be sure that someone has not made a claim against the property in the minutes or hours before the transfer. The closing is usually attended by everyone who participated in any way in the sale: parties, attorneys, real estate agent(s), bank representative, and so forth. And all states require that the deed must be signed and acknowledged before a notary public.

A postscript to the preceding is that, as of the date of this writing, present or planned consumer protection laws give the buyer a brief time (usually not more than three days) to "change his mind" if certain conditions exist. For example, if federal assistance involves such agencies as HUD, the buyer enjoys the option of changing his mind. The parties should check the possibilities of such laws which are pending or already on the books.

In recent years, various residential complexes with such designations as "condominiums" and "cooperatives" have been becoming increasingly popular. Let's take a look at them.

31
Cooperatives and Condominiums

THE EXPERIENCE OF LIVING in a condominium or a cooperative ranges from headaches to heaven, but once in, you cannot get out simply by buying aspirin or wings. If you contemplate buying a residence of this type, get a lawyer. You cannot afford not to. There are special problems associated with residence based on the principles of condominiums and cooperatives, such that under no circumstances should anyone consider either without obtaining the advice of a good lawyer. (And of course, you should also use the information in Chapter 30 when purchasing a house or residence of any kind).

THE QUESTION OF OWNERSHIP

While both condominiums and cooperatives are similar in that each involve joint or combined ownership or participation by several owners in specified units of a residential complex, such as apartments, houses, townhouses, and buildings of various kinds, there are important practical and legal differences between them. Oversimplifying it, and not touching on all the distinctions, in a condominium complex of (for example) 10 apartments, each participant has exclusive ownership of his own apartment and 1/10 ownership of the halls, passageways, and other areas that are commonly used by all the tenants. Whereas, if it were a cooperative, the 10 participants would have joint ownership of everything, including the individual apartment of each owner.

Technically, a "cooperative" is usually a kind of hybrid corporation which owns premises in which each "tenant" has stock and a lease of the particular unit he occupies. Thus he becomes a voting shareholder with a voice in making decisions that affect the cooperative. In the ordinary cooperative, the shareholders own the whole entity and the three-bedroom unit owner has one vote, as does the owner of a one-bedroom unit.

In both the cooperative and condominium one common rule is that no sale or change in any unit can be made without the consent of those who are operating the residential complex. Usually this is a board of trustees elected by the owners.

Obviously, there are all kinds of bylaws, rules, and regulations, some of which are highly legalistic and technical and can be of the utmost importance. For example, in some, legal changes can be made by the ruling board of trustees.

Speaking of "trustees" (or whatever the members of the ruling board are called in the particular case) there is considerable uncertainty as to what you, as the "owner" of one of the units in the condominium, can do if the trustees decide not to listen to your just complaint about some grievance. For example, I know of one unit owner who was unable to persuade the trustees to do anything about his leaking roof even though it was ruining his property. The Condominium Documents (Master Deed, Bylaws, etc.) very clearly said only the trustees had jurisdiction over the "common areas," including specifically the roof. When the trustees refused to act, my friend asked a lawyer to sue the trustees for the damage to his unit that had been caused by the refusal of the trustees to perform their duty. He was informed that there was no personal liability of any trustee and, as far as the liability of the trust was concerned, there was no money or property in the trust.

Caveat emptor (let the buyer beware); it is best to check very carefully to see what protection you have and what you can do if the trustees don't carry out their responsibilities. The Condominium Documents may say "The Trustees must repair," but it may also say they have no personal liability or give them some other protection. What can you do about it if they fail to carry out their responsibilities? Better find out before the situation arises.

IMPROVEMENT AND MAINTENANCE COSTS

Another point often overlooked is that the interests and desires of the individual owners may not be the same; and even if they

209

were identical for all when you bought, that does not mean they will continue to be the same. For example, when you bought into the condominium or cooperative, the cost of upkeep of the grounds was $1,000 a year, of which your 1/10 assessment would be $100. However, the trustees decided they wanted to beautify the grounds with flowerbeds, doubling the assessment on each owner. Another vote installed tennis courts and, although you don't play tennis, you're assessed for 1/10 of the cost. And so on, and so on. Majority rules, and it is simply your tough luck if you don't like or use what the majority has decided to incorporate into the premises.

Another possible headache is illustrated by a case pending in the Massachusetts courts at the date of this writing. The condominium bylaws in question required owners of the various units to pay the trustees $50 a month for maintenance and repair of the outside buildings. One owner wanted her roof repaired because it was leaking. The trustees told her to take it up with the builder of the condominium because, it being brand new, it was the builder's responsibility. However, the builder said he had no contract with her but only with the trustees. She went back to the trustees but they refused to take the builder to court. In the meantime, the roof was still leaking and beginning to damage the walls of her unit. She asked the trustees to at least have the roof repaired. They refused but insisted she keep up her $50 monthly maintenance payments to them, which they were using for maintenance and repairs to other apartments, but not hers. She has had to hire a lawyer to take the trustees and builder to court, and her roof is still leaking and she is still paying the trustees $50 a month for maintenance. If it were a single house and not a condominium, she would simply have used her $50 a month for the roof's repair; no lawyer, no court, and no leak. The only reason she cannot do that is because she is not in a single house but is in a condominium.

There are countless examples of how you may run into unanticipated problems in the condominium or cooperative type of residence. Some are social, others are practical, and all have legal overtones. If you are going to become involved in any way, get a lawyer. It may be expensive, true—but it can be even costlier if you don't.

As of this writing (and probably for many years still to come) the law concerning condominiums and cooperatives is not really "settled" in any state; the concept is too new and issues concerning them are either still pending in court or have not even been raised yet. Because of such uncertainties all kinds of lengthy (and expensive) legal problems and flare-ups will be coming between owners, trustees, builders, and others involved in such residential complexes.

SELLING THE CONDOMINIUM UNIT

One particularly troublesome problem is the usual provision that an owner cannot dispose of his unit without the consent of the other owners or trustees. That's really a comforting provision when the agent explains to you that it's for *your* protection so your neighbors can't just sell to anyone. Besides, if you want to transfer *your* apartment to anyone, you would obviously have a reasonably acceptable person. Who else could buy? And, anyway, you've met the neighbors, and of course such nice people wouldn't put any roadblocks in your way. Well, maybe they would and maybe they wouldn't; there have been occurrences of both kinds, so don't count on it.

However, the condominium unit owner who wants to sell usually does have some protection. When there's a "no sale without consent of other owners" provision, there's usually an escape clause added: the objectors must themselves purchase the unit if they reject the buyer the seller found.

What about other legal problems that might not even involve your neighbors, for example, inheritance. Let's say you have a worthless brother to whom you want to leave nothing, so you leave your condominium to a favorite cousin. Unfortunately, you have "disposed" of your unit without the consent of the trustees required by the bylaws of your complex. The worthless brother claims to inherit your condominium on the grounds that your legacy of it to your favorite cousin is void or can be set aside because of your noncompliance with the bylaws. He goes to court to enforce his claim as your only heir. Maybe your favorite cousin will win the case, but do you want even the risk of a loss? Or the difficulty of court action simply because condominium law is unsettled?

211

Or take another inheritance problem: you leave all your money (about $5,000) to sister A, who is quite wealthy, and your real estate (a condominium, worth about $100,000) to sister B, who is very poor. Looking down from heaven (where you can't do anything about it) you hear the trustees decide that they do not like sister B, to whom you "disposed" of your condominium without their consent. Under a bylaw that says the trustees have the right to purchase your unit for the $100,000 you paid for it if the person to whom you wanted to dispose it is unacceptable to them, they decide to exercise that right, taking your condominium and giving you (now, your estate) the agreed price of $100,000. Your estate is no longer a condominium and $5,000 cash, it is now all cash because the trustees have declared your disposal of the condominium invalid and they have given your estate the $100,000 for it. Your will said the money (you thought it was $5,000) would go to wealthy sister A and the condominium (worth $100,000) to your poor sister B. But now there is no condominium in your estate, only money, which the court probating your estate might rule goes to sister A under your will. Poor sister B is not only left out of the condominium; she's left out in the cold. And there's not a blessed thing you can do about it because you're gone and the only document speaking for you is your will. Legislatures and courts will be taking steps to prevent such results of course, but *your* state may not have corrected it as yet.

What's the situation if you become involved in bankruptcy? People do, you know. Let's say that you're in such desperate straits that you have to immediately sell your condominium. The ruling authorities of your condominium complex will not consent to your buyer (for whatever reason) but you sell it at a sacrifice, anyway. Several months later you go into bankruptcy. The trustee in bankruptcy is supposed to collect all your assets and the law says that any transfer of any asset within four months of the bankruptcy is presumed to be fraudulent to creditors. Your transfer of your condominium is all right, you think, because it was made more than four months ago. But the trustee in bankruptcy reads the bylaw that says the condominium owner cannot dispose of his unit without the consent of the other owners, and they did not give their consent. The trustee in bankruptcy moves to have the sale declared invalid, which means it becomes an asset of your estate and available to the creditors he represents. If you had done the identical thing with a single house, you would have been fully protected; in this case you have lost out all around because your residence is a condominium with such by-laws and regulations.

Can those bankruptcy and inheritance problems arise? Maybe yes, maybe no. I've discussed such matters with many lawyers (including specialists in Florida, a state which has had more experience than any other state with condominiums and co-operatives) and, while there are varying opinions on the result, they all agree that the law on such residential complexes is still so unsettled and uncertain that "anything is possible." And that would not be true of the identical situations with a single house or apartment.

BUY WITH CARE

Let me emphasize that I am not saying that you should not buy a condominium or cooperative type of residence. It might be just right for you. All I am saying is: if you decide that is what you want, have a lawyer go over all the details and advise you of what your legal rights and liabilities are. And be sure to ask the questions that have been asked here. Otherwise the lawyer may not think of them. I know because I have talked with many lawyers and most of them are not too familiar with the technicalities that can be involved in condominiums and coopera-tives. It's a new field, and any new field involves new law. You may want to become a part of history, but certainly not because of your name as the title of a case involving condominium or cooperative law. So play it safe, talk to a good lawyer before buying this type of residence.

Lastly, (and even lawyers, realtors, and other "experts" should do this) if you're going to have anything to do with a condominium (buying, selling, developing, promoting, legislating, etc.) write to the Real Estate Commission of the Department of Commerce of the state of Virginia and get a copy of the Virginia Condominium Act and the Condominium Regulations. As far as legislation is concerned, the Virginia Condominium Act is perhaps the best model for other states to follow. And the Virginia Real Estate Commission's "Condominium Regulations" has virtually a blueprint to be followed by anyone interested in starting or investing in a condominium.

The statutes of Florida are another good reference for anyone planning to become a developer or manager of condominiums. They may be obtained from that state's Division of Condominiums in Tallahassee, Florida.

32
Libel, Slander and the Right to Privacy

LIBEL OR SLANDER IS the publication of defamatory words, pictures, signs, drawings, or other similar means which expose the person to contempt, hatred, scorn, ridicule, or other disparagements, or tend to impair his standing in the community. In general, libel is written whereas slander is oral.

Slander connotes nonpermanence but libel connotes permanence; and slander is normally considered to have limited circulation whereas libel has wide circulation.

In libel, it is not necessary to show specific damages; but slander is not actionable in itself unless the words charge the injured person with a crime or loathsome disease or injure him in his business.

Truth is a defense to libel, unless the libel is published with malice. Truth is a complete defense to slander, whether the words were uttered maliciously or not.

Privilege may be a defense to slander or libel. The usual "privilege" situation arises when there is something more than a mere voluntary statement; where an employer has reasonable cause to believe an employee is stealing, and so charges him; or a statement without malice is made to the police in the course of an investigation; or a witness gives pertinent testimony in court; or someone gives a character reference without malice; and in comparable situations.

There can be some close cases in determining whether something is technically libel or slander. What is the situation when a person is hanged in effigy? A court decision has held that it constitutes libel.

The development of radio and television has created some difficult situations, too. What is a broadcast where only words are spoken? Does it make a difference if the spoken words are read

215

from a script? Today, if a television speaker uses a script, it is considered libel rather than slander.

Words that appear innocent on their face may be libelous under circumstances where an insinuation is included. A sign saying: "Mrs. Jones had a baby last night"—when everyone knows she had been married for less than a week—under certain circumstances might constitute libel if it were done with malice.

There is also group libel; but the group must be small enough and the plaintiff must be identifiable in it. For example: "Americans are thieves" is too broad; but "Women in that apartment are all prostitutes" might be actionable.

The "public figure" has virtually no protection at all against slander or libel. Unless he can prove malice or reckless disregard of the facts (which is usually impossible) the statement is not actionable. The theory is that the value of giving people free rein to criticize public officials far outweighs any harm to the individual. "Public figures" are usually high officials, famous athletes or entertainers, and people whose names are (or should be) well-known.

WHAT CONSTITUTES AN INVASION OF PRIVACY?

Closely allied to matters involving libel and slander is the "right of privacy." A person's privacy may have been violated even if the words or actions do not constitute libel or slander.

Even in the absence of statute, most states follow the Common Law recognition of the right to privacy. Some states also have statutes that guarantee the individual against any undue invasion of his or her privacy. Perhaps typical of both the Common Law and the statutory protection for the person's privacy is the Massachusetts statute, General Laws Chapter 214, Section 1B, which provides that a person shall have a right against unreasonable, substantial or serious interference with his privacy.

Whether based on Common Law or Statutory Law, an action for invasion of privacy is usually based on one or more of the following wrongs:

1) Intrusion against the plaintiff's physical solitude. This does not mean that a person has the right to be completely free from any invasion of his privacy. That would be impossible in today's complex world. But it does mean that a person's privacy must be respected unless there is some very good reason for interfering with him. The usual case that arises in the courts is where there is some

question about the propriety of the investigatory techniques used by a credit agency. 2) Publication of private matters violating the ordinary decencies. Of course not all matters are "private"; some are newsworthy. Another problem is that juries have conflicting ideas of what the "ordinary decencies" are. They may very well differ from community to community. 3) Publicly placing the plaintiff in a false position by attributing views to him that he does not hold. The false position does not necessarily have to be one that is of a defamatory nature; however, if it is a position that merits public approval it may be difficult for the plaintiff to show any damage to himself. 4) Invading privacy by using the plaintiff commercially without his consent. The usual case here is where a person's name or picture has been used in an advertisement without his consent. The state of Massachusetts even has a statute (General Laws Chapter 214, Section 3A) granting as much as treble damages for certain infringements upon privacy of this type.

An interesting case is the 1974 suit brought by a high school student accusing the Federal Bureau of Investigation of having invaded her privacy. As part of a school project, the student wrote to the Socialist Workers Party to inquire about its practices. The FBI, which had been keeping a "mail cover" on that party under its surveillance of possible subversive groups, intercepted the letter. An FBI investigator went to interview the student to ascertain the reason for her writing to the Socialist Workers Party. Incensed at this invasion of her privacy, the young lady sought the assistance of the American Civil Liberties Union—and eventually the matter landed in the court. The suit (which involves the invasion of privacy and a possible violation of First Amendment rights) had not been decided at the time of this writing.

There is another matter that may never be fully and finally decided: Women's Rights. Let's take a look at this subject.

33
Women's Rights

THE STATUS OF WOMEN has been receiving particular attention in recent years. It is, of course, a constantly recurring item on the agenda of every state agency fighting discrimination in employment and other fields. The federal and state governments have many kinds of statutes and judicial decisions that either "protect" women or "discriminate" against them, depending upon your point of view. They may be prevented from working long hours, being employed at night, lifting heavy weights, and so on. They may be barred or exempted from jury service, especially if they have minor children. The public is pretty familiar with most of the illustrations that have been widely publicized by debates on the Equal Rights Amendment.

For many years (long before E.R.A.) there have been statutes and judicial decisions in the law books that should be of interest. In addition to federal legislation and executive orders, your state may have statutes or decisions comparable to some of the following illustrations.

SEX DISCRIMINATION

Federally, the Civil Rights Act of 1964 (42 U.S.C. Sec. 2000e), in Title 7, forbids virtually every kind of discrimination based on race, creed, color, national origin, sex and so forth. Discrimination may include failing to hire women, assigning them different jobs or different rates of pay, failing to promote them, and other treatment that differs from that accorded to male employees. The courts have put teeth in the law by ruling that statistics may be used to show a pattern of different treatment of one sex, thus establishing a *prima facie* case of discrimination. The federal cases of *Parham v. South-*

218

western Bell Telephone Co. (433 F(2) 421), and *Jurinko v. Weigand Co.* (477 F(2) 1038) strongly support the right of women to equal treatment.

Any woman who feels discriminated against in any way should insist upon her rights. If they are being denied, she will not be alone in her attempts to get justice. Various groups stand ready, willing, and able to assist her morally, legally, and often even financially. They have different names in different places but, whatever the names, they are headed by militant feminists (sometimes aided by men, too) who are knowledgeable, capable, dedicated, and extremely resourceful—and brother (and I do mean "brother") they are itching for a fight! While the injured person may look and be poor, weak, and virtually defenseless, male chauvinists had better realize that her champions are well-financed, strong, have a well-stocked armory of weapons, and know what to do and when and how to do it. The "why" is simple: to make equal rights a reality.

While discrimination on any ground can be attacked, the favorite targets thus far have been in the fields of credit and employment. If banks, finance companies, and other credit agencies have different rules or standards for women than men—in applications for loans, mortgages, and other forms of credit—the courts are virtually certain to find that it is illegal discrimination. A lending institution that insists on the husband co-signing for the wife's application had better have a similar rule for husbands who apply. And employers who want to give preference to men in hiring or promoting are going to be penalized by legal decisions that give back pay *and* the position to women who take steps to correct such injustices. Courts, labor departments, Commissions against Discrimination, and other agencies (state and federal) all have made it clear that, at long last, women have truly been emancipated.

Under Title 7, the Equal Employment Opportunity Commission—the EEOC—sets guidelines that put teeth in enforcement of the Act. For example, the EEOC has ruled that "protective" laws in many states actually discriminate rather than protect. No longer can an employer escape a discrimination conviction by hiding behind permissive state legislation: the guidelines of the EEOC have eliminated such a defense.

The official message to male chauvinists is loud and clear: sex objects are still pretty and sex is still fun—but discrimination based on sex is too costly to be enjoyable.

WHY CAN'T WOMEN HOLD THESE JOBS?

There still are jobs or positions that can reasonably be held only by a male, of course. Statutes and judicial decisions refer to something called a Bona Fide Occupational Qualification (so common it is abbreviated to BFOQ). If the specifications or qualifications for a position do have standards or criteria that seem to favor male applicants, the courts will carefully scrutinize them to be sure it is a BFOQ—one that is made in good faith on reasonable grounds and is not arbitrary or capricious. And employers had better remember that they cannot get away with fictitious or out-of-date employment or promotion qualifications. For example, at one time an apparently reasonable qualification for the driver of a heavy truck might have been a certain degree of strength (that would be far beyond the average woman)—but the development of power steering and power brakes changed that. It's that sort of thing that is the reason for the BFOQ doctrine which is the basis for action by courts and agencies seeking to prevent discrimination based on sex. The writer of "Brother, Can You Spare a Dime?" is going to have to change the title to, "Brother or Sister, Can You Spare a Dime?" Sorry, fellows, but do you remember the pendulum we discussed in the early chapters on the Constitution, judicial interpretations, and climate of opinion? It's still swinging.

Incidentally, the law refers to *sex* discrimination: it protects men as well as women. In fact, there have been complaints by men against employers who advertised for a "female" receptionist, nurse, hairdresser, waitress or other employees in fields that have customarily been dominated by women. So even the chauvinists are not limited to one sex.

EQUAL PAY, MATERNITY LEAVE, AND GETTING CREDIT

The federal Equal Pay Act (29 U.S.C., Section 206) is enforced by the Wage and Hours Division of the Department of Labor. It has ruled that, where the pay scale is unequal between sexes for the same job, the man's pay cannot be reduced but the woman's must be increased to accomplish equal compensation for the same work.

The case of *Frontiero v. Richardson* condemned "romantic paternalism which, in practical effect, put women not on a pedestal but in a cage." By an eight-to-one decision the United States Supreme Court held that women members of the Armed Forces can claim spouses as dependents on the same basis as men.

There have been some important state decisions, as well as statutes, relating to two key points: pregnancy and credit. In Massachusetts, General Laws, Chapter 149, Section 105D protects a woman's job after maternity leave. And Chapter 151B, Section 14 makes it a discriminatory practice to refuse to extend credit because of sex or marital status. This statute not only allows actual damages but, if there are none, the person refused credit may be awarded special damages up to $1,000.

In *Phillips v. Martin Marietta Corp.* (404 U.S. 991) the United States Supreme Court held it was discrimination to fail to consider a woman for employment because she had pre-school age children.

The Federal Communications Commission and other agencies (both federal and state) have made favorable rulings for women who petitioned for assistance on the grounds that they were barred from certain top positions in an industry.

The layman should be aware of such statutes, cases, and rulings. He (or she) should also know about the agencies that have something to do with discrimination against women, such as the Department of Labor, and the Commission against Discrimination; and particularly with various women's groups which may give advice and aid in fighting cases of discrimination.

Most modern Americans agree that women should have their rights; the main disagreement at present seems to be whether the Equal Rights Amendment is a forward or backward step toward that goal.

In the meantime, perhaps we ought to come up with a few words that will be "neuter" enough to help bridge the gap between the two sexes. We need something better than "shim" or "his/her" or an apostrophe e ('e) for she/he (or makeshifts like "chairperson") for the writer or speaker who doesn't want to offend anyone.

I suggest that some terms might psychologically implement the Equal Rights Amendment by eliminating the letter "m" and substituting an apostrophe in its place in various words that end in "man." The apostrophe could represent either "m" or "wom" depending on whether the noun represented a male or a female. A few examples are:

alder'an	delivery'an	fore'an	patrol'an
chair'an	fire'an	garage'an	police'an
council'an	counter'an	mail'an	service'an

Perhaps you can think of some better terms to suggest equality between the sexes.

34
If You're Going to Do it Yourself

WE'RE ALMOST AT THE END of what the average person needs to know about law, as it applies to the kind of daily problems he is likely to face. That knowledge—no more and no less—was the aim of LAW FOR THE LAYMAN. The book was intentionally not entitled HOW TO BE YOUR OWN LAWYER because you should not be your own lawyer for serious legal problems; any more than you should be your own doctor for serious medical problems.

Lawyers have a saying: "A lawyer who represents himself has a fool for a client." There is good reason for this maxim. If doctors had a similar saying, I suppose it would be that a person who's his own doctor has a corpse for a patient. So this book is not intended to make you an Instant Lawyer: it is NOT a do-it-yourself legal kit. Rather, its role is perhaps comparable to that played by a first aid book in medicine, telling you what to do for everyday cuts, bruises, and minor ailments—when the services of a physician are not really essential—or giving you advice on emergency steps while waiting for the medical expert to arrive. LAW FOR THE LAYMAN tells you what to do for everyday legal problems (where you don't really need a lawyer) and it gives you information that you should have before consulting a lawyer (in those cases where you really should have one).

So before going on, let's summarize: (1) There are countless everyday situations where the only legal help you need is right in this book; (2) When you get into a serious legal situation, be sure to remember that even a lawyer who represents himself has a fool for a client.

Having said all that, what are some tips for the "amateur lawyer" who has "an everyday legal situation" that he should be able to handle with this book and his own common sense?

KNOWING THE LAW

Perhaps the first thing to keep in mind is that you want to impress your "opponent" (whoever you're arguing with) with the fact that you know what you're talking about; *you know the law,* and you have the law on your side. Let's try a couple of examples.

For example, suppose a bill collector is really strong-arming you with tactics that are improper or illegal in your state: perhaps you're being harassed with telephone calls at all hours of the day and night, or the creditor is threatening to tell your employer of the debt, or is using other improper means described in Chapter 20. What do you do? And how?

First of all, you put the harassing creditor on notice that *you know the law.* By way of a telephone call or (probably better) a letter to him, you say: "You have been harassing me by improper collection tactics that can subject you to penalties that will be enforced against you, by me, if you continue such improper tactics." Short, uncompromising, and to the point.

If you happen to know the state statute that contains the law on this point (see Chapter 20), just add another sentence: "If you are not familiar with the law in this state, it is found in Chapter 123 of the General Laws." This last is probably not necessary—the dunning creditor almost certainly already knows it, but is ignoring it because he doesn't think that you are aware of it. Your letter (whether it actually refers to a specific statute or not) is a forceful reminder to him that *you know the law.*

Suppose it doesn't stop him? If, in spite of your letter, he continues to use harassing collection methods, you may then avail yourself of some of the legal remedies described in Chapter 20.

Or perhaps you have been the victim of the "bait and switch" described in Chapter 22: you were lured into the X Department Store by an advertisement ("the bait"), and then the salesman sold you a more expensive item ("the switch"). When you and your spouse talked it over, you decided to return the article and get your money back, but the manager of the X Department Store refused. So you call or write: "Your 'bait and switch' tactics are improper and subject you to penalties that I shall take steps to enforce unless you refund my money immediately. In addition, if you do not, I shall report you to the Better Business Bureau and the Federal Trade Commission so that other customers may not be unfairly treated."

Again, that communication tells the manager of the X Department Store that *you know the law* and you know how to enforce your rights. And, again, if you happen to know the specific statute, you might quote it—not to inform the store of the law (they know it)—but to inform them that *you* know it.

If the manager of the X Department Store still doesn't see the light, hit him over the head (legally) with one or more of the remedies outlined for the consumer in Chapter 22.

Another common example: your landlord won't return your rental security deposit. The magic legal words: "I hereby demand the return of my rental deposit, with interest. If I do not receive it by return mail, I shall take steps to enforce the penalties provided by law." And, again, cite the specific law if you happen to know it; but, again, the landlord already knows it. The really important reason for your letter is to have the landlord realize that you do, too. It's always of paramount importance that your "opponent" be made to understand that *you know the law.*

Your letter should get immediate results—but suppose it doesn't? The best next step is probably the Small Claims Court mentioned on page 56. You go there, tell the clerk your story, pay a small fee to cover court costs (almost certainly less than $3.00 in most states); and within a couple of weeks you'll appear before the judge (no lawyer necessary). After the judge hears both sides, a decision will be forthcoming almost immediately. Quick, simple, inexpensive—if you know how to do it. Now you do.

The frosting on the cake is that you probably won't even have to go to court. When the landlord gets the notification, he'll probably return your deposit at once. Why? Because he realizes that *you know the law.*

Landlord and tenant examples spring up by the dozen (See Chapter 29). For instance. the Old Grouch is unreasonably stingy with heat. You can chill his blood colder than yours with a letter that shows *you know the law.* "Dear Sir: This is to put you on notice that your failure to provide adequate heat is deleterious to my health. Unless the situation is corrected *immediately*, I shall take steps to enforce legal penalties against you." (The word "deleterious" is a good one; it not only has five syllables, but he may not know what it means. He will be sure, however, that it's something bad.)

If you can cite the specific statute that spells out those penalties, (civil *and* criminal in many states), so much the better; but the omission won't matter too much because your landlord already is aware of them. Your letter is just to make him realize that you are, too. Once he understands that *you know the law,* you'll get heat.

But suppose you don't? Then turn the legal heat on him. Go to the proper court (it may be the Housing Court or the criminal side of the District Court or some other court, depending on your state) and report him. In some states, include an agency like the Board of Health, too. It won't cost you a cent to make the complaint. In addition, if your state provides money damages, you may also file a claim in Small Claims Court (assuming there has been no serious harm from the loss of heat; if there has been, you should get a lawyer).

There are dozens of other illustrations that can be given—but they all make the same point: let your "opponent" realize that *you know the law.* Once he is satisfied of this—either on his own or after his lawyer explains your communication—you'll probably win your point. After all, why should he fight you, hire a lawyer, and go to all that trouble and expense if the law is against him? Put yourself in his position and ask yourself what you would do if the law was against you, and your opponent knew the law. You'd pull in your horns. Right? And that's what your "opponent" will do—once you show him that *you know the law.*

There are more illustrations that can be given of situations where you don't really need a lawyer—provided you know the law. But be very wary of trying to "do it yourself" if it's a serious legal matter. A good rule of thumb to follow is this: if it is a matter that's going to court (other than Small Claims Court), you had better retain a lawyer. However, there is one probable exception to this: uncontested divorce.

UNCONTESTED DIVORCE

You may not need a lawyer to handle an uncontested divorce, if there are no children and no questions about property or alimony. Let me repeat the word "uncontested," because if the divorce is contested, it's imperative to have an attorney. And a person is simply a fool to go it without an attorney, if such questions as custody of children or division of property or alimony are involved. But if it's a plain and simple uncontested divorce, and solely the matter of dissolution of the union, you are pretty safe in being your own lawyer.

How do I proceed? First, read Chapter 23 carefully. Second, get the form on which an application for divorce is made. In most divorce courts, a printed form is filled in by the applicant. Those forms should be available either at the court or at a legal stationery store, depending upon the practice where you live. (If you're in a state that doesn't use forms, you'll have to follow the typed document used in a completed case with grounds similar to yours. Fill the form in lightly in pencil. Third, take it to the divorce court and talk to the clerk or registrar (the person responsible may have still another title; it differs from state to state). If the clerk or registrar has assistants or fellow-employees, they are probably sufficiently knowledgeable about divorce to answer the questions you should ask.

Your questions are fairly simple, but write them out and leave a space to fill in the answers you get. (1) Is my application filled out correctly? (It's still in pencil; but you explain that when you actually file it, you will have either typed it or printed it in ink.) (2) Have I lived here long enough for the court to have jurisdiction? (Most states have requirements about residence.) (3) Do I need any witness other than myself? (Some states may require a witness to establish the cause or service of the divorce papers, or for other reasons; it depends on the particular state.) (4) Do I need any documents? (For example, the marriage certificate) (5) Will I have to file some sort of paper stating that my spouse is not in the military service? (6) How do I serve the divorce papers on my spouse? (Probably by a sheriff or constable—again, it depends upon the practice in the particular state.) (7) After my spouse has been served with the divorce papers, what next? (The sheriff or constable will probably file them in court with his sworn statement that the process has been properly served; but it depends upon the practice in that state.) (8) Once serving and filing has been completed and the case is ready to be heard, what must I do to have the judge hear it? (You probably have to file a request that your case be put on the list for hearing.) (9) How will I be notified of what day to be in court? (Probably by a postcard or other notification from the divorce court clerk.) (10) How soon after the hearing does the divorce become final? (Some states have a waiting period.)

Now, of course there may be other questions and answers—it depends upon your curiosity and the clerk's patience. But the questions I have suggested are the minimum you should ask before finalizing your pencilled application by typing it or printing it in ink.

Incidentally, if you are a woman, there is one additional question that you must ask in some states: If I want to resume my maiden name, what do I do? (Some states may still have the requirement that you must ask and receive the permission of the divorce court.) But who knows? By the time you read this, the women's Lib Movement may have proceeded to the point where the man has to ask the court if *he* may resume *his* pre-marital name.

Once you have begun writing the questions, you may decide that it's worth a couple of hundred dollars to have a lawyer, after all. Keep your courage up: if you do decide to go it alone, the chances are a hundred-to-one that you can do it successfully without a lawyer—provided it's uncontested and there are no questions involving custody of children, division of property, or alimony.

There is one other possibility: free legal aid. More and more bar associations, governmental programs, and private groups are providing legal assistance of one type or another; however, it is generally in criminal cases or other matters where legal process of some kind is being brought *against* a person. The one seeking a divorce is the moving party *bringing* the action, so unless there has been a change by the time you read this, free legal assistance to the person seeking a divorce is probably not available in your state. However, it won't hurt to inquire before you start a do-it-yourself divorce: just call Legal Aid and ask.

JOB DISCRIMINATION

Another example involves discrimination, usually based on race, creed, color, sex, or age (there can be other grounds. of course, but these are the usual ones). Let's take one of the "examples" mentioned in Chapter 33.

You are a woman getting less pay than men doing the same job for the same employer. Of course you can begin by retaining a

227

lawyer or seeking the assistance of one of the groups or agencies mentioned on page 185. But let's assume you like your work; your boss is normally a "good fellow" (even though he is a male chauvinist pig); and you don't want to be a troublemaker who is running to "the law" and Feminist groups. What can you do?

You can reach into your do-it-yourself legal kit and come up with a letter (or oral request) that makes the powers-that-be aware of the fact that *you know the law*. "Now, Mr. Jones, I'm not the kind of person who wants to trot out Title VII for every little discrimination, but I *am* doing the same work as the men, even though my job description is 'helper' and theirs is 'inspector.' Don't you think we should get the same pay?" (My God! She even knows the title number!) Mr. Jones will probably get the message—that *you know the law*—and you'll probably get your pay increase.

However, if he doesn't, and you don't, then he really isn't a "good fellow," but is just a male chauvinist pig. He should be thrown into the toils of the Commission against Discrimination, as well as dragged into court for back pay and a change of job title and all the other official lacings he can be given by formal action. After all, you gave him his chance—didn't you?

The discrimination example is probably as good an illustration as any of the value of your legal knowledge and how and when you should use it as a legal do-it-yourself kit. First of all, know what the law is and how it applies to your situation. Secondly, convey this information to your "opponent" so that he realizes *you know the law*.

Those two steps alone may very well resolve the situation in your favor so that your problem is solved. However, if they do not, your knowledge of the law will tell you what the next step should be: where and how to obtain other free assistance from governmental agencies or private groups; or, perhaps as a last resort, to retain a lawyer because your case warrants it. You will take the right step and you will know what the right step is for one reason and one reason only: *you know the law*. That's basic and fundamental and it is the reason we have LAW FOR THE LAYMAN. It's not so much to enable you to be your own lawyer as it is to give you enough knowledge of the law to win your point without a lawyer, whether it be yourself or a real one. Doesn't that make sense?

GETTING THE MOST FOR YOUR MONEY

Speaking of sense, let's also talk dollars and cents in case you do get to the point where you need a lawyer: you want the most for your money. And, speaking now as a lawyer who's known all kinds of cases and all kinds of lawyers—it isn't only Heinz who has 57 varieties. There are lawyers and *lawyers*: good and bad, smart and dumb, honest and crooked, energetic and lazy, careful and careless—not 57, but 157 varieties. So be as careful in selecting one as you are when you choose a doctor (which is often done by such determinants as his availability or the parking facilities near his office). You can't do that with lawyers; for a prospective client, they're always available and they are willing to fix your parking tickets.

Before you shout disagreement, let me say that the availability and fixing apply only until the prospect becomes a client. Once you're a client, the lawyer doesn't want to see or hear from you; and fixing parking tickets becomes un-American. Most lawyers who represent the average person (not a business or a steady customer) want to be bothered by the client only when he chooses. And, in fairness to the lawyer, let me add that this is usually often enough for the needs of the case. But back to the business of selecting a lawyer.

Most bar associations or courthouses have some sort of referral list that will at least tell you the names of the lawyers that they believe to be ethical, but it probably doesn't tell you anything about their abilities or habits. Ask around among friends who have had cases of one kind or another. Try to talk to one or two attorneys and size them up for yourself. "Shop around": do what you do when you buy a car or a house or anything that means something to you. Whatever you do, it's still a gamble; but at least you've cut the cards.

Whoever you select, whatever his character, ability, and methods, you will get more for your money if the lawyer realizes that *you know the law.* That doesn't mean that you know as much as the lawyer or understand all the intricacies and technicalities of the law—it does mean that you have an understanding of the principles of law that apply to your case, and an appreciation of the kind of work the lawyer must do to carry it to a satisfactory conclusion. It doesn't mean that you only know those points of law that favor you—you're aware of the unfavorable ones, too. It doesn't mean that you want to try the case yourself or be a nuisance, but it does mean that you understand the problems to be faced and are willing to follow constructive suggestions that assist in overcoming those problems.

An automobile salesman won't talk knowingly about the value of the "framzis" if he's aware of your knowledge that the automobile doesn't have a "framzis"—a lawyer won't talk in mysterious Latin phrases if you know that the only real question is whether the policeman was justified in opening the trunk of your car.

Lawyers don't have all the knowledge at their fingertips or even in your file; you may have a lawyer who is taking a chance on memory rather than taking the time and trouble to go to the library and look it up. However, if you make a statement or simply ask a question that indicates that you have some knowledge of the law, the lawyer will see to it that he becomes accurately informed on the point.

There are literally dozens of simple illustrations: "Mr. Lawyer, I wonder about what the policeman will offer as 'probable cause' for making the search." "Mr. Lawyer, I have some question whether section 3 of the lease is void as against public policy." "Mr. Lawyer, isn't there a principal and agency question here?" "Mr. Lawyer, I know the automobile driver doesn't have insurance, but why might the automobile manufacturer not be responsible in a product liability case?" "Mr. Lawyer, are you planning to file interrogatories to the other party?" "Mr. Lawyer, has the case been marked up for hearing?" "Mr. Lawyer, under our right to discovery, can't we see such and such a document the other side has?" "Mr. Lawyer, I know the other side is saying the ticket stub from the parking lot said 'no responsibility,' but doesn't the law say fine print isn't controlling?"

Bring up a point or ask a question, but do it intelligently and not argumentatively. Let the lawyer know that you are aware of the possibility of such a point or the need for information on the question: believe me, he will look into it. He's going to want to know at least as much as *he thinks* you know, and he won't want to be caught in any erroneous answers. The more law you know, the more you'll get your money's worth from your lawyer; but be sure you do know what you're talking about. Remember, he knows what a "framzis" is, too.

230

Let me illustrate by an experience I had with a prospective client who was charged with desertion from the Army at the beginning of World War II. He came into my office after he had been missing from an East Coast camp for a year. He had been caught in a Midwest city He had taken an assumed name, married, and was working at a civilian job when the Military Police caught up with him. To me, it looked like a clear case of desertion— indeed, what else?

"No," he corrected me, "I'm just absent without leave. I'm just AWOL." Well, of course I knew better. "AWOL" or "absent" was when you missed a roll call or went temporarily over the hill on a weekend drunk. He was certainly more than just "absent" when he left his post of duty, went to a far-off city, took an assumed name, married, and worked for a year in a civilian job. Moreover, when a soldier was just absent, he always returned voluntarily—not so in this case. They searched for a year before they found him and then had to arrest him and take him back forcibly. To make it even worse, he also denied his true identity—until his fingerprints proved it.

"If all that doesn't prove desertion, I don't know what does," I told him.

"I always kept my Army uniform in the closet," he said.

"So?" I asked.

"So that proves I planned to return to the Army some day. And if I planned to return some day, it isn't desertion because there was no intention."

"Do you mean to tell me," I asked him, "that all a soldier has to do to beat a desertion charge is to keep his uniform? Not wear it, just keep it?"

"That's right," he said. "Then all it can be is absent without leave, AWOL, not desertion."

Well, of course that was absurd. And of course it was doubly absurd for me, a lawyer, to even discuss it with a layman. I didn't need to look anything up: the facts here were crystal clear. Leaving your duty post, taking an assumed name, running away and hiding in a far-off city, getting married under the new name, working a year as a civilian, denying identity until established by finger prints—all of these things showed me that it was obviously absurd to call it anything but desertion. And I wasn't going to make a fool of myself by representing a client with such a

231

ridiculous defense. And I didn't.

Naturally, he got another lawyer. And, naturally, the other lawyer looked up the point that the soldier had insisted was the law. And, naturally, the Court Martial Board ruled in his favor: it was a case of absence without leave, AWOL, and not desertion. (Maybe the Board was wrong, but that's the way it ruled.) That was the last time I failed to take the time and trouble to double check any point, no matter how absurd, raised by any client.

Any lawyer will tell you that a client who asks questions or raises points of law may be a nuisance, but he is really helping or forcing the lawyer to make a better preparation of the case. The lawyer either wants to know or he finds out in self-defense, if nothing else. The lawyer "looks it up," he works harder; he becomes better informed and better prepared; and the client gets more for his money. Why? Because the client raised a point or asked a question.

Simple? Yes. But—and this is an important *but*—the client had to know what question to ask or what point to raise. *The client had to know the law*. All the law? Of course not, but enough so that the lawyer is aware that the client understands the kind of legal situations with which the average person should be familiar. As we stated in the beginning, this is the aim of LAW FOR THE LAYMAN.

35
Retirement

RETIREMENT! YOU EITHER JUST retired or you're thinking about retiring—and what's at the end of the rainbow? Well, what's there depends to some extent on planning of course, but even if you have a pot of gold there, you're also going to find inflation and taxes quietly but very efficiently robbing your savings of its purchasing power.

Retirement is a comfortable word, but we're only kidding ourselves if we don't realize that retirement must be considered within the framework of the purchasing power of your dollar in the light of inflation and taxes.

Inflation works a special hardship on retired people because they usually live on fixed incomes. The average rate of inflation from 1975 in 1980 was 8.9%, beginning with 7% in 1975, dropping to 4.8% in 1976, then rising to 6.8% in 1977, 9% in 1978 and 13.4% in 1979, and finally ending at 12.4% in 1980. As we re-publish, the inflation rate in September of 1981 was 14.8%—with no relief in sight. While we hope inflation isn't here to stay, we have to expect it will be with us for a long time.

The average layman's plans of retirement usually are based on income from Social Security (or some similar pension plan) and savings in the form of stocks, bonds, insurance, bank savings accounts, and other such sources. So let's talk about the hard realities of inflation, taxes and purchasing power.

EARLY PLANNING FOR RETIREMENT

First of all, the time to plan for retirement is *now*—whether you're seventy years old or fifty or twenty. Why? Because now is probably when you're still earning money—and paying high income taxes on money that's coming to you in the form of wages, dividends, interest, or other such sources. You're in a high income tax bracket when you're working—at least, higher than you will be after you retire and stop working. So now is the time to start thinking about how you can have more income after retirement when, because you'll be in a lower tax bracket, you'll be giving less to Uncle Sam.

Other than returns from a business venture, the usual way to have retirement income (in addition to your Social Security or pension) is by investing in real estate, stocks, bonds, treasury bills, insurance, bank accounts, and the like. Since we're discussing retirement programs for the average layman, let's limit our analysis to these possibilities.

Before we try to find out where we're going at retirement, we must first determine where we are now. So, begin by conferring with your local Social Security Office and your company personnel or union office to ascertain exactly what you may count on from those programs. Among other questions, be sure to ask specifically: What length of service and what age must I attain before I become eligible for full pension benefits? What will determine the amount of money I get? When do my benefits "vest"? (Vesting means that after a specified period of time on the job the worker is entitled to benefits at retirement even though he has left to work elsewhere or simply stopped working. Different employers have different "vesting" times).

While Social Security payments and some government pensions are tied to the cost-of-living index, generally pension plans of private employers do not provide for such adjustments. Incidentally, if your employer doesn't have a pension plan for your retirement, a recent federal law lets you set aside a certain amount of your salary or wages under an approved Individual Retirement Account plan (IRA). You probably will need the advice of an expert like a banker, lawyer, accountant or life insurance agent for an IRA plan. The same is true of the H.R.-10 Plan, familiarly known as the Keogh Plan, if you are self-employed. Your own pension plan will leave you with fixed amounts which do not increase to offset inflation.

Before deciding what you'll do with your assets, you first have to figure out exactly what you've got. So the first step is to list—by a *written* list—every single item of value that you have or will have at the age when you plan to retire. That includes bank accounts, insurance, savings bonds, annuities, corporate stocks and bonds, governmental securities, real estate, interest in a business, jewelry and personal property, and assets of any kind. Then list any liabilities: mortgages, loans, and liens of every kind. Subtract the total liabilities from the total assets and you've got your net worth. Now we're ready to consider where, when, and how to invest any liquid assets.

INVESTING YOUR LIQUID ASSETS

The ideal investment should be safe, liquid (be readily convertible into cash) yield a relatively high rate of return, and escalate with the cost of living. Unfortunately, no single investment has all those characteristics. For example, it is a truism that the safer the investment, the less the return—while if you're looking for a 25 or 30 percent return on your money, you're going to be speculating with gold mines or shooting craps. So the prudent investor will probably want to have an inventory of investments (a portfolio) of various kinds ranging from slightly speculative to slightly conservative, but averaging out as basically "sound" from the point of view of safety, liquidity, yield, and inflation.

REAL ESTATE INVESTMENTS

Many experts believe that real estate is not only one of the best possible investments but is also the one investment least likely to be hurt by inflation. In addition a bill was recently passed by Congress permitting a person over 55 years old to sell his house without paying any tax on the first $100,000 of profit. So, of course, real estate must be given prime consideration in any retirement plan. It supposedly does very well in meeting the tests of safety, rate of return, and inflation—although the liquidity factor may not be as satisfactory as desirable. But there are other considerations.

Real estate is supposed to be a good investment, but do you want the headaches that go with ownership of real estate? What about painting, repair, upkeep of the grounds, and routine problems? If you own real estate you may have tenants who do not pay the rent. If you're willing to take the headaches, do you have enough money to buy real estate? And keep the payments for the mortgage, taxes, insurance and other expenses? And if you can, are you going to "babysit" the house after retirement? Or, if you don't want to be tied down to it, have you considered the problem of absentee ownership if you're going to retire to Florida, California or Shagri La? Yes, real estate may be a good investment, but even if the property tax doesn't go up, and do you know a place where it won't increase?, do you have a big enough chunk of money for even a down payment? And, if you do, do you want the headaches? Is that really your idea of a comfortable and relaxed retirement? No, it probably isn't. Probably you don't want the tensions and anxieties, the being tied down, that are "part of the territory" when you're an owner or landlord. So let's turn to the kind of investment that is at least equally safe but does not require constant supervision and resolution of problems. How do stocks, bonds, insurance, bank accounts, and annuities of various kinds "shape up" when tested under the impact of inflation and taxes.

"BLUE CHIP" STOCKS AND BONDS MAKE SOLID INVESTMENTS

Stocks and bonds are a common investment and—limiting our analysis to sound "blue chips" and not some fly-by-night gold mine ripoff—stocks and bonds can be a relatively sound investment. But instead of trying to guess what to buy, consult an expert—a banker, insurance agent, stockbroker, or financial consultant. (They may not be able to put you onto a moneymaker but they probably can keep you off "dogs" that read glamourously, but perform poorly.) You don't have to follow their advice which, incidentally, doesn't cost you anything unless you do—so what do you have to lose by getting advice for nothing?

Many stocks pay dividends and it is hoped that over a long period of time they will also appreciate in value, thus increasing the worth of a person's portfolio of stocks.

Over the past twenty-five years stock prices, despite periodic declines, have more than maintained the purchasing power of the prudent investor's dollar. Since 1952, the cost of living has doubled, while common stock prices, as measured by the Dow

Jones Average of 30 Industrial Stocks, have more than tripled. However, long term appreciation in value of stocks is likely to be less important to a retired person or person about to retire than the immediate prospect of increased dividends.

There are various kinds of bonds: municipal (state, county, and local), governmental (E, EE, H or HH bonds), and corporate, with yields that fluctuate reflecting economic conditions. Municipal bonds are tax-exempt, which is why they pay less interest than most federal government bonds.

Stocks have shown that they have a greater appreciation return, over a long period of time, than the return a person might realize on bond investments. On the other hand, bonds offer less risk of capital invested, although this will not protect against a loss in purchasing power. You can't have your cake and eat it too—so you pay your money and take your choice of security or return. The higher the return generally the greater the risk.

N.O.W. ACCOUNTS (Negotiated Order of Withdrawal)

Beginning with 1981, banks and savings and loan associations have been permitted to pay 5¼% on funds in interest bearing checking accounts. Savings and Loans are prohibited from paying more than 5½% on passbook accounts, banks more than 5¼%. The new tax law permits NOW accounts for business as well as for personal use.

ALL-SAVERS CERTIFICATES

Effective with tax years ending after September 30, 1981 and before January 1, 1983, commercial banks, mutual savings banks, savings and loan associations, and credit unions are authorized to issue these tax-exempt savings deposits. They will have a one year maturity, bear an investment yield equal to 70% of the average investment yield for 52 week U.S. Treasury bills auctioned the previous week, be made available in $500 denominations, and give a $1,000 lifetime tax-exempt exclusion ($2,000 in case of a joint return).

MONEY MARKET CERTIFICATES

They require a minimum investment of $10,000, offer a fixed rate of interest based on the U.S. Treasury bill rate, and mature in six months. Federal regulations require a penalty on principal withdrawn prior to maturity (equal to three months' earnings on certificates of one year or less).

TAXATION

With the exception of the All-Savers Certificates exclusion mentioned above, interest on NOW accounts, Money Market Certificates, and Certificates of Deposit is subject to both state and federal taxes.

U.S. TREASURY BILLS

These are stable instruments guaranteed by the federal government, and they are highly liquid. New issues of 3 month and 6 month T-Bills are auctioned weekly on Mondays; one-year maturities are offered every 4 weeks. The minimum purchase is $10,000, with increments of $5,000 above that. There is no transaction cost if purchased from the Federal Reserve, and if bought at a bank, a small service fee is charged.

U.S. TREASURY NOTES AND BONDS

Notes carry a fixed return, mature in one to ten years; bonds mature in ten to thirty years. Both are generally available in minimum denominations of $1,000 with interest paid semi-annually, The Treasury announces offerings several weeks before the issue date.

U.S. SERIES EE AND HH SAVINGS BONDS

These are available in increments from $25 to $5,000. Series EE bonds now pay 9% and under present law the Treasury Department can boost the rate by 1% every six months. Series HH bonds pay 8.5%.

FEDERAL AGENCY PAPER

These securities are available in maturities from one month to 25 years, with fixed yields. They usually provide higher yields than

Treasury issues because they are the liability of the issuing agency—Fannie Mae (Federal National Mortgage Association), Banks for Cooperatives, Federal Land Banks, and other agencies like World Bank Bonds—and are not the liability of the U.S. Government.

TAXATION

Interest on federal instruments is subject to federal income tax but is exempt from state and local taxes.

MUNICIPAL BONDS

These are debt obligations incurred by state and local governmental bodies to underwrite public programs. The interest is exempt from federal and state taxes. Issued in denominations of $1,000 to $5,000 generally, they usually pay interest annually in specified amounts over a period of years. Prices and interest rates are determined by the credit-worthiness of the issuer (the municipality or state, for example) and market acceptance of the bonds.

MONEY MARKET FUNDS

Money Market funds pool the assets of investors in short-term financial instruments like Treasury bills, Certificates of Deposit (CD's), and short-term corporate loans known as commercial paper. They allow the small saver to participate in the high yielding instruments that have long been available only to the large investor. Interest rates fluctuate daily. The minimum investment is generally $1,000. The high rate of return, high liquidity, and minimal risk make them popular investments. Most Money Market funds offer check-writing privileges with certain minimums required per check.

INDIVIDUAL RETIREMENT ACCOUNTS (IRA's)

An individual who is not an active participant in a qualified pension plan can make deductible contributions to an IRA. Under the old law, the contribution was limited to the lesser of 15% of compensation or $1500 a year. A non-working spouse was allowed an additional $250 deduction, but the total contribution had to be evenly split between the IRA of the individual and the IRA of the spouse. The new law raised the deduction level to the lesser of $2,000 or 100% of compensation; and, most importantly, there is no longer a requirement that the person not be an active participant in an employer-sponsored plan. The limit has been raised to $2250 where contributions are also made to the IRA of a non-working spouse. The former equal division requirement has been dropped, but not more than $2,000 can go to either account.

HR-10 KEOGH PLAN FOR THE SELF-EMPLOYED

In 1981, the limit a self-employed person could contribute to an HR-10 Plan was $7500, but no more than 15% of earned income. Starting in 1982, the contribution can be up to $15,000, but still limited to 15% of income. Self-employed people will also be eligible for an IRA Plan in addition to their HR-10 Plan.

BANK ACCOUNTS—SAVINGS AND TIME DEPOSITS

Bank accounts come in all shapes and sizes—ordinary savings, time deposits (also known as Certificates of Deposit) etc.—and carry different rates of interest. We can expect time deposits—where you cannot withdraw before the time stated (without a penalty)—will pay a greater rate of interest than that earned on ordinary savings accounts. Interest on all savings accounts is taxed in the year it is earned. Unlike Social Security payments which increase automatically as the cost of living increases, interest in savings accounts is not adjusted in relation to inflation.

The careful bank depositor will inquire as to how interest is computed (from day of deposit to day of withdrawal is usually best); how often it is credited and compounded (the more frequently the better); and does the institution require any minimum balance or the payment of fees or penalties for early or numerous withdrawals. The bank should also be asked what its practice is when a Certificate of Deposit matures—some banks transfer the funds to a lower interest paying savings account. Most savings accounts are insured by the Federal Government up to $40,000 (as of this writing)—but ask the particular bank to be sure. And of course government savings bonds and Treasury bills, notes, and bonds are guaranteed by the United States government. If you have in mind opening a bank savings account "and forgetting about it" for several years in order to let it build up, be very careful. Banks will take steps to forfeit "inactive" accounts—those where no deposit or withdrawal has been made for a period of time (for example, five years in New York and ten in

Massachusetts). The usual procedure is for the bank to advertise the bank book for some weeks before the funds escheat (revert to the state). If you have changed your place of residence, you probably will never see the advertisement or hear about it. The states have procedures (within time limits) by which the account can be reactivated or reinstated if the depositor takes the proper steps. Ask the bank (or the State Banking Department) just what the situation is in your state.

PRIVATE PENSIONS

Private pensions have not fully fared up to inflation. The Committee for Economic Development, a business study group, has warned us that future retirees may face "insecurity and hardship" unless Society Security is reformed and private pension plans find a way to expand benefits. Unlike Social Security, almost no private pension program automatically takes inflation into account in calculating post-retirement benefits, even though price increases can wipe out the value of a pension. An annual inflation rate of 10% will have the buying power of a retirement check in about seven years.

Take the individuals who just retired on a fixed income of $10,000; if inflation continues over the next ten years at just a 7% average per year, that $10,000 would only have $5,083 buying power ten years from today. In 20 years, that $10,000 would be reduced to $2,500 in purchasing power.

The average rate of inflation from 1975 to 1980 was 8.9%. Will you have adequate purchasing power to meet your financial objectives ten, twenty, or thirty years in the future?

Constance Gleason, an expert estate planner who is the Director of Variable Annuities for the John Hancock Insurance Company, has developed a "Retirement Test" which you may wish to take to learn how you are charting your own financial course. The test begins with questions about your financial objectives and about the value of the resources you've accumulated, whether your financial program will enable you to see your children through college, you through retirement and your family through all the big and little crises along the way.

Actual goals and priorities will vary with your circumstances. The important thing is to give serious thought to your goals and try to anticipate the expenses both short and long term. Your progress toward achieving these goals will help you attain your ultimate objective of "financial security."

Part of the test has been reproduced below:

ESTIMATE INCOME NEEDED AT RETIREMENT $ _____

ADJUST INCOME NEEDED FOR INFLATION (refer to chart below) $ _____

SOURCES OF ANNUAL RETIREMENT INCOME:

Estimate Income Unadjusted		Adjusted for Inflation*
$ _____	*Social Security (Based on current tables, adjust for inflation at same rate as INCOME NEEDED above)	$ _____
_____	Pension (Assume 4% factor to inflate pension)	_____
_____	Interest on Savings (Enter unadjusted amount in Column 2)	_____
_____	Dividend Income — Investments (Enter unadjusted amount in Column 2)	_____
_____	Insurance and/or Annuity Income	_____
_____	Other Income	_____
$ _____	Total EXPECTED INCOME Adjusted for Inflation	$ _____

ADDITIONAL INCOME NEEDED:
Subtract total EXPECTED INCOME as adjusted
for inflation, from INCOME NEEDED $ _____

*ADJUSTMENT FOR INFLATION

Years	4%	5%	6%	8%	Years	4%	5%	6%	8%
5	1.2	1.3	1.3	1.5	25	2.7	3.4	4.3	6.8
10	1.5	1.6	1.8	2.2	30	3.2	4.3	5.7	10.1
15	1.8	2.1	2.4	3.2	35	3.9	5.5	7.7	14.8
20	2.2	2.7	3.2	4.7	40	4.8	7.0	10.3	21.7

*Select percentage rate and multiply income needed at retirement by factor indicated for the number of years until retirement.

YOU HAVE PASSED THIS TEST ONLY IF YOUR EXPECTED INCOME EQUALS OR EXCEEDS YOUR NEEDED INCOME (AS ADJUSTED FOR INFLATION).

If you have been guilty of a lack of coordination of your finances, or if you have not taken the time to plan adequately, or if you have a serious need to build wealth while your income remains relatively high—you should sit down right now and develop a balanced financial plan. Begin right now! Don't procrastinate! The sooner you develop and follow a plan—whatever it is—the better are your chances of attaining your financial objectives.

CREDIT UNIONS

Credit Unions of various kinds (industrial, ethnic, social) have become popular because they usually pay a higher rate of interest than bank accounts, although they may not be as safe as banks.

INSURANCE AS AN INVESTMENT OPTION

Insurance—life, health, etc.—offers several investment possibilities that you should discuss with an insurance agent. Insurance dividends can also be accumulated and not taxed until the year they are paid or distributed—but (at the time of this writing) legislation is pending to tax it as of the year it is earned.

FIXED, VARIABLE AND COMBINATION ANNUITIES

Annuities also come in assorted financial packages—fixed, variable, combination, etc.—but the purpose of all is to provide the annuitant with an income for life by providing monthly payments called annuity installments. The fixed annuity pays a guaranteed rate of interest on the monies invested, the variable carries no guarantee, and a combination annuity combines the features of both.

Most people are not too familiar with variable annuities, a relatively new type of saving concept. It came into being about twenty-five years ago when financial experts were seeking a solution for the problems retirees were experiencing with taxes, inflation and purchasing power. They came up with a relatively simple answer: let the wage-earner have an investment on which he can postpone any income tax on the investment earnings until after his retirement—on the theory that the tax bracket a retiree would be in is of course considerably less than the one he is in while working. That sounds like a great solution, and it was—with one hitch: would the government allow the income tax to be postponed until after retirement? Well, to make a long story short, the government would—on the annuity principle. The wage-earner simply buys an annuity contract on which the income tax is deferred to a future time.

EXPERTS WHO WILL HELP WITH
RETIREMENT PLANNING

Of course there are scores of other investments—and the careful investor should consider them all in planning retirement. Then—and this is vital—you should discuss your planned program with experts in the field. Those experts will be found among investment brokers, insurance experts, lawyers, accountants, and financial counsellors. Libraries have many good books available on investments. And the following associations have publications and advice to give that should be helpful:

> Administration on Aging
> U. S. Dept. of Health, Education & Welfare
> Washington, D.C. 20201
>
> American Association of Retired Persons
> 1909 K St., N.W.
> Washington, D.C. 20049
>
> National Council of Senior Citizens
> 1511 K St., N.W.
> Washington, D.C. 20005
>
> National Council on the Aging
> 1828 L St., N.W.
> Washington, D.C. 20036
>
> Public Affairs Pamphlets
> 381 Park Avenue South
> New York, N.Y. 10016
>
> Retirement Living
> 150 E. 58th St.
> New York, New York 10022

Call or write to one or two of them. You have nothing to lose and everything to gain. If you apply your energies to making the best use of all your assets it should pay off in greater financial resources for retirement.

BALANCED FINANCIAL PLANNING MEANS
HAPPINESS AND SECURITY

Everyone planning retirement would do well to be familiar with a viewpoint expressed by Constance Gleason as one of the speakers at a seminar on families and estate planning I attended recently. She followed a child guidance counsellor who told the story of a parent who bought his precocious son the most difficult jigsaw puzzle in the store upon the clerk's assurance that no one could put it together in less than two hours. When completed, the jigsaw puzzle was a picture of the entire world; and to the father's amazement, his son put it together in less than five minutes.

"How did you do it?"

"Well," his son explained, "the box said the other side was a picture of a boy. So I tried that first. And you know what? When you put the boy together right, the whole world fell into place."

The next speaker, Miss Gleason, seized her opportunity: "That store had another equally difficult jigsaw puzzle," she began. Then she went on—and I later obtained a transcript of her remarks: "This one was even more difficult than the first one (The Boy and the World). It was a jigsaw puzzle called "Happiness and Security." We all have an idea of what those words mean—but what does a picture of Happiness and Security look like? How do you put together dozens of little jigsaw pieces of a picture puzzle that's supposed to represent *Happiness and Security?* I tried and tried—but I couldn't. Well, there was a way to do it—and you've probably guessed what it was. It was on the other side—where there was another picture puzzle. The other side was called "Balanced Financial Planning," and every piece in it was labelled. The names weren't intangible or undefinable like *Happiness and Security.* Oh, no! They were common, everyday words. Not intangible but tangible. Not indifinite but definite."

"Every estate planner or financial counselor knows exactly what every word on that other side means—exactly what it is and exactly what it does. Because they're *our* words—stocks, bonds, savings accounts, insurance, certificates of deposit, annuities, and so on."

"Every little piece of that picture puzzle called "Balanced Financial Planning" has a specific name, an exact place, and a definite function. They all fit together perfectly."

"And when they formed the picture, "Balanced Financial Planning," the other side, *Happiness and Security,* fell into place perfectly."

Well, as Miss Gleason said, if you have balanced financial planning, you'll have happiness and security. Lastly, always remember that—while you have nothing to say about when death, illness or disaster strikes—you *can* plan retirement. Are you going to steer your way into it? Or just drift? It's up to you.

245

36
Epilogue: Looking Forward

WHILE THERE IS NO end to the law, which is a continuing process through eternity, there is an end to any book—and here we are. But often the end is merely a beginning: so let it be with LAW FOR YOU.

The mythical Roman god Janus looked both backwards and forwards—and so should the layman who truly wants to understand law. The law, too, looks both to the past and the future: the past mirrors the future because it always will be prologue.

This book is not intended to be an all-inclusive and definitive treatise on the law or any of its myriad subjects. Its purpose is to give the non-lawyer a practical understanding of those legal matters that are apt to confront him in his daily life—and, in addition, to awaken interest in the legal process. Hopefully, now that you have been exposed to legal history, constitutions, statutes, trials, judicial decisions, and the makings and workings of our legal system, you will continue and deepen your interest in it.

The more sophisticated and complex a civilization, the more sophisticated and complex the law governing it. Yet, basically, the law is always very simple: insure fairness and justice. That has always been its touchstone and always will be.

Law is the vehicle by which society makes it easier for individuals to live together and enjoy the rights and privileges of civilization without interfering with others who want to exercise their own legal rights. It takes more than the expertise of legal specialists to accomplish this—it also demands the intelligence, compassion, tolerance, and understanding of the non-lawyer. Imparting that idea, too, has been a major aim of LAW FOR THE LAYMAN.

We hope the book has achieved its purposes.

Appendix

INDIVIDUAL TAX RATE REDUCTIONS

Under the prior law individual income tax rates ranged from 14% to 70%. Beginning with 1982, the top marginal tax rate has been reduced from 70% to 50%.

WITHHOLDING RATES REDUCED

Withholding rates have been reduced 5% on October 1, 1981; 10% on July 1, 1982; and 10% on July 1, 1983.

CAPITAL GAINS TAX RATE REDUCED

Prior to the new tax law individuals were taxed on 40% of their net capital gains. Under the 1981 law net capital gains are taxed at a maximum effective rate of 20%. For example, a capital gain of $10,000 will now be taxed at $2,000 instead of $4,000. The minimum tax rate, which had been 25%, has been reduced to 20%.

EXCLUSION OF GAINS ON SALE OF PRINCIPAL RESIDENCE

The one time exclusion from income of gain on the sale of a principal residence has been increased from $100,000 to $125,000 for sales or exchanges after July 20, 1981 for taxpayers age 55 or over. The holding period for buying a replacement home of equal or greater value has been increased for eighteen to twenty-four months.

ESTATE AND GIFT TAXES

Under the prior law (The Tax Reform Act of 1976), a single unified estate and gift tax credit of up to $47,000 was available.

There were no estate or gift taxes on an individual's transfers up to $175,625 during a lifetime or at death. The new 1981 Act gradually increases the amounts of the unified credit from $47,000 to $192,800 over a six year period beginning in 1982. By 1987, with a unified credit of $192,800, there will be no estate and gift tax transfers on transfers totaling $600,000 or less.

UNLIMITED MARITAL DEDUCTION

The maximum estate tax marital deduction has been the greater of $250,000 or one-half of the adjusted gross estate. The 1981 Act removed the limitation on the marital deduction for both estate and gift tax purposes. As a result, unlimited amounts of property can be transferred between spouses without the imposition of estate or gift taxes. (Be sure to check the section on "Wills" to see how this affects wills drawn before September 12, 1981).

ANNUAL GIFT TAX EXCLUSION

The old law allowed annual exclusions of $3,000 per donee for gifts of present interests in property. Under it, a married couple could give up to $6,000 per donee annually without any gift tax. The new Act increased the exclusion to $10,000 per donee, and a total of $20,000 for married couples.

AMERICANS LIVING ABROAD

For Americans working abroad, $75,000 a year of earnings becomes non-taxable—the non-taxable sum increasing in later years.

MARRIAGE PENALTY

Under the identical set of facts, the so-called "marriage penalty" imposed a greater tax on a married couple than on two unmarried persons who were living together. The 1981 tax law reduced that penalty by allowing two-earner couples a 5% deduction, up to $1500, on earnings of the lower paid spouse; and double that in later years.

CHILD CARE

If you have to hire someone to look out for your child while you're working, you may now be able to deduct 20% of the cost of the care—up to $400 for one child and $800 for two or more. There's a similar credit for care for a disabled dependent.

ADOPTION

If you've adopted a "hard to place" child (an older child or one from a minority group) you may now be able to deduct up to $1500 of adoption expenses.

Glossary

These words and phrases are found in many law books. The definitions are intended to give the layman a practical understanding of the words, not necessarily a technically exact one.

abatement: reduction or decrease

adjudication: judgment or decree

administrative law: law governing procedure before commissions, boards, agencies, and other departments of government

affidavit: a written sworn statement

arraignment: calling of the defendant to plead

bailment: temporary transfer of possession of personal property, but not the title to it

caveat emptor: let the buyer beware

certiorari: a Writ of Certiorari is usually the order from U.S. Supreme Court to a lower court, calling up the record for review

chattel: item of personal property

citation: reference to a case or statute or other legal authority

cite: to "cite a case" is to refer to a case as authority for a point

concurrent: running together; at the same time

construe: interpret or determine

de bene: for what it's worth. Evidence admitted "de bene" is evidence admitted "subject to connection"

defendant: the party defending; the one who has been sued or accused

demurrer: a pleading that in effect says, "Admitting the facts alleged, they are insufficient." It's a legal "So what?"

deposition: written testimony under oath

dictum: something said but not controlling

et als: and others

et uxor (et ux): and wife

ex parte: on our side; usually refers to a Judge hearing only one party

felony: a serious crime, one usually calling for a prison sentence ·

fiduciary: person holding property in trust for another

garnishment: attachment

habeas corpus: have the body; a writ by which a person in custody is brought before the Court

immaterial: doesn't matter, remote; unimportant

incompetent: inadequate; incapable; legally not qualified

indictment: accusation

infamous: shameful, disgraceful

in pari delicto: in equal fault

irrelevant: no bearing upon the matter; not appropriate to the situation

judicial notice: court takes notice without evidence being presented to prove the point

judgment-proof: no assets

jurisdiction: the power to hear and decide a case; geographic area

libel: a divorce action

lien: a charge or encumbrance upon a property (like a mortgage)

malum in se: bad in itself (such crimes as rape, murder, robbery, etc.)

malum prohibitum: bad because prohibited (jaywalking, etc.)

misdemeanor: a minor or less serious crime, one usually calling for a fine or jail sentence

mistrial: court trial ended without a decision because of some mishap (usually the case is tried again)

moral turpitude: baseness or depravity

motion to suppress: request to court to prevent evidence being used

nolo contendere: I do not wish to contest

nol pros (nolle prosequi): I do not wish to prosecute

per capita: by the head

petit jury (petty jury): the trial jury

plaintiff: the person suing; the claimant

pleading: papers filed in court stating a position

presumption: presume; assume; take for granted. A presumption calls for a certain result unless the party adversely affected overcomes it

prima facie: on first appearance. It is evidence that establishes the fact unless rebutted

251

probate: to prove

quasi: almost. A quasi-judicial board is almost a court

res gestae: the thing done; the subject matter; the transaction

res ipsa loquitur: the thing speaks for itself

res judicata (adjudicata): the thing judged or decided

stare decisis: to stand by decided cases; to follow decisions

statute: a law passed by a legislature

supplementary: additional

suppress: to prevent; to put a stop to; to prohibit

testator: the person making a will

tort: a wrong; a private or civil wrong

usury: excessive interest on a loan

venire: usually refers to the list of jurors from which trial jury is chosen

venue: usually refers to county or place where court is located

waiver: abandoning or relinquishing a right or claim

writ: a written order from a court authorizing someone to do something

Index

254

255